The Pursuit of Happiness

The Pursuit of Happiness BLACK WOMEN, DIASPORIC DREAMS, AND THE POLITICS OF EMOTIONAL TRANSNATIONALISM

Bianca C. Williams

Duke University Press   Durham and London   2018

Interior designed by Courtney Leigh Baker
Typeset in Garamond Premier Pro and Gill Sans by
Copperline Book Services

Library of Congress Cataloging-in-Publication Data
Names: Williams, Bianca C., [date] author.
Title: The pursuit of happiness : black women, diasporic dreams,
and the politics of emotional transnationalism / Bianca C. Williams.
Description: Duke University Press : Durham, 2018. | Includes
bibliographical references and index.
Identifiers: LCCN 2017036326 (print)
LCCN 2017044098 (ebook)
ISBN 9780822372134 (ebook)
ISBN 9780822370253 (hardcover : alk. paper)
ISBN 9780822370369 (pbk. : alk. paper)
Subjects: LCSH: African American women—Race identity—Jamaica. |
African American women—Race identity—United States. | African
American women—Travel—Jamaica.
Classification: LCC E185.86 (ebook) | LCC E185.86 .W555 2018 (print) |
DDC 305.48/896073—dc23
LC record available at https://lccn.loc.gov/2017036326

COVER ART: Photo by Mario Tama / Getty Images News /
Getty Images.

For my grandmother, Nerissa Viola Rose:
for all the seeds of love, family, and happiness you planted, from Westmoreland, Jamaica, to the United States, and back.

WE MISS YOU DEEPLY.

Contents

Acknowledgments

Since my grandmother passed away during my first preliminary research trip to Jamaica almost fifteen years ago, the country has provoked a complex web of feelings and emotions in me whenever I visit: gratitude for a homecoming filled with family members I've never known, but a familiar culture that I grew up with. Pleasure-inducing memories of amazing, fierce bonds with Black American women as they experience their best selves, and a mourning of lost connections once one leaves the field and returns to the complexities of real life. Joy associated with centering Black women in all their brilliance and glory, and the anxiety of being honest about the ways we are implicated in the systems we try to resist. The grief of ending one of your deepest friendships and loving relationships, and the (short-lived) excitement of creating a new, tumultuous one that crashes and burns. The exhaustive push and pull of home and the field, and the peaceful times when they feel like one and the same. The affirmation felt in a country where Black people are so clear about their agency and the ways we can determine our own destinies (expressed in film, song, dance, literature, and entrepreneurial endeavors), while being overwhelmed by evidence that larger systems of oppression work hard to limit our abilities. Jamaica holds a great deal of emotions for me, and I'm grateful for every lesson, experience, and opportunity for growth as it welcomed me in doing this research.

I have a profound sense of gratitude for the women of Girlfriend Tours International, especially Angelia Hairston and Marilyn Williams, for letting me into their lives and allowing me to follow them around while I asked a million questions about everything. I'm grateful for the stories you shared, for the things we experienced together, and for the lessons you taught me. You embodied #BlackGirlMagic before it became a hashtag. I send thanks to the members of Jamaicans.com (including the web-community creator Xavier Murphy), who construct a vibrant community daily and remind the world that Jamaican culture continues to have a global impact. I am thankful to Guardian, Humble Lion, Delia, all the members of my Mo Bay crew, the squad at Fisherman's Beach, and the staff at numerous hotels and residencies, including Sky Castles, who offered their own stories, shared great meals, showed me parts of "the bush," and kept a watchful eye on me. Last, I want to thank my uncle Noel, who took me in whenever I showed up on his doorstep needing a break from fieldwork, and who introduced me to parts of my family history I wouldn't have known if not for his patience and storytelling.

So many people provided love, support, gentle words, useful feedback sessions, hugs, and rejuvenating energy during the process of conceptualizing and writing this book. My heart and spirit are grateful for every kind gesture and constructive critique, including those I may no longer be able to name after all these years. Believe me—it made a difference. To the generous trifecta of Lee D. Baker, Deborah A. Thomas, and John L. Jackson, I offer a million thank-yous. You have been with me since the beginning of this project, and I appreciate all the ways your teachings and guidance have shaped this research. Thanks for affirming the way I do anthropology and for modeling what loving mentorship, intellectual innovation, and passionate teaching can look like. When I was at Duke University, Anne Allison, Tina Campt, Wahneema Lubiano, Mark Anthony Neal, and Charlie Piot all helped spark the flame I carry for anthropology, Africana studies, and Black feminist thought, and taught me how to ask good questions. Mark, thanks for telling me I'd get over the dissertation fatigue. You were right. Chandra Guinn, and the community at the Mary Lou Williams Center for Black Culture, provided a cozy home and brainstorming space for me when I was their first scholar-in-residence in 2010. Attiya Ahmad, Leigh Campoamor, Giles Harrison-Conwill, Dwayne Dixon, Erica Edwards, Micah Gilmer (the homie!), Alvaro Jarrin, Mara Kaufman, Treva Lindsey, Samantha Noel, Netta van Vliet, and Wang Yu helped by sharing their writing journeys and having long conversations with me about how to do the academy on our own terms. I am grateful for the multiple cohorts of the Bassett Squad and all my loved ones from Duke '02–'05, who still remind me to have fun, laugh from my belly, and engage in shenanigans that make life worth living.

Lauren Berlant, Faye V. Harrison, Jason Hendrickson, David Ikard, David Kennedy, Kerry Ann Rockquemore, Aimee Carillo Rowe, Karla Slocum, Ayden Saldana, Frank Tuitt, and Deborah E. Whaley provided crucial feedback and encouraging words during this process. Frank, thanks for the cinematic and musical distractions and for providing uplifting commentary on the scholar you see me becoming. Naomi Greyser—the best writing coach ever for anxious writers—held my hand physically and virtually through so many bouts of writer's block I lost count. Loretta Shaia and Karen Lenzi gave me tools for reflection and maintaining emotional wellness that were crucial to the writing process. Deirdre Royster, with great care, spent four hours during a trip to Italy listening to me speak my arguments out loud and helped guide this book into existence. A fantastic crew of Black women anthropologists—including Donna Auston, Riche Barnes, A. Lynn Bolles, Dana Ain Davis, Marla Frederick, Kamela Heyward-Rotimi, Leith Mullings, Tami Navarro, Jemima Pierre, Ashante Reese, Kaifa Roland, Cheryl Rodriguez, Savannah Shange, Christen Smith, and Erica Williams, among others—reminds me regularly that our work on Black people is important and that there is a legacy of antiracist, decolonizing, feminist anthropology to which those who came before us expect us to contribute. We roll deep. The writing of Sara Ahmed, Ruth Behar, Katherine Frank, Gina Ulysse, and Alisse Waterston sustains me and gives me the confidence to push and bend the boundaries of writing.

Donna Goldstein, Carla Jones, Carole McGranahan, and Kaifa Roland actively created a community with me/for me in the Department of Anthropology at the University of Colorado Boulder. I am ever grateful. Carole, thanks for your advocacy and for making me press "send." Thanks also go to Lorraine Bayard de Volo, Scarlet Bowen, Kwame Holmes, Danika Medak Saltzman, Deepti Misri, Emma Perez, Manushkka Sainvil, and Seema Sohi for their feedback and friendship during my time in Colorado. Over the past seven years, the students in my "Black Women, Popular Culture, and the Pursuit of Happiness" course have bravely and vulnerably engaged in discussions about affect, mental health crises and disorders, their own pursuits of happiness, and the influence of racism and sexism. The lessons you all have taught me are invaluable. Shout out to the Black Lives Matter 5280 crew (especially the visionary Amy E. Emery Brown and the accomplice, Renee Morgan) and to Marcus Littles and Ryan Bowers of Frontline Solutions, who taught me the importance of affect, emotional wellness, and emotional justice in community building, organizing, and philanthropy. #ALLBlackLivesMatter. Everywhere. Always.

I am thankful to Brian Baughan and Kelly Besecke for providing editorial assistance on this book in its early stages. I thank the whole team at Duke University Press for their wonderful work, especially Courtney Berger and Ken Wissoker, who believed in this project. Courtney, thanks for having my back and a wealth of patience. The anonymous readers for this book were kind, generous, and on point with their feedback. Their careful attention to the text helped me make the book better.

Finally, I am forever in debt to my friendship circle and family for all that they gave me while I wrote this manuscript. Pamela Thompson and Angela

Whitenhill prayed with me, and over me, speaking great things into existence before they were. Charisse Davis, Aliea Diaram, and Iyanna Holmes read drafts, sent me snacks in the mail, reminded me to practice self-care, and gently nudged me when they saw I was stalling. Jamaica Gilmer and Tami Navarro—words cannot express how much you mean to me. You know the inside and outside of this process more than most. On the really tough days, your girlfriendship and our ability to celebrate each other no matter what keep me going. I got you. Nerissa Johnson, I could feel you with me every step of this process. Thank you for taking all my calls when I was doing fieldwork in Jamaica—listening to the awesome and the not-so-good—and for always helping me keep the end goal in sight. I am extremely blessed to have your unconditional sister love. Markus Johnson, I'm grateful for each and every time you opened your home to me, for all the pep talks and mantras, and for giving me the best niece ever. I love you, Mari. To the Rose family—making you all beam with pride gives me joy. Thanks for always celebrating with me and reminding me from where, and from whom, I come. Dawn Williams, thank you for loving on me and telling Nerissa and I that we can do anything we put our minds to and move our feet toward. There have been numerous times throughout this process when I needed to believe those words to make it through. Thank you for all of your sacrifice and for helping us get to where we are. God, thank You for always dreaming bigger dreams for me than I ever can, for having plans to prosper me, for providing hope, for giving me a voice, and for teaching me how to use it.

INTRODUCTION. "Jamaica Crawled Into My Soul"
Black Women, Affect, and the Promise of Diaspora

Caring for myself is not self-indulgence, it is self-preservation,
and that is an act of political warfare. —AUDRE LORDE

Don't wait around for other people to be happy for you. Any happiness
you get you've got to make yourself. —ALICE WALKER

Perhaps it is peculiar to begin a book about happiness with a story centered on crying. While tears can have many meanings, they are not usually a central part of one's vacation narrative. Consequently, as I sat in silence on a cliff in Jamaica with the ladies of Girlfriend Tours International (GFT), each staring up at the starry sky and reflecting on our time in the country, I had to stop and ask myself, "What is all this crying about?"

The evening had begun with us filing into a sixteen-passenger van to make the ten-minute drive from our hotel on the beach to the cliffs of Negril's West End for dinner. It was the first night of the annual tour by GFT, a group of predominantly African American women from all over the United States, ranging in age from twenty-two to their early sixties. We held on to our seats as the driver sped through the twists and turns of the hills, following Jacqueline's instructions to "hurry up, before we miss the sunset!" With our hair disheveled but our lives still intact, we finally pulled up to the restaurant, 3 Dives. A large chalkboard advertised the long list of seafood and Jamaican cuisines the cooks specialized in, with the daily special—"CONCH SOUP"—written in bold, white block letters. Six picnic benches and round wooden tables painted bright red, yellow, and green marked the spot where we would break bread and begin our initiation into girlfriendship.

Marilyn Williams and Angelia Hairston, the founders of GFT, explained that they loved 3 Dives because there was space at the back of the restaurant to make a campfire. The proximity of the benches to the cliff's edge gave the impression that we were sitting directly over the water. The beauty of the vast blue ocean and the rhythmic crashing of waves against the cliffs served as an impressive introduction to Jamaica and provided a serene background for the founders to share their life stories with the Girlfriends. Every year, on the second night of the tour, Girlfriends were "initiated" into GFT on this cliff.

Each cliff initiation played out in a similar manner. After the group made small talk in the main eating area—where they were from, how long it had taken to get to Jamaica, and how many delays or obstacles the ladies had survived at various airports—Marilyn or Angie would welcome them to the tour group and tell them to enjoy the amazing cuisine. Shortly after the food orders were taken, Marilyn would whisper in the ear of one lady, "Girl, come here. I've got something to show you!" She would then escort the Girlfriend down the steps and over the dark dirt path to the edge of the cliff, holding her hand tightly so she would not fall, and seat her on the wooden bench near the campfire. Marilyn would sit down next to the Girlfriend, give her hand a tight squeeze, and encourage her to just look at the stars that lit up the sky, smell the ocean air, and take in Jamaica.

After a few moments of silence had passed, and Marilyn felt like the woman had dutifully followed her instructions and relaxed, she would smile and say in her Southern accent, "Welcome to Jamaica, Girlfriend." More often than not, this statement would immediately draw a few tears from the initiated Girlfriend's eyes, and she would thank Marilyn for bringing her there. After they sat in silence together for a few more moments, Marilyn would head back to the dining area to escort the next Girlfriend down. Eventually, all the Girlfriends would be sitting on the edge of that cliff together, each lost in her thoughts. Intermittently, they would begin to speak softly and share stories about their lives, their struggles, and why they had come to Jamaica.

I heard a diverse collection of life experiences when I first observed and participated in this initiation in 2004. I connected deeply with these women, and most are central to the rest of this book. Jacqueline, a fifty-four-year-old educator, had begun traveling to Jamaica to "get away from all the drama" in the United States. Gayle, a fifty-two-year-old professional, began her travels to Jamaica in 2000 after ending a long-term relationship with a boyfriend. Sitting next to her was Maya, a fifty-four-year-old civil service worker, who planned on retiring in two years to open her own bed-and-breakfast in Jamaica. Sasha, a thirty-five-year-old woman from DC, said that she had caught "Jamaica fever" from Jacqueline, whom she had met online. This was a standard episode of every GFT initiation: one by one, each Girlfriend would reveal a tiny piece of her story. Some shared more than others, but it was during this moment of life-sharing that, almost every year, the collective tears would begin.

Although I was an ethnographer interested in the affective dimensions of Black women's lived experiences, I had not considered what to do if an interlocutor began to cry.[1] In fact, as I accompanied these mostly middle-aged, African American women on their multiple vacations to Jamaica, back to their home-towns in the United States, and finally, on virtual "journeys" in their web community from 2003 to 2007, I was initially surprised, even dumbfounded, by the frequent display of tears throughout our trips and conversations. However, after four years of listening to their life narratives and combing through hundreds of discussion threads online, I came to understand that the shedding of tears was a form of individual and collective emotional release that was connected to larger stories about happiness, yearning, struggle, validation, escape, and love. These larger stories symbolize the complex webs of contradictory images, destructive stereotypes, and misrecognitions Black women experience as they live at the intersection of racism and sexism.

Unfortunately, popular myths about Black women as Jezebels, Sapphires, Mammies, and Strong Black Women along with deficit-based scholarship (research that focuses on what Black women lack and views them as a problem to be fixed) affect both the visibility of these women and the ways they are represented once they are made visible. As a result, when we see tears drop from the eyes of Black women, it is easy to draw on a familiar narrative that leads to a simplistic conclusion: Black women's lives are full of sadness and struggle, and these tears are what result when one strives to beat the odds. Because of historical and contemporary burdens of racism and sexism, struggle is undoubtedly an aspect of many Black women's lives; however, it has always been only a portion of our story. What about Black women and happiness? Pleasure? Leisure? During my years of fieldwork with the women of GFT, I documented how these Black women found ways to pursue and experience these things in the context of generations of racialized and gendered oppression.

When I first met some of the African American women of Girlfriend Tours International in Jamaica in 2003, it was their undeniable happiness that most impressed me. This tour group, composed predominantly of African American heterosexual cisgender women, featured some of the most lively, young-at-heart

Black women in their forties and fifties I had ever met. A few members were married or partnered, while most were divorced and/or single. They were dedicated to living life to the fullest and enjoying everything Jamaica had to offer, including the latest dancehall music and dance moves. Joy radiated off of each woman, and a sense of tranquility permeated the group. These women declared that they did not need husbands, boyfriends, or some other male escort to travel internationally; they were fine navigating unfamiliar streets on their own. In fact, it seemed that most of these self-proclaimed "Jamaicaholics" were enticed by the tour group's focus on women and the opportunity to build "girlfriend-ships," or deep female friendships.

It was the tears of happiness, restoration, and connection shared by the Black women of Girlfriend Tours International, along with their profound expressions of girlfriendship and sensuality in Jamaica, that led me to write this book. Something about the sense of Black womanhood they expressed felt freeing, and this freedom intrigued me. The shedding of tears is a metaphoric theme running throughout the chapters—one that connects the different emotional aspects of these women's transnationalism. As the vernacular notion "traveling while Black" suggests, race affects the emotional experience of international travel—as do gender, class, and national identity. I use the phrase "emotional transnationalism," originally coined by Diane Wolf, to capture this experience and to connect the Girlfriends' emotional lives with their transnational mobility. In her research on second-generation Filipinos, Wolf defines emotional transnationalism as the process of sustaining transnational connections through emotions and ideologies.[2] "Emotional transnationalism" conceptualizes the ambiguities and contradictions embedded in the Girlfriends' pursuit of happiness in the context of global racisms and patriarchies. This group's understanding of their racialized and gendered subjectivities is not contained by, or simply attached to, their nation-state, but rather is deeply connected to their participation in transnational processes and an engagement in what they envision as a diasporic community. These women's choices about whom to love, how to relax, and where to find personal acceptance and community tie together countries and cultures using technologies that are different from those of the past. New technologies often result in new forms of connectivity and belonging that link to historical racialized and gendered ideologies. As I observed their emotions and tracked their tears from the United States to Jamaica and back, I wondered what led Girlfriends to use these technologies and seek leisure experiences. The concept of emotional transnationalism offered a theoretical lens that enabled me to answer two central research questions: First, why do people like the Girlfriends seek out transnational and diasporic experience, and how might their desire for such experience reflect nationally specific affective and political economies of race and gender? Second, how might our understandings of the racialized, gendered, and emotional aspects of transnationalism shift if we place Black women at the center of our research?

This book is a multisited ethnographic study of a group of African American tourist women and their transnational pursuits of happiness. I explore the emotional journey these women encounter as they seek wellness and belonging in the context of national and diasporic differences. I also examine how these African American women make sense of the paradoxical nature of their hyphenated identities while traveling to Jamaica. Initially, like many tourists, they simply seek a leisurely escape from the stress of everyday life. But over time, the *repeated* trips of these self-proclaimed Jamaicaholics take on more meaning as they begin to use Jamaica as a site for dealing with and escaping from American racism and sexism. These African American women have established a complex concept of "happiness," one that can only be fulfilled by moving—both virtually and geographically—across national borders. To travel to Jamaica, Girlfriends need American economic, national, and social capital. At the same time, to remain hopeful and happy within the United States, they need a spiritual connection to their imagined second home of Jamaica and their imagined community of Jamaicans. I argue that their access to virtual and international travel enabled them to temporarily replace their experiences of hardship and invisibility in the United States with fantasies of happiness, intimacy, community, and connectivity in Jamaica.

The Pursuit of Happiness offers an understanding of Girlfriends' relationship to Jamaica that sheds light on multiple areas of anthropological inquiry. Methodologically, the virtual and transnational aspect of this multisited work expands the possibilities for ethnographically documenting imagined community and diasporic longings. Substantively, the focus on these women's affective lives illuminates the significant emotional costs of living as a racialized and gendered subject in the United States. This challenges discourses that belittle and deemphasize emotion, particularly Black people's feelings, as important nodes of data and sites of meaning-making. Additionally, here I highlight some transnational strategies people use to gain access to emotional wellness, leisure, and belonging. And last, while the ethnography centers on the perspectives of one group of African American women, as a whole it illuminates some of the power dynamics of participating in an imagined African diasporic community.

Emotional Transnationalism

Emotional transnationalism is central to my theorization of race, happiness, and diaspora. It enables a useful analysis of exercises of power and privilege, practices of reciprocity and solidarity, the transfer of cultural meanings, and the modification of the identity formations Black women construct and problematize as they create their transnational network and community. Girlfriends' access to class and geographic mobility and their movements in virtual and physical spaces challenge notions of happiness and wellness that mistakenly bind these pursuits to home or a nation-state. The fact that they are African American women, women who are the descendants of enslaved Africans whose movement changed the world, is significant. Their ancestors were forcibly removed from Africa, chained inside the bellies of ships, and sailed across the Atlantic against their will. Aware of this history and that their movement is different, Girlfriends recognize the profound sense of choice and free will they have as they move across national borders and engage in leisure that their ancestors could not. However, they also note how their mobility has been constrained by sexist notions that women should not travel on their own, or that it is abnormal for women to be sexual beings after the age of fifty, and by the particular ways Black women, happiness, and leisure often seem incongruent to many. While their narratives are interwoven with the trauma of the transatlantic slave trade, and a yearning for diasporic connectivity is a significant aspect of their pursuit of happiness, their emotional experiences are more complex than a singular origin story of the diaspora. Therefore, my use of emotional transnationalism is about mapping their desires for girlfriendship, diasporic connectivity, and pleasure and about the ways race and gender influence these desires.

Emotional transnationalism is important for understanding how these women have created a transnational emotional social field—a field that includes two countries that are geographically bounded but also constructed emotionally, culturally, and virtually. Researchers interested in transnationalism and globalization have theorized the fascinating ways goods, ideas, and people increasingly cross national borders and geographic boundaries. However, less attention has been paid to the transnational dynamics of emotions—how people carry emotions with them as they move, experiencing them individually and collectively and across time and space. David Harvey's concept of time-space compression transformation is useful here, as it allows a theorization of the temporal and spatial aspects of emotion. Harvey argues that processes of capitalist commodification and accumulation, alongside technological advances, can lead to a shrinking of distances, or a sense that different times and spaces are closer together than they appeared before.[3]

For the women of GFT, Jamaica and the United States are two countries with distinct cultures that offer essential components for their pursuits of happiness. Their emotions are linked to their experiences of racialized and cultural politics, which are connected to actual nation-states and geographic spaces. Within the group, many Girlfriends are Black women who feel they cannot experience happiness regularly within U.S. borders because of American racism and sexism. Subsequently, they begin to search for ways to fulfill their "inalienable right" by temporarily leaving the United States, drawing on diasporic connections and imaginings, and pursuing happiness and belonging in Jamaica. While it may be weird to cry on vacation, these women cry because they cannot fully disconnect from the emotional burdens of racism and sexism in the United States even as they search for a space where racism is not as prevalent. They also shed tears while experiencing joy and affirmation within the kinship of other Black American women. And as they virtually and physically travel between the two countries—cultivating deep connections to people, places, and their own understandings of self—time and space seem to compress and their crying takes on different meaning. The time between the past and the present compress as they experience diasporic nostalgia and long for a racial and cultural unity with Jamaicans that they imagine was prevalent in another ancestral time. Their happiness lies in the idea that although slavery was terrible for Black populations in both countries, it is a shared history that creates connection in the present. Girlfriends assume that their relationships with Jamaican men, and their more strained connection with Jamaican women, will be nourished by this shared history, a collective experience of racialized suffering and resilience. These women experience and explore their emotions in virtual and physical spaces that concurrently emphasize and blur each country's borders. Girlfriends' emotions simultaneously are experienced in the present, engage a previous diasporic moment, and embody a hope for a future. Through an examination of their emotions, the concept of emotional transnationalism enables us to recognize how certain ideas and feelings, particularly those connected to race and racism, are linked to spatiality and temporality.

The Significance of Imagined Community:
Race, Gender, and Diaspora

My analysis of the Girlfriends' relationships with one another, with Jamaica, and with Jamaicans draws on and contributes to theories about imagined community. To understand how imagined communities are influenced by technological advances, the deterritorialization of economic and political power, and increased movement and mobility, many engage Benedict Anderson's paramount theorization of nationalism and the nation-state in his book, *Imagined Communities*.[4] Anderson describes the nation-state as a unique form of political community shaped by historical forces and imaginings of commonality. He argues that a "community is imagined if its members will never know most of their fellow-members, meet them, or even hear of them, yet in the mind of each lives the image of their communion."[5] Community is often imagined "because, regardless of the actual inequality and exploitation that may prevail in each, the nation is always conceived as a deep, horizontal comradeship."[6] The imagined community created by GFT members is a rich site for illuminating the possibilities and limitations of Anderson's concept, because this imagined community is fraught with the dilemmas that arise as individuals navigate the complicated terrain of identity and community formations.

This story of imagined community takes up Anderson's emphasis on imagination, stretching his analysis to conceptualize some of the ways race, diaspora, and transnationality problematize our perception of community as a collectivity based on sameness and similarities. Anderson's theorization does not actively account for the racialized dimensions of imagined community and the tensions that different experiences and understandings of race (and racism) may generate. Anderson does, however, suggest that inequality, difference, and tensions are frequently embedded in imagined community. By using race as a tool for homing in on these differences, our understanding of community shifts, and we can take seriously the fantastical, imagined, and emotional aspects of racialized experiences within communities.

I also use Anderson's notion of an imagined community as an entry point for articulating how imaginings of African diasporic relationships (particularly African American imaginings) connect with or diverge from Anderson's interpretation of how community works. I deconstruct the narrative of diasporic community the ladies of GFT create in order to understand how members of the African diaspora may experience Blackness differently and how power differentials connected to gender, class, and nationality complicate the viability of diaspora as an imagined community. Since processes of racialization and diasporic subjectivity are inherently about power, mobility, and difference, one can conceive that these processes may act as dilemmas for imagined communities. Tensions may arise as an individual who imagines community one way is confronted with alternate realities when others perceived as community members do not share the same imagining. The community created by GFT members illuminates the possibilities of diasporic imaginings and potential ruptures generated by diasporic realities. How might imagined communities shift and transform if at times commonalities are viewed as shared and, at other times, this imagining of sameness is rejected?

I aim to frustrate particular notions about diasporic community by highlighting some of the power differentials within diasporic formations. By analyzing how affective transactions influence the creation and maintenance of diasporic relationships, particularly those in which national, economic, and gendered differences frequently become marked, I am using GFT as a lens to investigate diasporic diversity. Additionally, instead of anchoring the notion of diaspora in prevalent histories of pain and suffering, this book shows how people use leisure, laughter, and the pursuit of happiness to construct diaspora. While memories of slavery and discrimination definitely inform these women's constructions of Blackness and Black identities, their experiences of pleasure and leisure also ground their imaginings of diasporic community.

Finally, this ethnographic study of imagined community and emotional transnationalism shows how the women of GFT use transnational methods to create community and engage in affective transactions. In the past thirty years, it has become commonplace in disciplines such as anthropology and sociology to argue that many of our lived experiences are not limited by national borders but are, in fact, transnational. Studies of transnationalism have been conceptualized as political examinations of movement and mobility, recognizing that power and privilege are embedded in the ability to cross national borders and geographic lines. Identifying who has access to global movement and mobility (through people, goods, and ideas) frequently points to who has access to economic wealth and political capital. The transnational factors influencing relationships between African Americans and Jamaicans are also salient. The GFT members participate in various forms of movement, but their movement is different from that of the communities usually studied under the rubric of transnational studies. The chapters that follow describe the women's various methods of mobility, explain why these movements seem necessary to these tourists, and describe how their identities as Black American women affect the methods they use to become virtually, physically, and economically mobile. Their movements across national borders, and the new networks of friends and family that this mobility enables, drastically change how these women think of themselves as racialized and diasporic subjects. Their experience highlights specific ways that transnational forces complicate the formation and maintenance of imagined communities.

The Pursuit of Happiness focuses on both virtual and real-time communities in which the connections between race, gender, affect, and transnationalism are critical. Because Black women's lives demonstrate the dynamism of race and gender and speak to issues of power and privilege, their experiences are crucially important for understanding the tensions and exchanges that emerge in this transnational, increasingly globalized world. However, the experiences and narratives of Black women, particularly Black American women, are scarce in transnational studies.[7] Moreover, scholars and journalists who do address the lives of Black American women often limit their analyses and representations in three ways: (1) they present narratives that constrain these women's experiences to the national borders of the United States, neglecting to understand how their lives are influenced by transnational processes and various forms of mobility; (2) they discount the differently racialized and gendered experiences Black women have when engaging these transnational processes; and (3) they frequently offer a one-dimensional view of these women's struggles within spaces of institutional and social oppression, presenting them simply as sad, depressed women without also engaging their desires and ability to experience pleasure, leisure, and happiness.

This lack of attention to Black women's narratives and experiences is not unique to transnational studies. While there has been an explosion of affect studies that highlight affect's social and political dimensions, few of these studies theorize the ways that affect is also racial. But for those racialized as Black in the United States, the ways that affect is lived, experienced, and politicized are inextricable from its raciality. Black feminist scholars such as Faye V. Harrison, Patricia Hill Collins, Deborah Gray White, and Beverly Guy Sheftall have long argued that if we examine lived experiences and politics without engaging a racialized analysis, we miss critical dimensions of how power works. As just one example, public health studies describe how Black health is affected by microaggressions; this literature also links experiences of race and racism to high blood pressure, stress-induced diseases, and unhealthy coping mechanisms. Being seen as "different" or being discriminated against because of race can generate emotions that become profoundly significant not only to physical health but also to one's understanding of self and sense of belonging. Emotions are not limited to personal histories and individual anecdotes; they also bring otherwise abstract ideas of oppression and discrimination into stark relief for individual actors. Because of this, emotions are an excellent source of information about how intersectional oppressions become reified. To not insert race into the story of affect is to leave out a critical dimension necessary to an adequate understanding of how affect works, and to neglect the paramount role race plays for those who are racialized as Black in the United States. Additionally, to equate Blackness with masculinity or to assume that Black men's experiences are the same as Black women's experiences is to ignore the significance of gender in their everyday lives.

Critical race studies, diaspora studies, and gender studies have all made important contributions to the project of theorizing racialized and gendered subjectivities, but these studies frequently remain delinked and relegated to theoretical silos. Black feminist thought, by contrast, enables a better understanding of the links between emotion and transnationalism due to its emphasis on narrative, lived experience, and emotion as ultimate sites of meaning-making and empowerment. Black feminist thought anchors my examination of how processes of racialization and gendering are central to Black American women's lives, including their pursuits of happiness. I identify the methods Black women use to pursue happiness and emotional wellness in the context of American racism and sexism, and I show how the transnational is central to their pursuits of happiness.

This book lays out how the emotional journeys of Black women lead them to momentarily leave the spaces that many argue should make them happy—their families, their homes in their native country, and their jobs. What about these women's lives as Black women pushes them to repeatedly leave the "land of opportunity" to pursue happiness? What happens when Black American women begin to look beyond their nation's borders for happiness and fulfillment? More broadly, what can these tourist women's emotional journeys and participation in affective transactions tell us about race and gender in the contemporary moment of globalization and transnationalism?

Escaping John Henryism and Sojourner Syndrome: Research Motivations and Intersectionality

The African American women of Girlfriend Tours International employed multiple strategies to pursue happiness both at home and abroad. At home, they often addressed their social conditions by requesting that their government and their families make changes that would help them fulfill their pursuits of happiness. But they didn't stop there. These women (mostly of the civil rights generation) constructed a "do-something," action-oriented attitude toward fulfilling their pursuits. Their trips to Jamaica were an attempt to take advantage of their mobility and expand their lives in the United States. Over the course of my research, I came to recognize that neither the negative media images of Black women nor the women's own apparent joyfulness fully captured the reality of Girlfriends' lives. Instead, their lives were complex and sometimes full of contradictions, so it was necessary to adopt a both/and approach to understanding their life experiences and emotional expressions. There were moments when they encountered financial hardships and cried about feeling lonely. *And* they also experienced profound joy and pleasure, particularly when they could virtually or physically access Jamaica. I wanted to show their full selves, flaws and all, to emphasize their humanity as Black women.

As I began my research, I could not help but see these women's transnational pursuit of happiness as a strategy for escaping the threat of what public health researcher and epidemiologist Sherman James coined "John Henryism." According to legend, steel-driver John Henry died after winning a hammering race against a steam-powered hammer while building a railroad tunnel. To prove his worthiness, Henry essentially worked himself to death. In the 1970s, James used the term "John Henryism" to describe the behavior and strategies African Americans use to cope with long-term, psychosocial stressors they experience, such as social discrimination.[8] In a similar vein, anthropologist Leith Mullings offers the "Sojourner Syndrome" (named after Sojourner Truth) as an intersectional framework that addresses race, class, and gender as relational concepts and acknowledges the survival strategies African American women use to circumvent, resist, and work through racism, classism, and sexism.[9] In her article "Resistance and Resilience: The Sojourner Syndrome and the Social Context of Reproduction in Central Harlem," Mullings discusses the burdens that are associated with the prevalent "class exploitation, racial discrimination, and gender subordination" in the lives of the Black women in Harlem she observed. She argues that this framework encourages researchers to see the ways "race mediates both gender and class status" by recognizing, first, that "the consequences of race and gender—of being a Black woman—contribute to the instability of class status" and, second, that "race dilutes the protections of class."[10]

Mullings persuasively delineates how race acts as a mechanism for these gendered and classed experiences, stating,

> Middle-stratum Black women may have attained the achievements necessary for middle-class status, but they continue to suffer job and occupational discrimination; they are less likely to marry and more likely to become single heads of households because of the shortage of "mar-

riageable men," as a consequence of disproportionate unemployment and the prison-industrial complex. For middle-class women in the study who moved to a Black community to avoid racism, their class advantage was diluted by the structural discrimination and neglect to which Black communities are subject. All these factors have the potential to become sources of stress and chronic strain.[11]

In the same way that Black women in Harlem create strategies for resisting and working through the racialized, gendered, and classed systems of discrimination and disempowerment they confront daily, the women of GFT use their trips to Jamaica to lay down similar burdens. Instead of, or in addition to, moving to a Black community in the United States to avoid experiencing racism regularly, Girlfriends travel internationally to a predominantly Black country where they feel that their presence among a diasporic critical mass will protect them (even momentarily) from the tentacles of American racism, sexism, and ageism. While none of the GFT members I interviewed discussed John Henryism or Sojourner Syndrome by name, it was clear they were aware that Black Americans, particularly Black women, often worked themselves to death, not taking time to rejuvenate and restore the emotional resources necessary for physical and emotional wellness.

The physical, emotional, and spiritual struggles Black women have encountered throughout U.S. history are in some ways intergenerational and transhistorical; the generations that follow often feel the impact of the pain and struggle of those before them and frequently suffer at the hands of similar structural oppressions. However, the strategies Black women have used to experience happiness, intimacy, laughter—tools for rehumanizing yourself when the world states you do not deserve access to these experiences—are rarely discussed publicly. Instead of becoming their own versions of John Henry, these women prioritized leisure and relaxation, recognizing that all the labor they did at home (for their families and communities) came at an emotional cost. In this way, traveling to Jamaica was an attempt by Girlfriends to put on the proverbial airplane mask before they had to provide physical and emotional labor to the people and institutions that demanded it at home.

In line with Girlfriends' prioritization of happiness, Gina Dent theorizes pleasure and joy, emphasizing the ways that affect and emotions are always political and can be used as oppositional tools. She writes in her introduction to the *Black Popular Culture* reader that "pleasure under commodified conditions, tends to be inward. You take it with you, and it's a highly individualized unit.... But joy tries to cut across that. Joy tries to get at those non-market values—love, care, kindness, service, solidarity, the struggle for justice—values that provide the possibility of bringing people together."[12] In many ways the Girlfriends' trips to Jamaica demonstrate Dent's argument here—they seek individual pleasure and access to sexual autonomy in this foreign space, yet they often travel as a group so they can experience the joy and happiness that comes with the possibilities of bringing Black women together and potentially joining other diasporic kin. Dent continues,

> To extend the discussion of pleasure and joy into a black context is to shift back and forth continually between the political and ethical registers. It is to shift between the material domain in which our identities are constructed for us and where we play them out, and that "other side" where we play with the many possibilities of identification, where we possess the secret of joy.[13]

The women of GFT provided me with insight into the transnational coping strategies Black women use for dealing with American racism and sexism. As a result, I have grown ever more committed to studying the intersectionality of Black women's lives. Ethnography that focuses on Black women's lives can offer crucial information about the links between the affective and material dimensions of race, class, gender, sexuality, and age. These intersecting factors influence women's expectations of how and where they might satisfactorily be recognized as valuable human beings, viewed as community members, and find belonging. In this study, an intersectional approach illuminated the ways that the Girlfriends' yearning for diasporic belonging factored into their participation in emotional transnationalism. American realities led these Black women to travel to Jamaica and imagine that its people and its land would provide not only an escape but also, more importantly, a community of belonging. Their diasporic dreams were the fuel of their imagined community.

As these middle-aged African American women grew increasingly frustrated with feeling devalued and worthless because of their racialized, gendered, and generational social positions in the United States, they sought refuge in the comforts their American dollars could buy in Jamaica, including the companionship of a (sometimes) younger, Jamaican man or the comfort of a peaceful suite in a well-staffed hotel. By transforming themselves into internationally mobile African American women with access to (sometimes symbolic) economic status and social privilege in Jamaica, Girlfriends leveraged the African (read: "Black") and American parts of their identities to make the best of both worlds. Both their trips to Jamaica and their access to new forms of sociality through virtual experience served as strategies for critiquing and responding to the ageist, racist, and sexist discourses that marginalize them within the United States.

Stella and the Informal Industry of Romance Tourism in Jamaica

Frequently, when I present my research at conferences or tell people in conversations that I study Black women and happiness, they give me a puzzled look, as if these concepts are an oxymoron. Once we get to the role Jamaica plays in my research, the book/film *How Stella Got Her Groove Back* inevitably comes up.[14] In much of the popular discourse and scholarly world, it seems that traveling to the Caribbean as a woman has become synonymous with sex, romance tourism, and the search for a young Jamaican (male) lover. While Jamaican beaches, food, and music are cultural products the Jamaica Tourist Board uses to draw millions of travelers to their country annually, the informal industry of sex, romance, and intimacy for sale or gift exchange has become ever more popular. In other Caribbean and Latin American countries, such as Brazil, the Bahamas, and the Dominican Republic, it is common for residents and visitors to openly engage in transnational sexual exchanges. In these locations, men of a variety of races from the United States and Europe are usually the consumers of sex tourism, while women are the workers. In Jamaica, however, narratives of intimacy, seduction, and desire are central to the informal economy of romantic relationships, where sex may or may not take place. Women from the United States, Canada, and Europe are commonly seen as the consumers here, with Jamaican men providing much of the sexual and emotional labor. Here, the explicit exchange of money for intimacy, romance, or sex is frowned upon, although all involved and observing the practices recognize that money (or gifts in place of actual currency) eventually changes hands. While white European, Canadian, and American women have been participating in this industry in Jamaica for generations, the narrative of *Stella* is frequently cited as the cause for Black American women, particularly African American women, to make the exodus to Jamaica in search of romance, love, and happiness.

In *How Stella Got Her Groove Back*, Terry McMillan tells the story of Stella Payne, a divorced, forty-year-old African American businesswoman and mother who is encouraged by her girlfriends to take a vacation to Jamaica to relax, loosen up, and remember her life's purpose. Early in her trip, Stella meets Winston Shakespeare, a twenty-year-old Jamaican man, who romances her into letting go of her fears and falling in love with him. The book and resulting film depict Stella and Winston's fantastical love affair, with Jamaica's landscape, food, and music as background characters. Delilah Abraham, Stella's best friend who accompanies her on the trip, both encourages and calms her as Stella worries about the potential complexities of this relationship with a younger man. At a touching part of the story, Stella meets Delilah on her deathbed before cancer takes her away, and Delilah reminds her that life is short and she needs to live it to the fullest. Stella takes this warning seriously and reconsiders her decision not to pursue her relationship with Winston because of the various (gendered, aged, and nationalized) differences in their relationship. At another point in the narrative, Stella meets Winston's well-established Jamaican parents. His mother does not hide her disdain for the relationship, exclaiming that Stella should be ashamed of herself and that she will destroy Winston's dreams of becoming a doctor. Quincy, Stella's son, also expresses some concern about the relationship, worried that the young Jamaican man will break her heart. By the end of the film, Winston comes to the United States to support Stella during Delilah's wake, and the filmmaker offers the promise of their relationship carrying forward.

Since *Stella*'s film release in 1998, droves of Black American women have found their way to Jamaica to get their groove on and back, in dancehalls and on beaches. However, I knew from my time with Girlfriends that their travels were more complicated than a simple reenactment of *Stella*. Nevertheless, the specter of sex and romance tourism haunts this text and their happiness pursuits, as *Stella* and its cultural meanings were both embraced and challenged by Girlfriends. While no one ultimately confessed that finding their Jamaican soulmate was the impetus for their trips, neither could any deny the profound influence Terry McMillan's love story had on their imagining of Jamaica and its significance to them as Black women. Stella's narrative of finding love, girlfriendship, and an agentive sense of self inspired Girlfriends and gave them the courage and permission to go out and pursue different aspects of it for themselves.

An Introduction to the Field Sites and Methods

At its core, *The Pursuit of Happiness* is about a group of lower-middle-class African American women who use the Internet and tourism as methods for finding love, happiness, and girlfriendship across transnational lines and within the context of diasporic diversity. Acknowledging that racialized subjectivities are always simultaneously gendered, classed, and nationalized, I examine the construction of racial and gendered subjectivities within an imagined diasporic community. I focus on the ways Girlfriends work through the complex webs of meaning and experience that constitute Blackness(es). Additionally, I describe how these women individually and collectively explore racialized, gendered, and nationalized difference in Internet-based and real-world diasporic "contact zones." Instead of simply conceptualizing race as a dichotomous relationship between Blackness and whiteness and gender as a binary between masculinity and femininity, this book explores the complexity of racial and gendered subjectivities as they are constructed in a context where different Blacknesses and cross-gender relations are placed at the forefront.

Ethnographically, I addressed these questions and explored the transnational lives of the African American women of Girlfriend Tours International by observing and participating in group activities, conducting interviews, and analyzing online postings. My ethnographic research with members of GFT began in their virtual community in March 2003 and continued until September 2007, for a total of fifty-four months. I completed my research in multiple cities in Jamaica and the United States during the summers of 2003 and 2004 and throughout 2005–2007, for a total of twenty-two months of regional ethnographic research.

My four years of virtual fieldwork took place in the online web board at www.Jamaicans.com, a site many GFT members engaged with before, after, and during their trips to Jamaica. The Pan-African colors of red, green, and gold appeared all over Jamaicans.com, emphasizing Jamaica's prominence in the community, but also establishing a connection to the entire African diaspora. The online web community frequently acted as a driving force behind the trips of those associated with Girlfriend Tours. Claiming that they are "Out of Many, One People Online," Jamaicans.com members rearticulate Jamaica's national motto as a transnational credo, exhibiting one of the intriguing ways people use technology to reconfigure notions of nationhood and their subject positions within these global communities. Xavier Murphy, a Jamaican who wanted to increase communication between Jamaican diasporic peoples and international tourists, created Jamaicans.com in 1995. Murphy laid the foundation for a virtual community that now includes more than fifteen thousand people from countries all over the globe, including the United States, Poland, Sweden, Australia, the United Kingdom, and, of course, Jamaica.

In the website's twenty-nine discussion forums, conversations about cooking Jamaican food, speaking Jamaican patois, and parenting the "Jamaican" way take place twenty-four hours a day. Interested parties visit the site to receive information about current events in Jamaica and comment on political and economic issues by posting original articles, participating in online forum discussions, and sending private member-to-member messages. This book focuses on a small subsection of the website—the tourist travel forums—where predominantly American and women web-board members called "boardites" ask questions about accommodations and concerts on the island, make contact with Jamaican entrepreneurs, publish reports of their own leisure and educational experiences in Jamaica, and discuss their obsession with Jamaican culture with other Jamaicaholics. The women of GFT and their networks of online friends, family members, and favorite Jamaican merchants are frequently at the center of discussions in the tourist travel forums. The friendships and adversarial relationships formed between these American Girlfriends and Jamaicans throw into relief assumptions about race, class, gender, and nationality and influence the formation of relationships offline.

I initially found the Jamaicans.com website in March 2003 as I was making travel arrangements for an upcoming research trip to Jamaica during the summer. While sifting through at least thirty websites promoting dancehall concerts and festivals in the Caribbean, I finally came across a website that seemed to answer almost every question I had as a first-time visitor to the country. With a click of my mouse, I walked directly into the trip reports forum, where I virtually traveled to Jamaica vis-à-vis the words of recent visitors. In the travel forums, particularly in the Trip Reports section, these organic ethnographers provided detailed descriptions of the events that took place during their travel adventures, including the people they met, their activities, and the restaurants, beaches, and other places they visited.

The authors often posted colorful photographs to complement their storytelling, providing a more vivid experience of Jamaica for their readers. The photos also lent authenticity to their narratives, a way to state clearly "I was there." From the moment I began to read these trip reports by tourists from various parts of the United States and other countries, I could not help but notice how ethnographic these "field notes" seemed to be. Most of the boardites were not run-of-the-mill tourists—these authors seemed to have a vested interest in understanding what their trips to the island meant for Jamaican people and the Jamaican economy and in publicly reflecting on the profound effect Jamaica had on them as tourists and visitors. For the next three days I spent countless hours on the website, meeting new tourists, veteran visitors, and people who had never visited Jamaica but hoped to make the journey one day. While I devoted some of my time to getting recommendations for places to stay and eat during my upcoming trip, I spent most of my time learning about the various online networks of friends, enemies, and "frenemies" present on Jamaicans.com. One of the most prominent cliques in the virtual community seemed to be the U.S.-based network of Girlfriends.

It was the trip report of Jacqueline, celebrity Girlfriend and unofficial Queen

Jamaicaholic, that piqued my interest and compelled me to attend my first *bashment* (a Jamaican word for "party") in Negril in the summer of 2003. She held a captive audience with a trip report in which she described her love affair with Jamaica and her long-term boyfriend and reported on the comings and goings of everyone from fishermen to schoolchildren she had befriended. Jamaicans, Americans, and other international residents offered comments and critiques of her story, making her trip report and its accompanying commentary one of the longest in the Jamaicans.com archive at over three hundred pages long.

While reading Jacqueline's trip report, I realized that these online conversations about race, national belonging, and diasporic (dis)connections were very similar to the discussions scholars were having about these topics within the academy. Moreover, because these Jamaicans.com members and Girlfriends often expected to meet their virtual neighbors at annual bashments and possibly become real-life friends with their interlocutors, these trip reports and discussion forums drew my attention to the ways people integrate their online and offline worlds, as well as to when and how they police racial and cultural boundaries in both spaces. Jacqueline and I became close during this research, and since she was at the center of many of the community relationships in both the virtual and physical Jamaica, she became a central node in my recruitment practices for research participants. Throughout this book, I present the stories Jacqueline and other African American Girlfriends shared with me in order to explore how their American realities led them to pursue happiness, love, and diasporic connectivity in Jamaica.

Throughout my virtual research, I focused on observing and documenting how racialized subjectivities were transformed and diasporic relations maintained as members of GFT created their social networks. Employing a multisited methodology enabled me to observe how processes of racialization, gender-making, and diasporic relationship-building work differently in various geographical locations and virtual sites. By participating in this virtual world, I was able to understand more fully the transnational methods these women used to pursue happiness across national borders. I began my virtual ethnographic research among board members in the Jamaicans.com community by participating in private messaging conversations and forum discussions with boardites while tracking their online postings. For the next four and a half years, I saved each thread I came across that had a discussion related to the politics of race, tourism, or diaspora, creating a profile for each of my interlocutors. I created a hard copy and a digital archive of the most popular trip reports, because the web moderators sporadically deleted these since the website's archive filled up quickly. By the end of my fieldwork, I had at least fourteen large three-ring binders, and numerous PDF files on my laptop, all filled with the stories of love, happiness, success, sadness, death, and depression the ladies of GFT had generated and coauthored with their Jamaicans.com neighbors.

During the international phase of the research, I was based in Negril and Ocho Rios, the two cities Girlfriends and other boardites frequent the most. I attended four GFT-organized trips to Jamaica. Two of these trips were official annual tours to Negril, while another was to Ocho Rios. The fourth trip was an unofficial tour, part of a trip to Negril that the founders planned for a veteran Girlfriend and her coworkers. In the summer of 2007, I accompanied members of GFT on an around-the-island tour with stops in Treasure Beach, Kingston, and Mandeville. The U.S. phase of my research was conducted in cities such as Atlanta, Washington, DC, Memphis, and Fort Lauderdale, where many of the Girlfriends and other boardites reside.

In Jamaica, I accompanied Girlfriends while they visited with friends and family, attended music festivals with other web-board members, and volunteered at schools and orphanages. Jamaicans.com members also had "reunions" in Jamaica, where those who virtually engaged one another in the web community could meet each other in person for the first time or reconnect after previously meeting. While attending the website members' annual reunions, I made contact with at least one hundred boardites, engaged in the weeklong series of organized activities, accompanied them to Sumfest and Sunsplash music festivals, and became acquainted with around forty of their Jamaican friends.

It was during my first trip that I apprehended the important role the Internet played in mediating the creation and maintenance of relationships within this community. I noticed that these opportunities to physically connect with virtual neighbors in real time were as significant as the conversations that took place behind cyber firewalls. In fact, the possibility of seeing neighbors in the future seemed to fuel the relationships constructed within the virtual community. Boardites often began friendships by communicating through online posts; then progressed to private member-to-member messaging, phone calls, and e-mails; and then finally made arrangements to meet face-to-face in the United States or at a bashment in Jamaica. When meeting in person, boardites were often surprised when friends did not fit their preconceived images, which were based on virtual interactions. These moments of "identity crisis"—when the race, gender, or age of the individual befriended in the online community differed from what the person expected—generated new questions regarding visuality and its potential to change the contours of friendship and intimacy between boardites and their virtual neighbors.

After a couple of trips, I realized that these reunions served multiple purposes, including (1) giving members the opportunity to forge relationships with virtual neighbors while simultaneously taking a vacation to enjoy the country they love, and (2) providing a way to "give back" to Jamaica through the revenue these reunions generated for local merchants, the donations they brought from the United States, and the service-oriented activities they completed. During many of these conversations and interactions, I observed how Jamaicans and web-board members encouraged Americans to analyze their nationalized and racialized privileged positions.

After my first Jamaicans.com reunion in 2003, I continued to attend the reunions every year until 2007. From 2004 until the end of my research, I also visited Jamaica as a member of GFT's annual tour. Ultimately, I concentrated my study on this subset of Jamaicans.com board members. Although not every participant of GFT was a member of Jamaicans.com, many times these member-ships did overlap. Sometimes Girlfriends would decide to join the online com-munity after their summer trip ended so they could continue their Jamaican experiences virtually and stay connected with Girlfriends with whom they had bonded. Founded by two African American women, Marilyn and Angie, who had met through Jamaicans.com, GFT was a group of mostly Black American women who traveled to the country annually in search of sisterhood (among themselves and with Jamaican women) and enjoyed group vacations designed to promote bonding experiences among women. During these trips, I learned the social geography of the tourist industry in Negril and Ocho Rios, infor-mally interviewed the Jamaicans.com website's creator, and gathered informa-tion, which sometimes included gossip about social and intimate relationships between boardites that were not discussed in the public arena of the Internet.

I wanted to understand how visits to Jamaica and participation in this Jamaica-based website affected how members constructed and maintained community within and across national and racialized boundaries. To this end, I paid particular attention to the cultivation of friends or lovers on the island; changes in website participation (i.e., moving from "visitor" status to a board "citizen" with increased participation); face-to-face interactions with other boardites through intra- and interstate travel; increased attention to U.S. for-eign policy, especially immigration and international travel regulations related to Jamaica; and attempts to "bring Jamaica home" by cooking Jamaican food, speaking patois, and participating in social or political events in Caribbean communities in the United States.

This ethnographic research of emotional transnationalism usually took one of two forms. In the first scenario, in which the anthropologist follows the in-dividual, I would travel to meet up with Girlfriends and boardites and engage in activities that were on their itineraries. Either I would travel to Jamaica to join them on their visits (ranging from one to six weeks) and then leave the country to accompany them to their hometowns, or I would travel directly to their hometowns for a two- or three-day visit, gathering data for the domestic part of the project that analyzed race in the United States. This "following the individual" method allowed me to observe how members' views of Jamaica and themselves changed as time progressed and as they moved between locations. At other times, when participants were not vacationing in Jamaica, I resided in Jamaica for one to three months alone, interviewing and observing their Jamaican friends and companions, the hotel staff, taxi drivers, and businesspeople with whom they had interacted during their visits.

Occasionally, participants would have an interest in my activities in Jamaica, and they would either pay me a surprise visit or ask to reside with me for a short time. During these occasions, the ladies often shared an apartment with me in Jamaica for a period of one to eight weeks and took part in a semistructured method of "following the anthropologist." In response to frequent requests that I take them to the spots where I "did my work," I would enlist them to help me in several activities, including completing my daily observations of cruise-ship tourists at Margaritaville in Ocho Rios and actively recruiting people for me to interview at taxi parks, car washes, or local bars. This process of "following the anthropologist" pushed me to question how the research participants perceived me as a young, Black American woman anthropologist and to become aware of how and what they conceptualized as ethnographic work.

I also used formal and informal individual interviews to collect narratives of racially and nationally "marked" experiences from American participants. This international phase included twenty recorded interviews, two to four hours long, with several of the virtual community's web moderators and members (particularly Girlfriends) while in Jamaica. In these interviews, I asked participants to discuss their perceptions of Jamaica, their relationships and networks on the island, and the role Jamaicans.com played during their visits. I supplemented these accounts with interviews with Jamaican mates and spouses of boardites, hotel entertainment coordinators, restaurant owners, and local vendors about their experiences with American tourists, enabling an analysis of these transactions and interactions from other perspectives.

The domestic phase of interviewing focused on boardites' experiences as racialized and gendered subjects in the United States and the role the website played in their lives at home. While providing life histories that explicitly discussed how interviewees "came to be" racialized or participated in racializing others, members also compared "home" experiences of race, class, gender, and nationality with their experiences in Jamaica. For example, I asked these African American women to describe and define "Blackness," to state whether they identified as Black, and to explain what this racial identity meant to them. Other questions included the following: "Do you see yourself as a part of the African diaspora? Have you ever felt included/excluded or powerless/privileged because of your Blackness? How do you experience your Blackness differently in Jamaica than in the U.S.?" I completed interviews with friends and family of the interviewees to get a sense of how they felt about their loved ones' trips to Jamaica and how this travel affected their relationships. In total, I conducted forty-eight individual interviews. These transcribed interviews provided additional ethnographic data for an analysis of emotional transnationalism. In particular, they helped me understand how the Girlfriends' racial and diasporic experiences were similar and different when they were in direct contact with Jamaicans in Jamaica versus when they were separated by physical distance yet connected via the website.

After participating in several Jamaicans.com reunions in the United States and Jamaica, observing and participating in interactions between these travelers and their Jamaican interlocutors, and interviewing Girlfriends at home and during their vacations, I concluded that African Americans experience a new sense of themselves during these virtual and travel interactions. Some come to realize that similarities of skin color and a shared history of the transatlantic slave trade may not mean that Jamaicans experience life, or their Blackness, in the same ways. Many Jamaicans, online and on the island, repeatedly made Girlfriends aware of the ways their "American" identity, and the perceived economic, social, and political status attached to their nationality, placed them in drastically different racialized and classed positions. Jamaicans they interacted with often reminded them that while they may all be "Black," American Blackness was drastically different and made the travelers more privileged. It was in these moments that the concept of diaspora became an explicit part of the conversation around racialized and national difference. That is to say, although several members of Jamaicans.com and GFT were not of African descent, many of the African American and Jamaican participants did see the website and the country as diasporic spaces where racialized boundaries were problematized and modified and diasporic (dis)connections were continuously discussed. These cross-national, sometimes interracial interactions enabled African American women to explain in virtual and real-world settings the logic that undergirds the stereotypes, assumptions, and meanings associated with various aspects of racial identities.

Here, I must point to an important limitation of this study: While this book investigates the connections between race, gender, and affect within diasporic relationships, it is centered on the perspectives of the African American women of GFT. The multisitedness of the project enabled me to meet and speak with people from a variety of backgrounds and experiences in the United States and Jamaica. However, I chose to follow the journey of one group throughout multiple cities and virtual spaces to get a fuller view of their participation in emotional transnationalism. In a way, I switched ethnographic foci for this study. In contrast to traditional ethnography, in which the anthropologist stays embedded in one location for a long period of time and creates deep relationships with numerous people in that community, I chose to embed myself in this community, following them through their multisited, transnational journey. I cultivated deep relationships with them and those they came into contact with as they physically and virtually traveled. Readers will hear Jamaican and Jamaican American voices in this book, speaking to and speaking back on what is happening in this imagined community with GFT. I interviewed, observed, and connected with over fifty Jamaican men and women who interacted with GFT members. I asked them about their interactions with Girlfriends, their own experiences in the tourism industry, their perceptions of Americans in Jamaica more broadly, and the differences they saw between Jamaicans and Americans. Jamaican women were less present in these tourist spaces, less excited about befriending American tourist women for a host of reasons that I discuss in chapter 4, and less represented in the friendships GFT members initiated in Jamaica, therefore, they are not as present in this book.[15]

I decided to make the African American members of Girlfriend Tours the anchors in this research. In some ways this reinscribes the privileges and hegemony associated with African Americanness that Jamaicans spoke to in my interviews with them, and I bring attention to these politics of visibility elsewhere. I recognize that one must ask then for whom this community is imagined and whether all members imagine it and mobilize it in similar ways. It becomes clear throughout the book, especially in chapter 2, that Jamaicans and African Americans experience African diasporic connections differently. I also acknowledge that because of the different ways race and gender may operate in Jamaica, and how Black Americans and "Black" Jamaicans have differential access to power and mobility, Jamaicans may have different strategies for maintaining emotional wellness than their American counterparts do. Therefore, I admit that much of this book uses the experiences of the African American women in GFT as a starting point for the discussion about diasporic community, and this focus has undoubtedly influenced my analysis and the conclusions I draw about this imagined community. Nevertheless, one of my main goals in completing this research was to bring to the forefront the experiences and voices of Black American women, who are themselves oftentimes silenced, overlooked, and made invisible. I do my best to address the politics of multiple groups' invisibility and silence throughout the book.

Analyzing the experiences and life histories of Girlfriends provides some insight on the following questions: (1) Under which circumstances do these women interrogate the attributes and experiences that constitute "Blackness" and "Americanness," and how might their travels and interactions with racialized and nationalized "Others" on- and offline encourage reflexivity about their own participation and positionality within the African diaspora? (2) How do these older Black American women use their access to international travel and the Internet as resources for critiquing their marginalized subject positions within the United States, while simultaneously employing the social privilege and economic capital attached to their American identities? (3) How do these privileges associated with being American situate African Americans as privileged outcasts in the African diasporic imaginary? What does this mean for African American pursuits of happiness and the experience of emotions transnationally? Ultimately, *The Pursuit of Happiness* is about emotional transnationalism and the construction of affect across diasporic difference. I bring together the literature on transnationalism, Black feminism, and diaspora to explain how the Girlfriends cultivate a sense of belonging and pursue happiness while moving across virtual and national boundaries. I complicate the narratives around Black women's affective experiences by exploring how the tears they shed on that cliff in Jamaica were entangled with transnational and diasporic processes that influence not only this group's pursuit of happiness but also the ways we all search for community and belonging.

And now we'll get back to the collective tears.

"Come, Bianca. Come sit next to me."

The details of that bright, sunny day in June 2003 are a little hazy, because I didn't go into it thinking that it would be significant. My grandmother had been sick ever since I was a little girl, diagnosed with diabetes and plagued with the many ailments that often accompany this disease, including cataracts and kidney failure. As years went by, and the benefits of her weekly dialysis began to wane, I became somewhat accustomed to her frequent hospital stays. Although each time she regained her strength, the fight with diabetes left her a little weaker, and the signs of the toll began to show on her face, in her shaking hands, and in her decreasing eyesight. But she had bounced back from the struggle every time, and I didn't expect this time to be any different.

I hate hospitals; I guess most people do. I hate the oppressive smell of disinfectants, the sterile, cold hallways, the look of agony patients have as their bodies twist in pain, and the overwhelming feeling that Death is right around the corner. However, I was in New York for a quick visit and decided to entertain my grandmother for a while before heading to Jamaica for a fieldwork trip. As usual, she turned the tables around and entertained me. I remember her joking about the woman in the bed across from her passing away that morning ("I woke up, and she had CROAKED!"), filling me in on the latest plot twists in her favorite soap operas, and complaining about the horrible food she was being served by hospital attendants. Although she looked a little tired and had quite a few black-and-blue bruises from the needles the nurses kept poking her with, my grandmother was in high spirits. She felt so fine, in fact, that she had resumed her favorite pastimes of worrying and lecturing me about my life.

She made a little room for me on her hospital bed, and I sat down with a sigh. At once, my grandmother began bombarding me with a litany of questions about my upcoming trip. "You're going by yourself? Which part are you going to? How long are you going to be there? Do you have enough money?"

"Grandma, I'll be fine. I know how to take care of myself," I replied in a voice tinged with exasperation.

Other than a very brief cruise, this was going to be my first time outside of the United States. I was traveling solo to Jamaica, the place of my grandmother's and mother's births, to begin preliminary research for a project on tourists and the consumption of Blackness at reggae festivals. I was excited, but I could tell from her many questions that my grandmother's mind was busy with worry. She knew I was a graduate student with very little money, but what really seemed to bug her was the idea that I was traveling by myself. "A *woman* traveling alone?" Something about that did not sit well with her, and she was not afraid to make her opinion known.

I tried to ease her mind by giving her as many details about the trip as I could, but I was also slightly annoyed and impatient, the way young people often are with their elders. I thought her warnings and worries were a bit ridiculous, especially since I was only going to be gone for two weeks. And of course I didn't appreciate her perpetuating the sexist idea that women couldn't travel on their own.

At the time, I didn't realize that behind the "ridiculousness," my grandmother was trying to share with me lessons she had learned as a woman growing up on an island that she both loved and hated. For her, Jamaica was full of memories of hard times, including poverty, abuse at the hands of men, and terrible acts of hatred by other women in her family. Although there was definitely a haunting silence surrounding my grandmother's life as a young woman in Jamaica, I also grew up understanding that it was the place she saw as her home. Throughout my childhood I remember her sporadically sharing pleasurable memories of her life there, especially when good fruit would make her suck her teeth from its sweetness, or some old-school reggae vibes would make her body groove with happiness. My grandmother loved Jamaica and seemed sad that her health wouldn't allow her to go back as often as she would've liked. Reflecting on that day in the hospital, I now see that my grandmother was proud that I was finally going "home" but also a little worried about what I might find, and what might find me. She was worried for my safety, a little apprehensive about her granddaughter being grown enough to travel the world by herself, and possibly afraid that the hardships that made her leave her beloved home would somehow find me two generations later.

"How are you going to get around the island?" she asked.

"I don't know. I'll probably walk or take a taxi. Don't worry, Grandma. I'll figure it out."

Her wrinkled hands grabbed mine and slowly rubbed my fingers. "Bianca, don't ride the bus. It's dangerous and you'll get mugged. You won't even know your money is gone. They're slick, ya know?"

"Okay, Grandma," I said and chuckled.

I stayed a little longer while she entertained me with stories about her adventures on the bus in Jamaica and reminded me to make some time to visit family members she hadn't seen in years. I finally gathered myself to leave.

"Bye, Grandma. I'll see you when I get back," I said. I bent to kiss her cheek and gave her a quick half-hug.

"Alright BB, be careful."

As I walked toward the door, she yelled after me, "And don't ride the bus!" I turned, shook my head at her, grinned, and waved goodbye. I didn't know that those would be the last words my grandmother would ever speak to me.

SOON AFTER THIS hospital visit with my grandmother, I left for my first trip to Jamaica. I spent ten days exploring the country my grandmother had such an ambiguous relationship with. As I interacted with Jamaican taxi drivers, tour guides, hotel workers, and merchants, I began to appreciate a little more her perspective on life. I understood why we often bumped heads—she was a Jamaican immigrant who loved the United States for the opportunities it provided her family, but she called another place "home." And I was a first-generation African American who did not understand why there were always barrels in our garage to send things to people that we never saw ("family," in her words). I did not fully comprehend the complexities of my grandmother's lived experience as a transnational subject. However, as I spent more time doing research and speaking to whomever would listen about my project in the United States and Jamaica, dozens of questions about my family's history plagued me: How did my grandmother feel as she left Jamaica? Why did it remain at the forefront of her mind, even though she had not been back in years? Were the dreams she had for success and prosperity in the United States ever fulfilled?

I received the phone call that my grandmother had passed away a few days before I was to return to the United States. As I held the phone, I could hear the crickets loudly announcing their presence over the silence that rung in the air. I felt such a great sense of loss—not only that my grandmother was no longer present on Earth, but also that a part of my family's history was gone forever. As I cut my trip short and jumped on the plane to New York for my grandmother's funeral, I realized that all the questions I had excitedly turned over in my head about who we were, where we came from, and what Jamaica was like when she was there would never be answered. The haunting silence surrounding Jamaica that I had felt as a child seemed to expand. It would stay with me forever because the one person who could answer my questions was now gone. I yearned for a history that was lost. And I felt guilty for not having tried to understand her better, for not having understood the strength it must have taken for her to do what she did for herself and our family. Now it seemed like Jamaica would always remain a place of both homecoming and loss, for I had gone "home" only to lose the crucial link that made it home.

My longing for answers to these questions is quite possibly part of the reason I was so intrigued by the women of Girlfriend Tours International and the boardites on Jamaicans.com during that first research trip. Although the Americans in this group and at the bashment were of various ages, socioeconomic backgrounds, regions of the United States, and racial groups, it seemed that we were all searching for something, and somehow Jamaica seemed to hold the answers. Although most of us were not born there, at times we felt like strangers in a place that felt like home. Over the next four years, I would spend countless hours with these individuals, listening to their life stories and documenting their travels between their three "homes"—the United States, Jamaica, and the Jamaicans.com web community. Simultaneously, tales from my own family's past would present themselves unexpectedly, making me feel as if I were engaging in a fortuitous pilgrimage "back" to my grandmother's home.

I

More Than a Groove
Pursuing Happiness as a Political Project

When W. E. B. Du Bois poignantly asked in his book *The Souls of Black Folk*, "How does it feel to be a problem?" he provided a useful starting point for interrogating Black Americans' lived experiences within the context of American racism.[1] I am sure he knew that there were a variety of answers to this question since Black Americans had suffered and survived amazingly diverse experiences of oppression by the time he wrote this question. Some could speak about what problemhood felt like in the sweltering cotton fields of the South, while others might have described how they were seen as problems in the grimy, stone-filled streets of the North. Photography documenting problemhood shows Black people hanging from trees like strange fruit, while Negro spirituals narrate the journey Black-people-seen-as-problems endured as they traveled on the Underground Railroad.

Using multiple genres in *Souls*, Du Bois does a brilliant job bringing the (white) reading audience behind the veil. He shares narratives (sometimes autobiographical) of living simultaneously as a Black person and an American in a country where many see Black folks as simply commodified, laboring bodies, savages to be saved and/or policed, while others who acknowledge Black peoples' humanity still deem it dangerous. Although Du Bois wrote this pivotal book over one hundred years ago, many of us find ourselves revisiting the text, interrogating how this perception of "Blackness" as a problem may or may not have changed since the book's publication. We continue to wonder whether the twoness Du Bois describes as "double-consciousness," the frequently in tension, conflicting notions of self one feels as a Black person and an American, may have changed with gains in access to political power, educational and job opportunities, and class mobility. The need to declare that #BlackLivesMatter in this moment would suggest that while some things have changed, others remain the same. Therefore, the narratives and theoretical tools Du Bois offers in this text are still useful for analyzing the racialized, social, and political experiences of Black peoples in the United States. However, each time I revisit the text, a voice in my head increasingly demands to know, "How does it feel to be a Black *woman* in the United States?"

Black feminist activists and women writers such as Anna Julia Cooper, Angela Davis, Paula Giddings, Deborah Gray White, Beverly Guy-Sheftall, and Barbara Smith have dedicated much of their time and life's labor contributing to Black women's studies and herstory, subsequently filling in the gendered gap in Du Bois's *Souls*.[2] Legal scholar and Black feminist Kimberlé Crenshaw coined the concept of "intersectionality," centering Black women's experiences in an effort to understand how multiple forms of oppressions intersect and work together to disempower and exclude.[3] Providing powerful descriptions of Black women's experiences, while persuading others to pay attention to what life at the intersection of racism(s) and sexism(s) looks and feels like, these scholars teach us about how power works. They make Black women visible, illuminating their positionalities in systems of oppression and helping us understand how elusive forces work to make power appear invisible. Here, I follow their lead, recognizing and making visible the range of emotional experiences and expressions Black women have while living within the context of racism and sexism. Given their intersectional lived experiences, Black women's emotional journeys are political, especially because they live in a nation that consistently fights to misrecognize or deny the fullness of their humanity.

Thus, this chapter asks, "How do racism and sexism influence Black American women's pursuits of happiness?" Here, I detail the numerous activities in the United States and Jamaica that members of Girlfriend Tours International engage in in order to demonstrate that for them, the pursuit of happiness is a process—one that is not without emotional labor and costs, and one where cultivating a sense of belonging is essential. In their travels to Jamaica to effectively become visible as Black American women, two of my primary research participants, Queen Jamaicaholic Jacqueline and fabulous GFT member Gayle, are at the center of this chapter. I present their stories as archetypes for the kind of experiences other Girlfriends shared. I focus primarily on their trips and experiences to decipher what their affective experiences tell us about the relationship between affect and the intersectionality of race and gender. How might we understand their pursuits of happiness as a process filled with "political" decisions, including how to represent one's self or how to find spaces of safety and comfort? What could we learn if we framed pursuits of happiness as political acts for Black women, or even as acts of resistance? How might we see the creation of affirming spaces, or "safe spaces," for Black women as one of these political acts? This chapter exposes the process behind Jacqueline's and Gayle's pursuits of happiness, showing that matters of emotion are social and political and are embedded in histories of racism and survival.

By describing the emotional roller coaster Girlfriends experience as they endure criticism for their "Jamaicaholism" and gain praise from Jamaican men, I draw attention to the affective costs and benefits of their visits, detailing how these women *feel* as they navigate the affective dimensions of power within their virtual and geographic communities.[4] I highlight the collective and processual aspects of their happiness, which shows the continuous sacrifice and effort they put into their pursuits. This, in addition to the complex web of emotions they feel while seeking diasporic connectivity with Jamaicans, complicates the one-dimensional view of these African American women as "Stellas" simply seeking to get their grooves back.

The Politics of (Mis)Recognition

Cultural studies theorist Stuart Hall spent his life writing about the politics of representation, particularly those in the media. Whereas some focus on whether media images are authentic or distorted representations, Hall pushes us to understand how all images are creative and active and, therefore, more productive than we frequently give them credit for. In many of his texts, Hall argues that images in media are powerful because they influence our understandings and imaginings of the world—who we are as a group of people, and how we interpret the events around us—and are connected to hegemonic discourses in each society.[5] Consequently, even when they do not lead us to the conclusions they were created to push us toward, images and representations are always linked to the ways power is operating in a culture, in a community, and in the government.

In her popular book, *Sister Citizen: Shame, Stereotypes, and Black Women in America*, political scientist Melissa Harris-Perry astutely describes the "crooked room," a concept that falls in line with Hall's explication of how the media and its images are productive.[6] Harris-Perry uses the term "crooked room" to highlight the multiple spaces and ways in which Black women negotiate the forces of misrecognition that influence how others see them and how they see themselves. As these women twist, turn, and bend, trying to align themselves with the stereotypical images U.S. society has of Black womanhood, they experience psychological and physiological forms of shame. While trying to pursue happiness, these Americans often struggle to access economic and political opportunities that would ensure physical and emotional wellness and safety. Because of American racism, most experience institutional obstacles on their journeys to experience happiness regularly. Their ability to freely experience joy, peace, leisure, intimacy, and recreation are hampered by American patriarchy and its burdensome gendered expectations.

Harris-Perry spends a significant portion of the book explaining how Black women (specifically those viewed as American citizens) are *structurally positioned* to experience racialized and gendered hardships in the United States that produce feelings of shame. She writes,

> African American women are structurally positioned to experience shame more frequently than others. As a group they posses[s] a number of stigmatized identities and life circumstances: they are more likely to be poor, to be unmarried, to parent children alone, to be overweight, to be physically ill, and to be undereducated and underemployed. Black women who escape many of these circumstances must still contend with damaging racial and gender stereotypes. They are aware that others see them through a distorted lens that renders them socially unacceptable. This sense of social rejection and undesirability may express itself in experiences of chronic shame, with both psychological and physiological effects. . . . In this sense, shame is the psychological and physical effect of repeated acts of misrecognition.[7]

Here, Harris-Perry describes the difficult time African American women have being seen and recognized within the United States. She points to the economic, political, and emotional difficulties these women endure as American citizens, arguing that these experiences may lead to profound feelings of shame.

Throughout *Sister Citizen*, Harris-Perry demonstrates that Black women do not magically find themselves in positions of economic, social, and political disenfranchisement; these situations are created strategically, and sometimes intentionally, by institutions and oppressive processes in the United States. Second, even if Black American women find ways to overcome these obstacles, they must still negotiate a sense of triple-consciousness—an awareness that these racialized, gendered, and nationalized oppressions influence not only their access to various forms of power but also how they construct their understandings of self and how others read their identities. In fact, it seems that the misrecognition of Black women, their identities and their affective lives, is central to multiple U.S. projects of oppression. Consequently, pursuing happiness in the context of American racism and sexism can be difficult, particularly for African American women. Therefore, I use the transnational pursuits of happiness of the ladies of Girlfriend Tours International to argue that this process of pursuing happiness is a political project for Black women. It is a process that requires a sense of determination and strong dedication to self-definition in the face of the psychological warfare and emotional strife caused by social and institutionalized forms of inequity.

In this way, one can understand why the controlling images and representations of Black women as Jezebels, Sapphires, Mammies, and Strong Black Women are important to pay attention to. These narrow and destructive depictions of Black women's lives in mainstream media and academic scholarship are frequently driven by a lack of appreciation for the complexities of living as both a Black person and a woman at the intersection of American racism and patriarchy. When one connects this to the discussion of happiness, we begin to see how media representations, and systems of oppression that work through them, attempt to limit and influence the emotional expressions of Black women. Many consuming these media images do not even expect Black women to ever appear happy, as they are conditioned to see them as ashamed, angry, and sad. For some, Black women's anger is seen as a source of strength that keeps them safe and pushing through racism and sexism. Referring to the frequently depicted Angry Black Woman, Harris-Perry writes, "But this no-nonsense, take-no-prisoners woman offers no expectation that the black woman is supposed to be happy, content, or fulfilled. Her sometimes explosive anger is part of what distinguishes her from the ideal of white femininity. This right to own and express anger is among the more potentially powerful psychological and political elements of the construction of black women's strength."[8] For Girlfriends, Jamaica provides a space where they don't have to be angry and where their strength is seen and respected.

Furthermore, as Harris-Perry and others note, race and gender, or more specifically, racism and sexism, can drastically influence one's affective life, particularly one's emotional wellness. In *Ordinary Affects*, anthropologist Kathleen Stewart offers a provocative discussion about stress, claiming that it can "tell the story of inclusion or exclusion, mainstreaming or marginality. But its widespread power to articulate something stems not from a meaning it harbors inside but from its actual circulations through forces and trajectories of all kinds."[9] Later, Stewart writes, "Racism can be a live texture in the composition of a subject."[10] While I do not mean to imply that being, becoming, and feeling

Black are only about one's experience of racism, I do mean to encourage scholars to investigate how racism, and the resulting stress of it, may profoundly impact one's emotional wellness, including one's definition of joy, sadness, and happiness. Stewart's discussion of stress and racism are useful for thinking through the ways some Black Americans are constantly engaged in an internal and communal discussion about power and agency and how this is reflected affectively.

In this chapter, I provide insight into the multiple ways race and gender affect one's access to happiness by putting the experiences of GFT members into conversation with Black feminist thought about race and gender in the United States. For example, Harris-Perry argues that the "internal, psychological, emotional, and personal experiences of black women are inherently political" because the "derogatory assumptions about their character and identity . . . shape the social world that black women must accommodate or resist in an effort to preserve their authentic selves and to secure recognition as citizens."[11] If we understand this to be true, then the documentation and analysis of the affective experiences of Black American women frequently leaving the United States in search of an escape from racism and sexism could tell us a great deal about what it means to be Black, American, and a woman. As these women encounter the oft-contentious relationship between "Blackness" and "Americanness" while traveling (virtually and physically) to Jamaica, they find ways to interrogate and expand notions of Black American womanhood.

Here, I expand stereotypical depictions and one-dimensional narratives of Black women in order to "fuck with the grays," as feminist theorist Joan Morgan encourages.[12] Black women's lives, like everyone else's, are complex and contradictory, are a combination of both/ands instead of either/ors. And as a result of the contradictory and intersecting ways racism and sexism work in the United States, one would expect Black women's lives to be complicated and multifaceted. These complexities and contradictions do not have to be viewed as negative but can be a liberating space of possibility, pleasure, leisure, and even happiness.

Race, Emotional Knowledges, and Affective Knowing

In the last decade, with the affective turn in multiple disciplines, many are embracing the idea that affective experiences are important, and even central, to understanding human life. Additionally, the notion that affect is both social and political is a common argument. However, if affect is social, then it must also be a process, and one that is undoubtedly influenced by historical and contemporary processes of racialization. Furthermore, if affect is social and racialized, then we must take into account how racism influences affect. While theorists such as Lauren Berlant and Ann Cvetkovich acknowledge the intimate relationship between affect and power, few interrogate how individuals and groups relegated to less powerful positions through systemic oppression may experience and articulate affect differently (although scholars like Rebecca Wanzo and Jose Munoz provide us with initial tools to do this work).[13] In *The Promise of Happiness*, Sara Ahmed reminds us that emotions are not simply private things but are constructed in publics, with technologies, and in the context of social conditions, and are therefore political.[14]

My argument here is that for those racialized and gendered as Black women in the United States, race is central to their affective experiences and therefore significant for what they view as social and political. For many Black women, something may not become political or social until race is taken into account. The literature and analyses of affect must reflect this or risk omitting significant aspects of the examination of affect. Additionally, an omission of Black women's experiences in the literature keeps us from understanding why a group like GFT sees race, and even diaspora, as important to how they define and experience leisure and pleasure. I suggest that GFT's frequent travel to Jamaica provides insight into the complex politics of Black American women's happiness, and it highlights how these women actively participate in their pursuits of happiness while negotiating the affective dimensions of diasporic relationships.

By framing this examination of African American experience through emotion, I call attention to the ways Girlfriends negotiate their identities and navigate the affective dimensions of power within their virtual and geographic communities. Here, I focus specifically on "happiness" as a rubric for thinking through the ways the women of Girlfriend Tours International experience processes of racialization and gendering, and I document how they understand themselves within these discourses. Recognizing the significant contributions theorists of intersectionality have made to the analysis of power and subject formation, this chapter builds on that work by proposing that emotions and feelings may be productive analytics for examining how race and gender not only intersect but are always inextricably linked.

Feeling, emotion, and affect are forms of knowledge. They provide ways of knowing the world and figuring out how to navigate it. The women of GFT do not distinguish between these three terms as some researchers do—they feel something, it generates a sensation or emotional response or reflection, and then they choose to act or not act. And sometimes all of these occur simultaneously. For this reason, I am less interested in distinguishing between these three forms of emotional knowledges and more interested in understanding the connections between this affective knowing, racialized and gendered experiences, and power. My theorization of affect here is in line with Shaka McGlotten's suggestion that "personhood is not necessarily constituted by what one does, but by how one feels, and by the ways one names those feelings (or doesn't) and puts them into relationship (or doesn't) with larger social histories of difference or national belonging.[15] Affect allows you to recognize when you are accepted or simply being tolerated. It helps you understand when you are experiencing racialized trauma and gendered shame, or when you are accepted wholly for who you are. Emotions let you know when there is a longing for something, even if words do not allow you to describe the "what" or "why" you are longing for it. Feeling these various forms of emotional knowledges is sometimes a knowing that is larger than words. And the affective lives of Black women enable us to learn about experiences with race and gender that have often been marginalized or denigrated because they (both Black women and their emotions) are not valued as significant forms of theoretical knowledge.

Even before the affective turn, Black feminist scholars such as Audre Lorde—who theorized shame and anger—implored scholars to pay attention to the information, the data, that is present in the emotional aspects of Black peoples' lived experiences, especially women. They have argued for decades that how we feel, how we understand our emotional selves, is influenced by politics and specifically systems of oppression. Taking race (and racism) into account when theorizing affect ensures that we do not neglect a significant part of Black women's stories. Without including the racial, we cannot adequately understand what Black women see and feel as political and social subjects. If one takes emotion out of the racialized context for Black women, especially these women of GFT, then one does not understand their pursuit of happiness and the strategies they use to experience happiness regularly. Taking into account the Girlfriends' Blackness helps one to see the ways their travel and participation in their virtual community are attempts to escape the tentacles of U.S. racism. Additionally, examining both their racialized identity and their affective experiences allows researchers to further understand how pursuing happiness can be a political project for Black women and how they create community and find belonging. Girlfriends make their political and social choices, even as they travel with a diasporic heart, based on their understanding of their racial identification and that of others. Their desire to connect across national boundaries with those they see as diasporic kin is based on their hope that those boundaries are permeable.

Happiness Declarations

Sitting in a neighborhood bar in Ocho Rios, Jamaica, Jacqueline and I watched the 2006 World Cup on a big-screen television with what seemed like the entire town. Hotel workers from the all-inclusive across the street, cab drivers from the corner, schoolchildren in uniforms, businessmen networking over drinks, and tourists from Europe, the Caribbean, and the United States all filled the available tables and chairs, everyone careful not to block another's view of the match. During one of the commercials, Jacqueline tapped me on the shoulder and exclaimed, "Bianca, I am happy!" grinning from ear-to-ear.

In the years I conducted research on African American women tourists and their relationships with Jamaica, I heard Jacqueline make this declaration several times. Sometimes she would whisper it as we watched the sunset on the beach, or shout it over music while dancing at a local club. During this period, neither she nor I knew I would end up focusing this study on happiness. So most times I would nod or affirm her declarations without giving them a significant amount of thought. However, the intensity behind Jacqueline's words on this particular day made me pause and take notice. Since she was not an avid fan of soccer and had not been paying much attention to the game itself, I understood immediately that her statement was not about the match. Quizzically, I looked around to search out the source of her bliss. Was it the fourth shot of Appleton rum she held in her hand? Was it the bar full of men paying her plenty of attention? Was it my company? Again, I shot her a confused look, and she laughed. "Bianca, I *feel* happy! I feel at peace. I haven't felt this happy in forever!" she shouted, as if saying the words made her experience the emotion even more.

This vignette recounting Jacqueline's declaration of happiness is an apt starting place for discussing the affective dimensions of her trips to Jamaica and investigating how the country becomes central to her pursuit of happiness. I offer that Jacqueline's frequent travel to Jamaica provides some insight into the complex politics of Black American women's happiness and the significant connections between affect, race, and gender. By framing this examination of African American experience through the question of emotion, I call attention to the ways Jacqueline, and other Girlfriends like Gayle, actively participate in the process of pursuing happiness as they negotiate their identities and navigate the affective dimensions of their nationalized privilege.

Here, I point to three key aspects of the Girlfriends' pursuit of happiness. The first is that for these Black American women, happiness is most frequently experienced in communal spaces with other Black people, providing them with a sense of racialized belonging that has significant emotional benefits. As they travel to Jamaica to find temporary relief from the stressors of U.S. racism, the possibility of finding acceptance and a sense of racialized and diasporic belonging among American Girlfriends and Jamaicans becomes ever more important for their pursuit of happiness. The second premise is that Girlfriends' pursuit of happiness is a process that requires planning, labor, and sacrifice, which results in some emotional costs. As essential family caretakers and community participants responsible for significant emotional and physical labor at home, many Black women like Jacqueline and Gayle pursuing leisure, recreation, and happiness find themselves getting pushback from family, friends, and community members who depend on their labor or who see these pursuits as neglecting racialized and gendered responsibilities. Finally, as GFT ladies travel throughout Jamaica, they experience moments where people "feel" them and understand them, but also moments when their sense of belonging is disrupted and their nationalized privilege is marked. Although difficult to endure at times, this process of affective exchange and learning is key to the Girlfriends' pursuit of happiness. As Jacqueline and Gayle exercise their inalienable right to pursue happiness (although outside of U.S. borders), they participate in affective experiences where racialized, gendered, and diasporic performances and discourses are interrogated.

Becoming Girlfriends: Happiness as Process

Most veteran travelers and repeat visitors with Girlfriend Tours International eventually became close friends with GFT cofounders Marilyn Williams and Angelia Hairston.[16] Marilyn and Angie became friends after several months of electronic correspondence on Jamaicans.com and decided to go into business together. In fact, the first time they met in person was after they decided to create GFT. Marilyn, who hails from Memphis, Tennessee, and Angelia, from Atlanta, Georgia, began by sharing stories about their love for Jamaica, discussing their relationships with their Jamaican boyfriends, and complaining about the expensive single supplements tourists had to pay at all-inclusives when they traveled alone. Eventually, Angie's and Marilyn's frustration with their U.S. girlfriends backing out of vacations at the last minute (leaving them to hold the bill), coupled with the Caribbean all-inclusive tourist industry's preference for (heterosexual) couples, pushed them to create a tour group for women who wanted to travel to Jamaica but could not find travel partners.[17] By the time I accompanied Marilyn and Angie on their tour in 2004, they had already completed three successful tours with women from all over the United States and had built a large network of business connections with Jamaicans who enjoyed residual benefits from their company. Over the years, the founders organized several different types of semi-customized trips for their racially diverse clientele of American women; however, their signature tour was an annual trip to Jamaica that usually was composed of predominantly African American women. This five-day tour began the Thursday after the American Independence Day and was held in Negril every year except for one, when it was held in Ocho Rios. Jacqueline and Gayle attended the three GFT annual tours I observed during my research.

Each year, before the ladies of GFT landed in Jamaica, several activities had already taken place in the virtual Jamaica constructed on Jamaicans.com. For months before their visit, these women and their Jamaicans.com virtual neighbors have in-depth conversations about, and post pictures of, the clothes they are ordering from different catalogs to wear on their trip, the colors they are wearing at particular events, their vacation hairstyles, the places they are going to visit, the hotels on their itinerary, roommate arrangements, and the drivers they are going to employ. In forum postings, member-to-member private messaging, and emails, they have discussed the dos and don'ts of going through customs and other lessons learned from previous trip reports written and posted by community members. These online conversations may spark lively disagreements resulting in warring cliques or initiate connections that become the foundation for friendships maintained on- and offline.

In order to gain insight into the processes involved in creating a sense of belonging and community among the ladies of GFT, I provide a brief overview of the annual tour. While the tour itinerary was pretty similar every year, the interests and desires of the individuals participating in the tour could push the founders to add an event or two. Additionally, the chemistry between the tour members affected the success of various events. The first day of meeting and greeting was always simultaneously exciting and exhausting. While the process of becoming Girlfriends had already begun through virtual communication in e-mail and on Jamaicans.com, the process continued as women arrived at Sangster International Airport from their respective U.S. hometowns. Girlfriends hugged each other tightly, with a few tears appearing as they met each other in person, sometimes for the first time. The ladies rode to the resort town of Negril together in an air-conditioned van or bus with television screens and an entertaining driver. For the annual tour, the drivers were usually men whom the cofounders of GFT had already "auditioned" during previous trips to the island. Marilyn and Angie looked for a driver who would make the ninety-minute drive to Negril from Montego Bay an experience their clients would remember, which often meant that he had to have a good sense of humor; had to know a good deal about Jamaica's history and the sights they would see along the way; provide snacks and drinks to his passengers; and had to know how to make newcomers, particularly women, feel comfortable. Additionally, it helped if the women thought he was good-looking and charming.

During the drive, GFT ladies transitioned into "Jamaica mode" by enjoying a Red Stripe (Jamaica's famous beer) and eating beef patties with coco bread. As they listened to the grooving vibes of familiar artists such as Bob Marley, Maxi Priest, Tanya Stephens, Beres Hammond, and Gregory Isaacs, the women looked out the windows of the bus and watched the landscape change from the concrete streets of Montego Bay to the sandy beach coast of Negril. Oftentimes, the bus was filled with conversation about where each person was from and how many times she had been to Jamaica, and numerous questions for the founders about what was in store for the five-day tour.

As the women arrived at the small, locally owned hotel, they were usually welcomed by the staff and shown to their rooms. The beds in each of the guest rooms had a gift bag from the founders of GFT, which included their signature T-shirt (with a picture of a caramel-colored lady in a sun hat lying out on the beach), some snacks, and a journal the women could use to write down their reflections during the trip.[18] The ladies dropped off their luggage and headed straight for the beach to take in the view of the beautiful coastline from the hotel's beach restaurant. Sometimes this view would invoke a few tears as some of the ladies realized they had finally made it to Jamaica. It was also during these first few moments on the beach that many of the newcomers got their first chance to mingle with Jamaicans on a one-on-one basis, without following the lead of veteran tourists. As their feet took in the heat of the sand, vendors, drug dealers, and men offering companionship called on them almost instantly. "Empress! Stella! Sista!"—these were the names sometimes used to hail Girl-friends as older tourist women, potential participants in romance tourism, or diasporic kin, respectively. The women would usually listen and laugh, make introductions, then head back to their rooms to unpack, take a nap, and get dressed for the evening's events.

Dinner was on the hotel's property and often included a feast of Jamaican foods to satisfy the women's palates, including jerk chicken, rice and peas, and callaloo. On Thursday night, the first night of every GFT, Girlfriends headed to the Jungle, the town's premier dance club. The Jungle is the only club and casino in the city, with three bars, a VIP area, two dance floors and deejay booths (one inside, one outside), an eatery, and a portable stage in the parking lot for those nights when artists such as Beenie Man and Ludacris entertain the crowd with live sets. Thursday night was Ladies Night, which meant that all of the Girlfriends received free admission, and the crowd was packed with men vying for their attention. Despite the fact that almost all the ladies were older than the crowd, most were pleased while taking in the fashions and getting lessons from locals on the new dancehall moves. However, it was not everyone's cup of tea to dance in a club filled with people half their age, listening to the "noise" of the latest hip-hop, pop, and dancehall.[19] On a regular basis, there were at least four ladies who left the club early, while others danced the night away and were entertained by the lyrics the young men threw at them in the club.[20] Although the GFT cofounders knew that there would be a few women who would not love the Jungle, they kept it on the itinerary every year, encouraging Girlfriends to experience an "authentic" part of Jamaica and be bold as they pushed out of their comfort zones.

Day two of the tour started with breakfast at the hotel at nine o'clock. Despite my personal preference for sleeping until noon, during the first tour I learned not to miss breakfast, as this was the time when Girlfriends exchanged gossip about events the night before or conversed about any men who may have provided entertaining lyrics and praise. It was also at breakfast, during the sunset hours after dinner, and right before bedtime that the ladies would often open up as they discussed their experiences with love, sex, motherhood, friendship, womanhood, and race. These moments of communal sharing were crucial for crystallizing the friendships between Girlfriends. There would be tears and laughter as Girlfriends began to see and hear themselves in another's stories about their lives at home in the United States and encounters in Jamaica.

By noon on the second day of each tour, the Girlfriends would relax on the beach while reading or listening to music, swim, and receive Angie's and Marilyn's introductions to some of the area's Jamaican vendors and business owners. In the evening, dinner was at 3 Dives, where the annual initiation into girlfriendship took place.[21] After the Girlfriend bonding session up in the cliffs, the party continued at Alfred's, a beach bar that entertained the Friday night crowd with a mixture of live band performances and a deejay spinning the latest dancehall. Since the bands usually opened by playing roots reggae and covers of American R&B songs, the crowd at Alfred's was mixed, including hotel workers, tourists, a few middle-aged Jamaican businessmen, and men some Jamaicans described as "gigolos." Many Jamaicans present seemed to have connections to the romance trade or the hotel tourist industry, worked at the bar, were there to celebrate a national holiday, or were part of local dance crews looking to practice and show off their moves. At Alfred's the GFT ladies were usually swarmed by offers to dance, enjoy a free drink, go on a date, or have sex, from men of all ages. Once in a while a woman would sneak off to have quiet time or a walk along the beach with a man who had caught her interest, but generally the ladies enjoyed a few dances and walked home as a group.

On the third day of the tour, those who were bored with relaxing on the beach went snorkeling at Booby Cay in a glass-bottom boat or went into town to shop for souvenirs. Sometimes Angie and Marilyn would schedule a climb to the top of a waterfall to encourage the ladies to try something new and get a little closer to nature. Lunch took place around noon at a local restaurant owned by a Jamaican businesswoman, a friend of the tour's founders. After lunch, a couple of the ladies went on dates or excursions with men they had met during the previous two days, while others relaxed with Girlfriends in their rooms or on the beach. Everyone returned to the hotel restaurant for dinner, where the owner and his staff threw a catered private dinner and hired a deejay for the group. Dinner usually ended with the American women learning dance moves from the young Jamaican women on staff at the hotel. The Girlfriends who enjoyed the Jungle on Thursday often invited these young women to return to the club with them on Saturday night, so they could perform their newly acquired dance moves in public. The invitations were usually accepted, resulting in a fabulous multigenerational parade of Black American and Jamaican women dressed to the nines walking from the hotel to the Jungle, punctuated by loud bursts of laughter and jubilation. Saturday night at the Jungle was a favorite of the local Negril community, as it was publicized as a hardcore dancehall event where tourists were the minority following the lead of locals, who ruled the dance floor and influenced the deejay's musical selection.

After breakfast on day four, the ladies and I would make the thirty-five-minute drive to Jackie's on the Reef Spa for an oceanside massage, manicures, pedicures, and all-day lounging. Jackie, the owner of the spa, would often be there to welcome the group, give a brief tour, and get everyone settled. This day of relaxation lasted for about five or six hours, as there were usually only two women to administer the massages and at least twelve Girlfriends requesting them. It rained every year during our time at Jackie's, laying a quiet, tranquil vibe over the day's activities. Each Girlfriend took some alone time, finding a corner with a hammock or bed to sleep, write in her journal, or read a magazine. The trip to Jackie's often included the most silent hours of the whole tour, with Girlfriends sometimes becoming lost in their thoughts and relaxing in solitude for hours at a time. After eating their prepared box lunches, a few ladies walked through the gardens to carry on a quiet conversation, while others walked the coast collecting seashells to take home. This time at Jackie's was especially treasured by the ladies, since many claimed they never took the time to spoil or treat themselves to these services in the United States, or to simply find time for reflection. Jackie's was treated as a sacred, women-only space. Similar to the Girlfriend initiation on the cliffs at 3 Dives, it was one of the spaces where Girlfriends centered themselves and ensured that they had time to connect with one another. The fact that Oprah was known for coming to Jackie's for her own relaxation time when in Negril always seemed to add a little more meaning to the pleasure these women experienced there. After dinner on their own, the ladies headed to Roots Bamboo, another beach bar, to hear some music.

Day five, the last day of the tour, was dedicated to soaking up as much sun on the beach as possible, getting in last-minute shopping, and saying goodbye to any friends, lovers, or companions the ladies might have acquired during the short trip. Each year there were at least two or three women who acquired male companions during their time in Negril, through either the informal romance economy or general flirtations with hospitality workers and other Jamaican men. As the closing event of the tour, the ladies went on a sunset cruise up and down the seven-mile beach on the hotel owner's yacht. For this special event, the women dressed all in black and posed for the annual GFT picture. The sight of twelve to eighteen Black women in black dresses, drinking champagne, dancing to reggae music, and waving from a yacht attracted much attention from other tourists and Jamaicans on land and in nearby boats.[22] A couple of the ladies would choose to invite their Jamaican lovers and companions onto the cruise (which costs an extra $25) so they could share the cruise experience with their mate and introduce him to the Girlfriends. After the cruise, those who were involved in a relationship would go "missing" for the evening, while other Girlfriends would carry on conversations with new Jamaican friends, hotel staff, and other tourists they had met during the week.

In the morning, Marilyn and Angie would gather the women after breakfast to give away prizes to certain members: the woman who paid for her tour first; the week's "Miss Congeniality"; the Girlfriend with the most GFT tours under her belt; the woman with the best nickname in the group; and others. After their luggage was placed in the lobby, some ladies would sit on the beach to say their goodbyes to Girlfriends, while others would try to prolong these last moments with their Jamaican companions.

I would watch as each woman said goodbye to Jamaica in her own way, whether it was by walking down the beach alone, spending a few moments letting the ocean wash over her toes, saying goodbye to the vendors lining the coast, sneaking last kisses with a lover, or writing in her journal at the hotel bar. As the drivers arrived to take those who were leaving Jamaica to the airport or to carry those who were staying in Jamaica to their next destination, the collective tears would begin. Usually one person would tear up, and then a few moments later tears were streaming down everyone's faces. There were promises to join Jamaicans.com (if they were not already members of the virtual community), exchange pictures through e-mail, post trip reports, stay in touch by phone, and return with the tour group the following year. Tight hugs were given and received as all said goodbye to one another and the island they loved.

The annual Girlfriend Tour provided what feminist sociologist Patricia Hill Collins calls a "safe space" for these Black American women.[23] Angie and Marilyn's careful design of a girlfriend-centered vacation that included time dedicated to relaxation, conversation, reflection, and affirmation enabled Girlfriends to build relationships with one another in a country that values Black American women, finds them desirable, and allows them to actively pursue leisure. As each woman offered pieces of her story on the cliff, during breakfast, in the hotel room with her roommate, and during massages at Jackie's, other Black women listened, acknowledged that they understood her life story and even share parts of it. Collins cites Audre Lorde in her book *Black Feminist Thought* to emphasize the significance of this listening and affirmation. She writes, "Audre Lorde describes the importance that the expression of individual voice within collective context of Black women's communities can have for self-affirmation. . . . For African-American women the listener most able to pierce the invisibility created by Black women's objectification is another Black woman. This process of trusting one another can seem dangerous because only Black women know what it means to be Black women. But if we will not listen to one another, then who will?"[24] In this safe space, Girlfriends created bonds of trust that helped make them visible and affirmed not only what they were looking and yearning for in Jamaica but also what they experienced back home. Their travel to Jamaica as a group allowed Girlfriends to find refuge they could not find in the United States among the various racialized and gendered expectations and forms of discrimination they encountered, inside and outside their homes.

Throughout my time with the Girlfriends, I saw them utilize three strategies to pursue happiness and create multiple safe spaces for themselves in the United States and Jamaica. Most with the economic ability and time to physically visit Jamaica did their best to do so, disrupting the popular notion that (older) Black women do not travel. As described, these trips and annual tours provided opportunities for relaxation and the creation of deep friendships in spaces conducive to leisure, as they were able to temporarily shift their focus from the stresses of home toward themselves and each other. When Girlfriends returned from their trips, could not travel physically, or were not able to afford visits to Jamaica, many virtually traveled to Jamaica through Jamaicans.com. This second strategy of pursing happiness enabled them to live vicariously through the trip reports of other Girlfriends and boardites; to learn about Jamaican culture and become familiar with it in an accessible medium; to connect with Jamaicans and veteran travelers, who provided tips for future trips and fueled traveling fantasies; and to commiserate with other Black women who wanted to go to Jamaica but could not for a variety of reasons. This virtual Jamaica tided them over until they could return or until they could afford their first trip. Since Jamaicans.com was a public space with members of various racial, gendered, classed, and nationalized backgrounds, there was less safe space here. However, in niches in the web community or through e-mail and private messaging, Black women could connect with, affirm, and dream with one another. The third strategy Girlfriends implemented was to have U.S.-based retreats or meetups in various cities. These allowed Girlfriends to see each other in person and connect in ways that weren't possible virtually. These retreats supplemented their group trips to Jamaica, allowed time for reminiscing about past trips, and encouraged those who hadn't visited yet to take the plunge.

Whether in physical Jamaica, in virtual Jamaica, or at Jamaica-centered U.S. retreats, Girlfriends were always encouraged to indulge in self-care, take time for restoration, and participate in solo and group reflection about their lives and how they were feeling at that moment. These temporary safe spaces allowed the ladies to compartmentalize—to escape and go to a place where they could have affective experiences without feeling shame. They provided each other with support and validation in the ways each needed, and they received something they did not often get in their everyday lives. Generational, individual, and social sentiments were transferred during these interactions and gatherings, and the connections created and the affirmation received was often more than words could capture.

Desiring Happiness in Jamaica: Emotional Costs

Oftentimes at the center of the Girlfriend-bonding and affirmation processes was Jacqueline. At the time of my research, Jacqueline had visited Jamaica seventeen times in the past eight years. For this, she will tell you, she has been both blessed and cursed. Jacqueline has visited Jamaica as part of the Girlfriend Tours International group but also as a traveler with one or two additional friends. She claimed to be regularly chided for her "Jamaicaholism," especially once people found out that she spent most of her waking hours (when not at work) talking to people around the world who shared her obsession with Jamaica. She was legendary for letting parts of her house go without repair for a while to fund her frequent trips to Jamaica.[25]

A single mom from the South with a college-age daughter, Jacqueline was one of the few Girlfriends I spoke with who came from a familial line of women who had traveled both on their own and as members of travel groups to different parts of the world. Most of the other Girlfriends either were first-generation leisure travelers in their family or came from families in which women traveling solo was looked down upon. This previous history of leisure travel didn't necessarily protect Jacqueline, however. Many of her family members were not fans of her Jamaica obsession, some even going so far as to write her out of two wills, fearful that she would take the money to visit Jamaica and "marry one of those Rasta guys and bring him to America," or "give money to the Rastafarian society and start a school for Rastafarian children or something." Their fear and frustration were about her frequent travel but was especially activated by her dedication to visiting Jamaica specifically over and over again. They could not figure out what it was about Jamaica and, according to Jacqueline, did not listen or understand when she tried to explain it. I know from conversations with Jacqueline and other Girlfriends that potential sex with Jamaican men was sometimes a factor in the pushback they received from friends and family. M. Jacqui Alexander writes in her article on tourism in the Bahamas, that "women's sexual agency, our sexual and our erotic autonomy have always been troublesome for the state. They pose a challenge to the ideological anchor of an original nuclear family, a source of legitimation for the state, which perpetuates the fiction that the family is the cornerstone of society. Erotic autonomy signals danger to the heterosexual family and the nation."[26] In the critiques Girlfriends receive from their families, we observe the types of policing that Black women experience around sexual agency and autonomy, not only from the state but also from their communities. When Jacqueline decided to ignore the critiques and make trips to Jamaica every three months to "keep herself from going crazy in Babylon," family members accused her of abandoning her daughter and not being a good role model for her. At times, this isolation and ridicule from her family and friends brought tears of loneliness to Jacqueline's eyes.

In contrast, the friendships she found in the virtual community of Jamaicans.com and in Jamaica were blessings to her. Online, Jacqueline was well known, introducing new tourists to veteran board members, policing web etiquette as a forum moderator, orchestrating online love connections, and providing boardites with all the information they needed to have weddings, birthdays, and fabulous vacations in Jamaica. In turn, her virtual friends supported her during her annual exercise programs to lose weight for upcoming trips, flew to her home to keep her company when she did not have the money to make it to Jamaica, and comforted her during the passing of her mother.

In Jamaica, she was a local celebrity, welcomed by almost everyone—fishermen, hotel staff, taxi drivers, businessmen, and restaurant owners alike. She knew most people and many knew her by name. One afternoon in our apartment in Jamaica, I asked Jacqueline if she could explain to me her deep connection to the country and her reasons for returning despite the fact that her Jamaican addiction kept her even more isolated from some individuals back home, particularly her family. In response, she described her first trip to Jamaica, which is when she believes the bond between her, Jamaica, and Jamaicans was created.

On the fifth night, it was time to go and I was *fit* to be tied. [Jamaica] did not get my girlfriend like it got me. A guy who was on the entertainment staff was taking $20 from us to take us out at night, sneak us off the property. But when we were getting ready to come back it was just like everywhere [*she sits up on the couch, voice filled with excitement, eyes bulging with the memory of that night*], up and down the main street all these barbecue grills broke out and there were people *ev-ery-where*. Uh, traffic and folks out on the street, little children running up and down the street, it was just like the Fourth of damn July!

And I was like, "What's going on?" And he said [*imitates driver's nonchalant tone*], "Nothing. This is every night here." And I said "What!?!" I wanted to do a swan dive out of the bus [*uses her hands to imitate this*] and go out and get among the people. I wanted to do this so bad. And he said, "No! I have to take you back to [the hotel]. I brought you out, I have to take you back in one piece. I can't leave you here." I thought I was *going to die* if I didn't get out that van and get into that perpetual cookout that I felt was going on.

And I will admit to you that I did meet somebody on that first trip, and I was *completely* enamored. But more so than him, it was a doubleedged thing. I wanted to get back and see him, but I also had a goal of getting off of the hotel's property and get *out* into the real Jamaica. And on my second trip, as a matter of fact, I did stay at the same place, but I got out into Ocho Rios proper and that was it! I mean from that point on, it was like a love affair.

And I don't know how I can explain to you what it is. It's just so different from where I'm from. If you found the same thing that you find where you live, then why travel? You're looking for something different. And you're looking for adventure. And you're looking for different culture.

Different rules and regulations and different way of doing things. That's what I found when I came here and it was like I couldn't get enough of it. I wanted some more. Jamaica crawled into my soul.

In this interview excerpt, Jacqueline describes her deep yearning for community and excitement, something that she thought she was missing at the all-inclusive and needed to get into the "real" Jamaica to experience. She is clear that she also feels as if she can't get this excitement and community feeling at home in the United States.

Hers was not the only story I heard about experiencing an intimate connection with Jamaica. Gayle, another woman in her early fifties and a single mother of two daughters, mused about her connection to Jamaica in an interview at her U.S. home.

It is peaceful for me. Very peaceful. People embrace you in the U.S. based on the person they think you are, or need you to be. Jamaica is the one place that I've been so far that anyone that likes me, they like Gayle. . . . Yeah, anyone that I know that actually likes me, they like the bare me. The me with no trimming, no anything. It's me. That's me. I'm not trying to be Corporate Gayle, I'm not trying to be Momma Gayle. I'm just me. The way I was born to be. That's me. So yeah, that's the difference. [My daughters] always say, "Yes, we know. Jamaica *embraces* you." I say, "Yes, it does. It embraces ME."

Like Jacqueline's, Gayle's connection to Jamaica reflects a deep desire to be part of a community—one that is accepting of who she truly is underneath the façade and roles she must play in the United States. As a professional administrator in a large organization in the South, Gayle spent much of her day making tough decisions about policy and money that influenced others' ability to do their jobs. Her eight trips to Jamaica were some of the few times she was able to focus and enjoy herself, by herself. At the end of the interview Gayle reiterated, "Jamaica is for *Gayle*. It's not for Mommy [Gayle]. It's not for Sister Gayle. It's for Gayle." In fact, Gayle was so adamant about Jamaica being her own personal space that she told me she usually tried to travel to Jamaica alone or with only one friend. Although she encouraged family members and friends to experience Jamaica for themselves, she purposely did not ask family to accompany her on her trips because she wanted to be selfish with Jamaica and keep that time for herself.

Gayle also echoed Jacqueline's feelings of isolation and sadness related to her family's and some friends' disdain of her fondness for Jamaica. Gayle's parents, in particular, disapproved of her frequent trips to Jamaica, suggesting that her Jamaica obsession distracted her from taking care of them and her children.

GAYLE: I would go away to Jamaica for two weeks, and I would call maybe two or three times. That was difficult for [my parents]. 'Cause they're accustom [sic] to hearing my voice everyday. And they *needed* to hear it everyday. It just bothered them that I had another outlet other than them. Although I always have, but it's different when you're in the States versus over there [in Jamaica]. And they didn't like the idea that I left [my daughters] alone.

BW: And what did your daughters say?

GAYLE: At first, they didn't mind. But then when I started going a lot, they didn't like it. Because again, it took away from their attention.

Most Girlfriends suggested that this burden of responsibility as daughter, mother, and caregiver for the family was a strong motivation behind their frequent trips to Jamaica.[27] Even though they faced constant criticism from friends and family for being selfish and taking "too much" leisure time, many felt they deserved a break from the demands of their daily lives. The notion that African American women should be able to handle all domestic, professional, and community-based responsibilities while sacrificing their personal pleasures was quite prevalent in Girlfriends' accounts of the pushback they received about their trips to Jamaica.

Gayle and Jacqueline explained that while it was clear that their labor as mothers, grandmothers, and other forms of caregiving was essential, family and community members often overlooked and invisibilized Black women's labor. Girlfriends felt their labor was crucial to how their families and communities operated, but it was also taken for granted. Additionally, family and community members did not appear to think of older Black women as people desiring recreational, pleasurable, intimate, or sexual lives. It seemed that the older Girlfriends got, the less those around them expected Black women over fifty to live full and exciting lives. Girlfriends discussed the normalized gendered and racialized roles within households and communities they were expected to fulfill and felt pressure for them not to want much more than this. In contrast, as Black American tourist women in Jamaica, most of the Jamaicans the Girlfriends interacted with assumed they wanted to have fun and sought pleasure and did not expect the same form of caregiving required at home. Moreover, Girlfriends had the time and money to participate in activities they did not do regularly in the United States, including hosting dinner parties, sailing, and dancing at clubs, which allowed them to enjoy social and pleasurable aspects of themselves that were ignored or repressed at home.

In her interview, Gayle stated that Jamaicans loved her for her true essence—for who she is without all the trimmings. While I observed the sense of peace and acceptance in Jamaica that was difficult for Gayle and other Girlfriends to find in the United States, I also noted that for some the process of getting happy (both before and during their trips to Jamaica) took a significant amount of work. Despite Gayle's claim that she was loved for being "bare" Gayle in Jamaica, Girlfriends engaged in numerous activities that complicated this statement, including dieting and exercising to lose weight for their trips to Jamaica; buying new wardrobes for swimming, clubbing, attracting male attention, and lounging; and paying for a change in hairstyle, including exquisite weaves and hair braiding. While in Jamaica with Gayle a few months after her U.S. interview, I mentioned that the ability to experience acceptance for one's true essence seemed to come at the expense of multiple forms of labor. She replied that for her, changing her hairstyles and clothing in Jamaica offered a sense of freedom and experimentation, and it made her feel as though Jamaica was about being young, whereas the United States was about being formal, rigid, and old.

Gayle's longing for connection and a space where she could be her authentic self is one that Charisse Jones and Kumea Shorter-Gooden discuss in their book, *Shifting: The Double Lives of Black Women in America*. They offer "shifting" as a concept to describe a strategy of performance and behavior modification Black women employ in order to cope with racialized, gendered, and sexualized discrimination. Using data from surveys of 333 Black women as part of the African American Women's Voices Project, Jones and Shorter-Gooden outline six strategies participants used to navigate the double burden of racism and sexism and to resist destructive myths about Black womanhood. Each of these strategies allowed participants to shift between contradicting expectations that family, friends, and colleagues had for Black women and the multiple roles they were required to fill at home, work, church, and in other spaces. Jones and Shorter-Gooden write, "Black women are relentlessly pushed to serve and satisfy others and made to hide their true selves to placate White colleagues, Black men, and other segments of the community. They shift to accommodate differences in class as well as gender and ethnicity. From one moment to the next, they change their outward behavior, attitude, or tone, shifting 'White,' then shifting 'Black' again, shifting 'corporate,' shifting 'cool.'"[28] The authors describe the mental, emotional, and physical costs of shifting, which often result in mental health disorders, physical distress, and a general sense of low self-esteem, worthlessness, and loneliness. The cost of trying to be everything for everyone frequently comes at a high price.

Both Jones and Shorter-Gooden's valuable research and Collins's theorization of safe space provide context for Gayle's desire to escape the pressures of her family to a place where she can be her true self. In *Black Feminist Thought*, Collins argues that, historically, "extended families, churches, and African-American community organizations are important locations where safe discourse potentially can occur" for Black women, as they use "family networks and Black community institutions as sites for countering [destructive] images. On the one hand, these Black community institutions have been vitally important in developing strategies of resistance. . . . On the other hand, many of these same institutions of Black civil society have also perpetuated racist, sexist, elitist, and homophobic ideologies."[29] Gayle and Jacqueline both viewed their families and communities as essential to their well-being in the face of racism, particularly as Black women living in the U.S. South. However, they also understood that as (older) Black women, they were responsible for a significant amount of the labor that created and kept extended families, churches, and community organizations running. They were also aware that as women, they were expected to perform particular forms of domestic labor and carework to maintain these communities that Black men were not expected to perform. Both noted that their travel would probably be okay, or at least tolerated, if they were men traveling, since men weren't often responsible for these forms of labor.

Consequently, Girlfriends used their trips to Jamaica as a transnational coping mechanism for the stress they experienced at home, a temporary escape from the costly burdens of shifting in response to U.S.-based discrimination and familial/community labor expectations. The shifting that took place in their everyday lives, and some of the shifting they participated in as they prepared for their trips, highlights the ways Black women are constantly contorting themselves—their bodies, their appearance, and their emotions—to fit into or make peace with the diverse expectations others have for them and with those they have for themselves. Nevertheless, the often fleeting moments of acceptance, freedom, escape, and happiness Girlfriends experienced in Jamaica kept them coming back. For most Girlfriends, the labor was worth it. They affirmed one another's beauty and praised results from months of working out as they showed off their wardrobes on sailing excursions, at dancehalls, and at various locations throughout the trip.

In addition to their relationships with one another, Girlfriends' interactions and relationships with Jamaican men were important during their pursuits of happiness. Some Girlfriends reported they were unable to find "marriageable men" in the United States, or ones they deemed appropriate to date, and these trips to Jamaica helped ease their loneliness. They had discovered a place where their (perceived) class status and economic success provided them with access to men who demonstrated appreciation for them with sweet words, slow dances, and romantic fantasies. In her interview Gayle said,

> The other day Jacqueline asked me what was the thing that I appreciated most about Jamaica. Besides the ocean, which I appreciate on so many levels. But I've also had the best romantic moments in Jamaica. In my *entire* life. It has not been with only one person. It has been by a multitude of different guys. And it's like, just really cool romantic persons. You may not be interested in the person, but you could've put the moment that happened in a movie.

Even if Girlfriends did not actually want to have sex or romance with Jamaican men, simply being the desirable object of his passing gaze and come-ons was often thrilling, affirming, and enjoyable enough. It meant that they were being seen and desired, and some Girlfriends saw the demonstration as a source of entertainment. When asked about whether she encourages other women to visit Jamaica, Gayle responded:

> I especially encourage my single friends that don't have an outlet [to go]. The ones that don't have boyfriends or that I know they're not going to get a boyfriend any time soon. Although I know it's bullshit you hear from those guys there, every woman deserves to hear a little bit of bullshit. Don't believe it! But enjoy it. I encourage them to go. Because for Malik [a Jamaican man Girlfriends met on a previous trip] it's not bullshit. He is a woman's man. That man *loves* women. And he means it to every. Single. Last. One of them [*laughs*].

The gaze of Jamaican men—and sometimes romance, sex, and intimacy with them—played a role in how many Girlfriends experienced and imagined what acceptance would look like during their pursuits of happiness and diasporic connection. Although their trips were not simply about getting their "groove back" like Stella, the potential to be seen as desirable in the eyes of a Jamaican man was part of their pursuit.

At the same time, the need to be an object of desire required balance. There were numerous moments when Girlfriends were offended by a Jamaican man being too forward or felt that the constant attention was exhausting. Some women wore their own wedding bands or pretend marriage symbols prominently to ward off some of the constant attention. Miriam, a Girlfriend from Washington, DC, would repeatedly tell Jamaican men sending lyrics her way that she "had a boyfriend from Kingston" to fend them off. Because Kingston has a reputation for being a violent part of the country, and men from that city are known for their tempers and assumed to have access to weapons, this usually kept men from Negril and Ocho Rios from pushing further, if they believed her. However, those wearing wedding bands who admitted to having American husbands were not as successful. Frequently the Jamaican man pursuing them replied along the lines of "Even better! Now I know you're good enough and wonderful enough for someone else to want you."

In the end, Girlfriends labored to "just be themselves" while visiting Jamaica, in order to experience community, seek leisure, and become visible in this space. It made me wonder if they were able to be their true selves in either country, or if the selves they were in Jamaica were who they would be if the United States did not hold so many contradicting and laborious expectations of them as Black women. And while their trips caused some tensions and frustrations within their families and communities, Girlfriends frequently expressed that these emotional costs were worth their pursuits of happiness in Jamaica. Nevertheless, some of these African American women still felt inner conflict about the fact that their repeat travels made them appear selfish and neglectful in the eyes of some friends and family. However, they were adamant that they could simultaneously be good mothers and daughters and fulfill other requirements as Black women in the United States, while still pursuing happiness in Jamaica. In fact, many argued that their trips to Jamaica, their momentary escapes, enabled them to better fulfill their responsibilities at home. They understood that time for relaxation and rejuvenation away from private and public work helped them be more present for their families and communities when they returned home.

Happiness and Its Tensions

The tensions created by Girlfriends' happiness pursuits were not only apparent within their families and communities in the United States. At times, Girlfriends felt tension as they recognized how their pursuit of happiness often came at the cost, or at least the labor, of Jamaicans. Chapter 2 discusses in more detail how nationalized and classed differences were illuminated in these diasporic interactions and relationships. However, here I want to focus specifically on Jacqueline's pursuit of happiness in Jamaica and how she negotiated the costs and tensions surrounding her wants and desires.

Jacqueline was one of the few visitors I saw pay particular attention to the ways in which the economic status and social privilege attached to her American dollars and citizenship constructed her as a "privileged Black" in the eyes of some

Jamaicans. Jacqueline consistently tried to engage in conversations with others that could teach her more about how Jamaicans viewed her. She was aware that although she had love for Jamaica and many Jamaicans, this love might not always be reciprocated. Through moments of frustration, misunderstanding, and nervous laughter, Jacqueline learned about the points of disconnect between her and those she envisioned as diasporic kin. Whereas she felt connected to Jamaicans because of the experiences she believed they shared in the global history of racism, some Jamaicans—particularly women—persistently informed her that although she understood racism, she could never understand the experiences of Jamaicans fully because of her American status and privilege.

This was highlighted during a conversation Jacqueline had with one of her favorite drivers and close friend Kevon. Kevon came by to visit Jacqueline and me at our apartment after a long day of trying to get work as a tour guide for visitors in the area. Jacqueline had decided to make him a late lunch, and he contributed some wonderful homemade carrot juice to the meal. We were sitting around the table sharing the latest gossip we'd heard around town when Jacqueline asked Kevon about his children. Since they had known each other for years, Jacqueline had met his kids and inquired about how they were doing in school.

"They're doing well," he said. "Getting big, quick with the mind, and trying not to give their teachers a hard time." This led to a brief discussion about what the children were learning in class. Jacqueline nostalgically began to share memories of her daughter when she was in elementary and middle school. She turned to Kevon and asked, "What does your daughter want to be when she grows up?"

"Oh, I don't know. I think a teacher or a principal. I tell her she needs to do something that will make her money and allow her to take care of herself."

Jacqueline responded, "I used to tell my daughter, and I tell my students now, that they can be whatever they want. A doctor, a lawyer. They can be president of the United States. I think it's important for them to dream big. And even if they haven't seen a Black president yet, I think it's important that they believe it can happen. Don't you agree?"[30]

Kevon was quiet for a moment, and I could tell that he was weighing whether or not he wanted to say what he was thinking. After a pause he said, "That may make sense in the U.S. You're American. It's different there. But in Jamaica, our prime ministers are often corrupt, and don't have much power. Depending on which party and dons are in control, JLP or PNP, the prime minister is responsible for taking care of certain communities, especially the dons that they get support from. I don't want my daughter caught up in that. I'd rather her get a nice job, stay close to home, and stay safe."[31]

Throughout her visits, I observed Jacqueline enjoying her leisurely vacation, but I would also see her ears perk up and her mind take mental notes during conversations like this. Whenever someone was willing to tell her, in subtle or even aggressive tones, that the way she experienced race, gender, and class was not at all how Jamaicans experienced the world, she would pause and take it in. In this conversation with Kevon, I could see she was having a hard time accepting Kevon's disagreement with the notion that every child, especially every Black child, should have the dream of being president, and every parent should teach them that they could attain it. It was as if her understanding of race and government in the United States was running into something that just did not compute. She was enjoying this conversation with someone she saw as diasporic kin and wanted to learn more about how Jamaica worked, but Kevon's genuine comfort with his daughter being "just" a teacher and his lack of enthusiasm about the highest political office in Jamaica left her unsettled. She took a sip of her carrot juice, looked out the window at the ocean for a few moments, and said quietly, "Yes, things are different here." And then the conversation quickly moved on to other topics.

After instances where Jamaicans emphasized the difference between Black experiences in Jamaica and in the United States, or other troubling moments of disconnect, Jacqueline and I would sometimes go back to our room and process these conversations, sifting through to find the gems that she would journal or write a trip report about. Although she listened to her Jamaican interlocutors and appreciated their candor, later she would tell me these conversations sometimes caused her great sadness. It was in these moments that she recognized her "outsider" status in a community of which she desperately wanted to be a part. It was as if they were saying to her, "You may spend your money here, you may look like me, but you will never fully understand me."

In this vein, Jacqueline's relationships with Jamaican women were particularly complex and nuanced. Some Girlfriends were adamant that Jamaican women did not like them and that the assumption that they were coming to Jamaica to have sex with or "steal" Jamaican men from Jamaican women was a huge part of the dislike. While Girlfriends were steadfast in their expressed longing to build girlfriendships with Jamaican women, they also stated that their actual or potential participation in romance tourism, their desire to draw the gazes of Jamaican men, and even their presence as Black American tourist women acted as barriers to these relationships. Jacqueline was not in denial about why many Jamaican women felt as if she were not a part of their community. Nonetheless, the opportunity to be appreciated and made visible in Jamaica was worth the disdain and scrutiny she endured from some Jamaican women.

It was also worth the economic sacrifices she made to pay for the trips. On several occasions Jacqueline stated that happiness is not free, and she was willing to pay the price for the lyrical praises and sexual attention she received from men in Jamaica. "I know it may not be genuine," she said, "but Air Jamaica can have my money on a regular basis as long as these men here keep making me feel like a beautiful, Black woman. Where else am I going to get attention like this? At home? Girl, please! There, I'm invisible. Here, I can be seen. I'll pay money to be seen and appreciated." In another interview, Jacqueline further expressed how she felt visible in Jamaica and that it was about not only the sexual attention she received from men but also the sense of community she felt just by being present and walking the streets. She said,

> I've had people that've said very nice things to me. Like that I look fit. I look beautiful, etc. And have a nice day. It's not, "Can I have your telephone number?" "Can I get with you later?" "Where are you staying?" It's just a pure simple, compliment that I think is genuine.
>
> And you don't get that at home. [*Her voice rises.*] At home, you're invisible. At home, nobody notices you. You're not in settings where you're even around your own people. If you don't go to a mall, a family gathering, or a prescribed event, you're not around people in America like you are here on a daily basis. All you gotta do at five o'clock is go down by that clock tower [in Ocho Rios's town center]. And the world is coming off work and trying to get to their respective parishes. And there are people all up and down the streets. And you know, [Americans] don't walk and mingle with each other, and be among each other like they do here.
>
> *That's* what I love about Jamaica. *That's* what I love. That's what I crave. I'm going to be honest with you. I *crave* the recognition. I *crave* somebody just saying hello to me. I *crave* someone saying, "Have a nice day." I *crave* someone saying, "I like your tan." Or, "I like your hair." Or just saying *something* to me. Just recognizing that I'm here on the Earth. Yeah! I crave that. I miss that when I go back home. When I go back home [*snaps fingers*], I immediately become invisible. Nobody says a damn thing to me. We're scared to talk to each other anymore. We're *afraid* of each other. In the U.S. we don't talk to our brothers and sisters. We don't say nothing to nobody. You just walk and you just pray that you don't get stabbed in the back, you know.

Here, Jacqueline acknowledges a fear of other Black people that some hold in U.S. Black communities, describing how people are afraid to acknowledge each other and make one another visible. Scholars such as Harris-Perry, Shorter-Gooden, and Jones write about the ways Black people sometimes internalize shame and fear related to Blackness, as it is imagined as ugly, dangerous, criminal, and abnormal within white supremacist systems of power. All of these Black women scholars describe techniques of distancing that some Black people engage in to disconnect from other Black people they deem dangerous, or from whom they want to be distinguished in order to gain access to privilege. Jacqueline's need to become visible in Jamaica, and to connect to other Black people, keeps her coming back; it is this craving for community and belonging that is satisfied when she visits. For Jacqueline, traveling to Jamaica is about more than sex or romance; it is about a feeling of racial and diasporic belonging that she does not experience in the United States.

As I reflected on Jacqueline's frequent happiness declarations during our trips, I realized happiness for Jacqueline was a result of multiple factors as she traveled to and from Jamaica. Her happiness derived from being in a place where other Black people surrounded her. It was connected to her feeling like a part of the community. It was about the comfort friendship with me and other Girlfriends gave her. It was her recognizing that the conversations about Jamaica, and all the saving and planning it took to organize her trip, led to moments of pleasure, release, and escape from the burdens she felt at home. When Jacqueline sat in the bar watching the soccer game that opened this chapter, she was looking forward to the next few weeks in Jamaica and saw that her sacrifices of labor, time, and money were paying off as she experienced moments of happiness and connectivity in return. She was seen and recognized as a Black woman in this space, appreciated not only by the men surrounding her but by her GFT Girlfriends also, new and old.

Conclusion

As mentioned earlier in the chapter, individual and collective tears were present throughout GFT tours and other trips to Jamaica. Girlfriends shed tears of happiness when they met one another for the first time or reconnected. There was crying as Jamaica's beauty and serenity awed the ladies—its beaches, green spaces, and smells of fruit in the air triggering tears. There was crying when a woman got her heart broken or had to leave a Jamaican man who praised his way into her heart. I witnessed joyful tears as the plane landed in Jamaica. There was always crying the night before a Girlfriend left, the day of, and sometimes during the ride to the airport as one made the return home. And there were tears as some resisted the idea of going back to the everyday, frequently resulting in a changed flight itinerary, postponing the departure if only for one more day. There were tears of joy, validation, heartbreak, affirmation, and dread.

The night before a Girlfriend leaves Jamaica is almost always emotionally intense. If the Girlfriend was returning to the United States on her own while the rest of the group stayed for a day or two more, everyone wanted to show the person leaving the best night ever. The night could include a fancy dinner where everyone wore their best dressy outfit, or an all-night conversation in one Girlfriend's room, where everyone wore their pajamas and had a drink in hand. But it was this night when all Girlfriends realized their leisure and relaxing time was quickly coming to an end, and they were sometimes frantic about returning home. The Girlfriends staying longer tried to support the person leaving. It's as if the entire room helped the departing Girlfriend put her armor back on—slowly, piece by piece—while supporting her with the newfound friendship they created. They showered her with hugs and reminders to take care of herself as she ventured back into the racism, sexism, and endless responsibilities waiting for her at home. One Girlfriend from Washington, DC, said to me, "I never let someone cry alone," and this seemed to be the mantra for many women in the group. Numbers were exchanged and promises to visit each other's homes in the United States were made. They promised to contact each other on Jamaicans.com and share pictures from the trip.

A driver sensitive to the feelings of the departing Girlfriend was chosen carefully and was responsible for soothing her and making the ninety-minute ride to the airport as comfortable as possible. Usually the departing Girlfriend made this ride alone, as no one staying on the island wanted to interrupt their trip with the somberness of the drive to the airport.[32] That ride forced an ending or at least a disruption to the fantasy of the escape, and most did not volunteer for that. Each woman would have to deal with that reality in due time. At the airport the Girlfriend would wipe her tears, get out of the car, pay and the driver, hug him goodbye, and thank him for his comfort. And as she walked away with her baggage, one could sometimes see the physical and emotional recognition of what she was going back home to—a re-sensitization toward the weight of racism and sexism when one is leaving a space of belonging and home they never knew, to return to a too-familiar home one will never completely be settled in.

In this chapter I have offered some ways that we can think of Black women's leisure and travel in the pursuit of happiness as a political process that highlights connections between affect, race, gender, power, and privilege. The multiple meanings associated with Girlfriends' tears point to the ways their leisure trips to Jamaica temporarily lighten the burdens of American racism and sexism, while also enabling Girlfriends to seek safe spaces and affirmation from other African American women; experience desirability and belonging through romantic relationships and friendships with Jamaicans; and develop acceptance for who they feel they really are at their core. As part of the Girlfriend Tours annual trip, they partake in emotional bonding experiences with other Black American women, crossing national borders to speak their individual stories and participate in collective analysis of Black womanhood outside of crisis mode. They act as mirrors for one another—providing affirmation and validation and making themselves visible in newly formed friendships interpersonally and as a collective.

Their trips allow them to become visible in ways that they often feel invisible in the United States. Recognizing that sexism and racism influence their home and community spaces, they understand the stress of shifting and that they are required as Black women to do a significant amount of labor to maintain these spaces for family, friends, and loved ones. Additionally, some of the Girlfriends are aware of how age compounds this stress and invisibility, because people expect them to live less sexual, social, and leisurely lives as they age. As a coping strategy for this lack of visibility, acceptance, and desire they feel in the United States, Girlfriends travel to enjoy the gaze of Jamaican men while also being in the company of Girlfriends. This simultaneous feeling of desire and affirmation is central to the Girlfriend Tour. Jamaica allowed them to see their lives in the United States more clearly—what was limiting their happiness, and the steps they could take to experience it more regularly.

Additionally, a focus on race and gender during their travels helps us understand that for Black women, particularly the ladies of GFT, pursuing happiness, leisure, and recreation is about more than just getting their grooves back; it is about accessing a certain form of privilege and community they do not feel they have in the everyday. At the same time as they are demonstrating privilege, we see in the following chapters that their travel and leisure is often about escaping the burden of oppressive powers such as racism. I offer that the political process of obtaining happiness is not restricted by national boundaries because their racialized and gendered experiences are not constrained by these borders either. Their experiences of emotional transnationalism call researchers and scholars back to the ground, forcing us to deal with the fact that affect cannot simply be theorized as social and political but is always about the reality of its racialized textures, contours, and imprints.

For Black women in GFT engaging in this form of emotional transnationalism, affect—particularly their pursuit of happiness—is intimately connected to their understanding of race and racism. For them, how they feel Black, how they become Black, how they live as Black is frequently haunted by racism. They feel the racism from the past—the experiences of racism their ancestors or previous generations endured, stories passed down through the years. They feel the racism in the present, an experience they are currently having on the job, in school, in church, or in their neighborhood. They feel the racism in the future, a potential danger or crisis that may be experienced next year or in twenty years. It is difficult for these women to feel Black without feeling and engaging all the things that accompany race when racism—as specter or burdensome reality—is present in their lives. While these women desire pleasure and leisure, and understand the significance of these pursuits, they also are aware that even their happiness is in conversation with or in resistance to the ever-present reality of potential racism they face as African Americans. In this way, affect for them is deeply empirical, firmly grounded, because race and racism have real-life ramifications. They do not have the pleasure or privilege of thinking about feeling, emotion, or affect as abstract ideas that one can pontificate or theorize about for sport. Their engagement with transnational and diasporic processes in their pursuits of happiness is about praxis, and not simply about the theoretical.

Finally, exposing the labor behind Girlfriends' pursuits of happiness and the need to export parts of these pursuits outside of their nation's borders is important. The desires and trips of these Black women demonstrate that happiness is not an inalienable right. The labor embedded in their trips to Jamaica denaturalize the so-called right to the pursuit of happiness, showing how and why some Black people search for a literal, as well as psychic, space outside of U.S. racism. The added labor, burden, and distance traveled to find happiness shows that not everyone has the same access to the "right" of happiness; but it involves more labor for some, and the history of race/racism has everything to do with this. Girlfriends' experiences in the United States and Jamaica show us the complex politics of happiness as well as the importance of affect studies, as some understand that emotions are not only political but also embedded histories of racism and its survival.

I slowly walk down the alleyway that connects the beach to the street near my wooden cabin in Negril, careful not to cut my feet on the gravel along the way. I try to calm my belly as it turns with excitement and nervousness. What do you say to someone who shares your blood but is a stranger? How will I even know what he looks like? Over the phone, I forgot to tell my uncle Noel what I was wearing or get details about what he looks like so we would be able to recognize one another during this first meeting. How am I going to pick him out from anyone else on the road?

There isn't any need for me to worry. As soon as I walk onto the road I come across a chocolate-colored man who looks exactly like a mix of my grandfather Norman, my aunt Shelly, and her son Johnathan. At first glance I knew he was family. It's a bit of an eerie feeling meeting a complete stranger (especially in a country that's not your home) who looks like so many of your other family members. Noel could've joined us at Christmas dinner, and he would've fit in perfectly among all the different hues and accents sitting at the family table. Besides the tight-curled hair that my grandfather has, the brown oval-shaped eyes of my aunt, and the roundness of my cousin's face, my uncle also possessed the one thing that completely gave his family membership away—he had the oversized forehead that almost everyone in my family has, lovingly referred to as the "Rose Forehead" (after my grandfather's surname) or the "Five Head" (so big that it's bigger than a *fore*head) by family members and friends.

Noel looks me up and down, from the tips of my toes to the top of my head, taking in my flip-flops, shorts, tank top, light-brown skin, long legs, skinny frame, and shoulder-length hair all in one quick glance. "Where did you get that white man's nose?" he asks.

Shocked, I am silent for a moment. I question whether I've heard him correctly. Is he seriously asking about my nose? Certainly this is not the first thing he wanted to say to me. I mean I didn't expect this at all. How was I supposed to respond to a question like that? I felt myself getting a little defensive about the racial categorization of my biracial father, and I thought it wasn't polite to bring up race when just getting to know someone. I immediately recognized the irony of my reaction, as I was the anthropologist repeatedly interrupting people's vacations by annoying them with questions about race and racism.

2

"Giving Back" to Jamaica

Experiencing Community and Conflict While Traveling with Diasporic Heart

Each time I traveled with the women of Girlfriend Tours International, it was abundantly clear that the bonds they had with one another were not the only significant relationships during these trips. I realized that their sometimes tense yet sought-after connections with Jamaicans were also paramount. The tourism practices they participated in, and the sites the women decided to visit, took place within the context of what I call "diasporic contact zones." In spaces like airports, hotels, restaurants, and the beach, Girlfriends and their Jamaican interlocutors were able to test the elasticity of shared notions of Blackness, while also interrogating power differentials within African diasporic relationships.

In this chapter, I expand Mary Louise Pratt's concept of a "contact zone" to examine moments where the imagined diasporic community Girlfriends hold on to is both fortified and fractured.[1] These encounters demonstrate the multiple ways race, class, gender, and nationality are salient in imaginings of the African diaspora. As an example of these imaginings, I highlight the Girlfriends' attempt to "give back to Jamaica," engaging in a form of strategic tourist consumption with the intention of economically cooperating with Jamaicans, all of whom they view as diasporic kin. Additionally, I present one Jamaican interviewee's notion of the "master's complex"—a critique of African American participation in Jamaica's tourism economy and an analysis of nationalized and classed differences within the African diaspora. This discussion draws attention to how the Girlfriends' ability to travel, their access to American dollars, and their assumptions about (American) Blackness mark and emphasize asymmetries in their diasporic connections.

When I inquired as to why first-time travelers had such strong desires to visit Jamaica, or why these tourists repeatedly returned, I noted that many of the Girlfriends held on to three important ideas regarding race, diaspora, and their travels. The first was that because Jamaica is a country with a predominately Black population, many of the tourists saw it as a geographic escape from U.S.-based racism. Traveling to Jamaica was akin to visiting a Black paradise, where they could connect with other Black peoples and Blacknesses while enjoying the sun, beach, great food, and good music. Girlfriends' relationship to Jamaica as a Black paradise is discussed further in chapter 3.

The second notion was that for many of the Girlfriends, and some Jamaicans .com members, the Jamaica Tourist Board's call to "Come Back to Jamaica" was truly a beckoning to "return" to an imagined homeland filled with diasporic kin. Although one or two of my interviewees searched their family tree in hopes of finding Jamaican heritage, none of the African American women I studied had any Jamaican family ties. However, in their interviews and group discussions, it became obvious that they felt a deep sense of diasporic connection and kinship to Jamaicans and expected that because most of them were Black, Jamaicans felt the same. Girlfriends assumed that Jamaicans experienced similar bouts with institutional racism and racialized prejudice, and they saw this as indisputably connected to the ever-present history of African enslavement and exploitation of labor that African Americans and Jamaicans shared.

Last, I observed that Girlfriends traveled with what I call a "diasporic heart." As African Americans who sought belonging and shared identity with Jamaicans, they desired to "give back" to their diasporic kin. Their choice to travel to Jamaica, and their decision to repeatedly return, was based in the notion that their U.S. dollars could impact Jamaican lives, if that money was targeted and invested in the right places. They understood that their American citizenship allowed them to be mobile in ways some Jamaicans could not and to have access to economic resources they assumed many Jamaicans did not have. In this way, Girlfriends attempted to acknowledge and address the power and status differences embedded in their diasporic encounters, while holding on to a deep sense of connectedness to Jamaicans as Black people and members of the African diaspora. Still, they were often stunned when their notion of a shared connection was troubled or disavowed by Jamaicans.

In *Imperial Eyes: Travel Writing and Transculturation*, Mary Louise Pratt analyzes the descriptions of non-European areas of the world (such as the Caribbean and Central Africa) in the travel writings of European tourists and conquerors from the mid-sixteenth century through the late twentieth century.[2] She defines "contact zones" as "social spaces where disparate cultures meet, clash, and grapple with each other, often in highly asymmetrical relations of domination and subordination—like colonialism, slavery, or their aftermaths as they are lived out across the globe today."[3] Several scholars interested in the politics surrounding transculturation, border crossings, migration, and other forms of local and transnational interactions have engaged Pratt's idea of "contact zones" to investigate the relationships between power, cultural exchanges, and identity formation.

Pratt argues that in these spaces, where "peoples [who have been] geographically and historically separated come into contact with each other and establish ongoing relations, usually involving conditions of coercion, radical inequality, and intractable conflict," both non-European and European identities are produced.[4] Although Europeans focused on their imaginings of the "rest of the world" in these travel writings, Pratt points out that these narratives actually display how Europeans constructed and reconfigured their *own* identities through interactions with "Others."[5] She asks, "How have Europe's constructions of subordinated others been shaped by those others, by the constructions of themselves and their habitats that they presented to the Europeans?"[6] Pratt answers this question by concluding that "the entity called Europe was constructed from the outside in as much as from the inside out."[7] Here, she points to the long history of cultural transformation (for both the oppressor and oppressed) that results as groups define themselves in opposition to one another during acts of conquest and colonialism.

Similar to Pratt's commentary on European conquests, much of the research on contact zones focuses primarily on the power dynamics between people racialized as "white" (Europeans or North Americans) and those "Others" racialized as Black, Asian, or Latino ("non-Europeans").[8] However, I employ Pratt's concept of "contact zones" to explore what Tina Campt and Deborah Thomas call "diasporic hegemonies."[9] Campt and Thomas apply a feminist transnational analysis to the African diaspora, drawing attention to the ways racialized, classed, gendered, and nationalized differences are marked and interrogated within African diasporic communities. I contend that Girlfriend Tours, and the Jamaican tourist industry in general, are useful for investigating how African Americans hold on to hegemonic ideas of Blackness that provide insight into how they see themselves and how they imagine their diasporic kin. Brent Hayes Edwards points out in *The Practice of Diaspora* that the diaspora is configured and reconfigured through miscommunication and untranslatability.[10] Diasporic contact zones enable us to examine those critical moments when individuals are aware of "the ways transnational Black groupings are fractured by nation, class, gender, sexuality, and language," and to observe how these disidentifications or misidentifications are constitutive of diasporic subjectivities.[11] Subsequently, I offer this theorization of "diasporic contact zones" to examine how African Americans and Jamaicans express their understandings of racialized subjectivities (indexed by nation, class, and gender), in spaces where interlocutors are simultaneously imagined as diasporic community members *and* nationalized "Others." In this way, I attempt to move anthropologists away from conceptualizing diaspora as communities of similarities toward one of communities working with, and through, difference.

During my fieldwork, it became evident that the diasporic contact zones highlighted during GFT's tours were rich sites for demonstrating how both connections *and* fractures, similarities *and* differences, harmony *and* conflict, are embedded in African diasporic relationships. Diasporic contact zones, such as the hotel, the beach, and the airport in this research, are complex tourist sites where the forces at work are more than just the historical and contemporary structures that create the spaces, the cultures, and the groups present. The shared and divergent imaginings of community—the fantasies and ruptures of diasporic connection—are also at play. On the tours, Jamaicans and Americans mobilize Blackness and the African diaspora as concepts to shine light on difference and desires for unity. However, in many of these encounters, African American tourists and Jamaican hosts are not coming to the interaction with similar positionings within systems of power or with unified notions of what the diasporic community means to them. Subsequently, this imagined community is fraught with the dilemmas that arise as individuals navigate the increasingly complicated terrain of identity and community formations. I pay close attention to how one's access to travel and participation in tourism mark and emphasize these asymmetries. By focusing on these contact zones and Girlfriends' commitment to traveling with diasporic heart, I examine two specific questions: First, what might African Americans learn about race, diaspora, and difference as they encounter Jamaicans in tourist spaces? Second, how do their nationalized understandings and performances of Blackness inhibit or facilitate the creation of diasporic community and connectivity?

Giving Back: Traveling with a Diasporic Heart

I was intrigued by what the Girlfriends decided to spend money on during their trips to Jamaica. Most of them were lower middle class or middle class, working jobs such as high school guidance counselors or postal workers in the

United States. The common assumption by many Jamaicans and other Americans I spoke with was that the women were wealthy, and this was how they could afford to travel to Jamaica so often; however, this was not true. To pay for individual and group trips, many of the ladies made economic sacrifices, including working extra hours at their jobs or taking on a part-time job just to pay for their trips. Some women did without fixing their homes and major appliances—remodeling their kitchens or using their heat only if absolutely necessary—until they could pay for another trip to Jamaica. Others avoided social-life expenses in the United States, choosing to devote their entertainment budgets and "disposable" income for leisure costs in Jamaica. Finally, some made a vow not to travel domestically or to countries besides Jamaica.

Every year, the women of Girlfriend Tours International paid a significant amount of money to pursue happiness in Jamaica. To participate in the official, five-day annual Girlfriend Tour each woman paid $1,600–$2,400.[12] This price included hotel accommodations, airfare, local transportation, entrance fees for various tourist sites, and food. The total cost differed for each individual since it depended on how much alcohol she drank, whether she bought souvenirs, where she chose to dine during her free time, and if she paid for gifts for a boyfriend or sexual or romantic partner. Of course, ladies who returned to Jamaica every three to four months for longer trips (ranging from a week to an entire summer) spent thousands of dollars more annually. A one-bedroom apartment at an apartment complex in Ocho Rios frequented by many of the women charged $1,000–$1,500 a month, whereas a week in the same apartment amounted to $560, since there was a daily charge. Taxi rides around Negril or Ocho Rios for tourists can cost anywhere from $3 to $10 each. Chartering a car or van for a ride to the airport ranges from $60 to $125. Additionally, many of the ladies spend money on new clothes, gifts for Jamaican friends, and other miscellaneous expenses. And every trip, without exception, one or two of the ladies decide that they just cannot leave Jamaica on the scheduled day of departure and call the airlines to delay their flight for an additional day or two at a cost of up to $100 per day.

Most of the Girlfriends understood the economic value their American dollars had in Jamaica, and they believed that making smart consumer decisions as tourists not only saved them money but also enabled them to empower those they felt they could most effectively help. In fact, they viewed their decision to repeatedly return to Jamaica instead of visiting other Caribbean countries as a way to support individuals in the Jamaican economy. This strategic form of tourist consumption and spending practices is what I call traveling with a "diasporic heart." After several conversations about "giving back," I surmised that Girlfriends included the word "back" for two reasons: First, some of the women expressed a desire to pay Jamaica back for feelings of comfort, happiness, and affirmation they could not find at home in the United States. Subsequently, they sought out opportunities to put as much money as they could afford directly into the hands of those they thought needed it. I noticed that they often gave money to those who facilitated and encouraged the fantasy of Jamaica as second home or Black paradise. Drivers who embraced the Girlfriends' obsession with Jamaica or servers at hotels who enthusiastically welcomed them back benefited from big tips or GFT members' return business. Jamaicans who provided a sense of belonging and made the women feel seen (countering their invisibility in the United States) oftentimes benefited more from "giving back" practices.

Additionally, their diasporic hearts felt a responsibility to give to other Black people as frequently as they could. Girlfriends' choices about where to stay and from whom to buy were intentional political choices connected to racial identification and their desire to "help other Black people out." They saw their attempts to economically support Jamaicans as cultivating a sense of diasporic connectivity and addressing the classed and nationalized privilege they had as American citizens. Instead of residing at all-inclusives that were frequently owned by American and European foreigners, Girlfriends usually stayed at hotels locally owned by Jamaicans. They ate at locally owned establishments and used Jamaican-owned transportation companies, putting money into the hands of those they viewed as diasporic kin. It was during this practice of "giving back" that I saw Girlfriends interact the most with other Jamaican women, filling their suitcases at home with toiletries, necessities, and clothing for women staff at the places where they stayed or ate; the moms and sisters of their Jamaican male friends; or local orphanages or specific families they had built relationships with. They also sought out businesses owned by Jamaican women, which were sometimes few and far between depending on the city they were vacationing in.

In an interview, I asked Jacqueline, a veteran American traveler, why she kept returning to Jamaica and how she came to make decisions about where to put her money. She stated,

> I don't care what anybody says, you could go somewhere else, or you could just stay home. The minute you step in this country you impact the economy. The minute you come here you've contributed a little bit. Whose hands it falls in is not really under your control, but you are coming, you are a repeat visitor. All the Jamaicans I talk to, when they find out how many times I've been here, they seem to appreciate that I come back, and back, and back. I think it's good for the economy.

According to the Caribbean Tourism Organization's website, Jacqueline's sentiments are right. In 2004, Jamaica depended on U.S. tourists for 70.4 percent of their tourism market, which continues to contribute significantly to the country's gross national product.[13] The practice of giving back was an attempt by Jacqueline and other Girlfriends to engage in strategic consumption and have some control over whom their tourist dollars empowered. In particular, their decisions related to transportation and tipping are useful for demonstrating and examining diasporic heart, as these spaces are also prime diasporic contact zones in the tourist industry.

THE AIRPORT

For some of the Girlfriends, Sangster International Airport, located in Montego Bay, is considered the first "tourist" site they visit in Jamaica. Girlfriends often chose to fly into Sangster (one of the two major airports in the country) because it is closest to Negril, their most frequented destination. Sangster also became the first site of "giving back" for some visitors, as they donated money to the (mostly women) singers who welcomed them or decided which vendors and drivers (mostly men) they wanted to support. In many of her trip reports, Jacqueline would gush over the singing ladies who welcomed her back to Jamaica each trip. The group of four to six women would sing songs and entertain tourists as they deplaned and headed to customs. Dressed in clothing similar to the traditional wear of Black peoples who labored on plantations in Jamaica's past, these women would draw the attention of some visitors, who would stay for a few minutes and enjoy the music, while others moved quickly past them. After seeing these performances a couple of times and being disappointed with the insufficient tips that the singers received, Jacqueline began to put money away for them while she was in the United States. When she returned to Jamaica and deplaned, she would place an envelope of bills into each singer's hand. To provide the group with publicity, she also began to post pictures of their performances in the virtual community of which many Girlfriends were members, describing her ritual of giving back and thanking the women for making her feel so welcome.

As other tourists took notice of the singers in these virtual trip reports and during their own vacations, several Girlfriends and web-board members began to take part in Jacqueline's efforts, giving their own donations and gifts to the ladies when they traveled. Some of the Girlfriends made this their first stop on the GFT tour, pausing to talk to the singers, thanking them for the nice welcome, and taking pictures. The singers became an integral part of the homecoming experience for Girlfriends and acted as catalysts for a ritualized form of giving back during each visit.

DRIVERS AND TOUR GUIDES

For many Girlfriends, choosing the "right" driver/tour guide for their trip was significant for several reasons: First, having a driver who arrived on time, would wait through flight delays, and knew how to get directly to their hotel meant Girlfriends could begin their trip without the hassles and mishaps that other tourists often dealt with. Additionally, because some of the women were traveling alone, they were concerned about having a driver who owned a reliable vehicle and drove safely. Knowing that they were in good hands made many of the women feel welcome and more comfortable entering a foreign space. In some ways, the drivers and tour guides acted as social and cultural ambassadors for Jamaica, introducing visitors to the country if it was their first trip, or helping them discover new things if it was a return trip.

Second, the decision to put their American dollars directly into the hands of a particular driver or tour guide was one that most visitors saw as another method of giving back. For example, Angelia, one of the cofounders of Girlfriend Tours, told me the owners made a conscious decision to utilize a certain Jamaican tour guide or driver for a consecutive number of group tours in order to provide him with their consistent business for multiple years.[14] This enabled him to buy a van or an additional vehicle and build up his business by employing other Jamaicans. After Angelia and Marilyn felt that he was well established, they would move on to supporting another person's tour company. In this way, they saw themselves contributing economically to diasporic kin, providing that person with sustainability, and choosing how their American tourists dollars impacted a small sector of the Jamaican economy.

Oftentimes the arrangements for a driver were made online or on the telephone while Girlfriends were in the States, after the person received referrals for drivers from Marilyn, Angelia, or other Girlfriends. Most of the drivers hired were not part of a formal transport service (such as the popular Jamaican Union of Travellers Association, or JUTA), because the women felt they could avoid bureaucracy and decide whose hands their money reached directly. On rare occasions when women did not arrange a driver's service before arriving in Jamaica, she would pick a driver from outside of baggage claim. In those situations she would often choose a driver who was *not* affiliated with JUTA—a practice that went directly against the advice of the Jamaica Tourist Board and guides like *Lonely Planet*, which suggested tourists only use drivers with JUTA certification and the signature red license plates. Again, this was a way Girlfriends felt they could give back to Jamaicans who could not afford the expensive fees required to become a part of the union or to own their transportation vehicles outright.

TIPPING

Each visit to Jamaica included frequent discussions about how to tip employees servicing Girlfriends at hotels and restaurants. The tipping discussion was part of the first-time visitors' "training," (an informal dinner orientation) as veteran travelers made it a point to repeatedly mention that hotel staff made much less than the U.S. minimum wage. Veterans also encouraged first-timers to bring gifts for hotel staff as another way to give back if they were in accommodations that discouraged tipping. Because all-inclusive resorts do not allow tipping and will sometimes terminate an employee who receives a tip, Girlfriends did their best not to patronize those hotels. Before each GFT tour, Girlfriends would remind each other to get one hundred American dollar bills from their banks at home, so they could tip drivers and other service workers without having to give the less valuable Jamaican money. This decision to tip with American dollars countered the "get the most for your American dollar" mentality that I saw some other American tourists use when exchanging money or acquiring services. Since African Americans have the reputation of being horrible tippers in Jamaica, Girlfriends worked diligently to fight against this stereotype.

Discussions about tipping and other forms of giving back sometimes unveiled the nationalized and classed assumptions underlining these money practices. Both Jamaicans and Americans noted the widespread assumption that Americans had money, or at least more money than Jamaicans, and life was economically easier for them. This was the assumption that often drove the idea of strategic tourist consumption and giving back. However, the notion that there was class diversity in Jamaica, and that some Jamaicans had significantly more money than Americans often went unrecognized. Jennifer, an African American woman in her early forties from the West Coast, was a friend of some members of Girlfriend Tours International and a Jamaicans.com boardite. While discussing stereotypes of Jamaicans as beggars and hustlers in an interview she says:

> You see, that's why I always tell people "Go somewhere [other than Negril and Ocho Rios] in Jamaica." 'Cause there are places like Mandeville where Jamaicans are just going to assume we [Americans] don't have as much as they do. A lot of people will come to [Jamaica] and they'll say "Oh, I've been to Jamaica fifty times. I know Jamaica so well." They don't know the rich Jamaica. I think that's important because some of the [Americans]

believe, Black or white, that everybody here is begging for something. Well there are a lot of communities that are not tourist communities where they are poor, but still would never beg. But Americans have no idea how much wealth is in parts of Jamaica.

Here Jennifer points to the lack of knowledge American tourists of all races (including veteran travelers) may have about Jamaicans. She encourages them to diversify the locations on their travel itineraries and get out of the tourist sectors, so they can get a better sense of the different classed experiences Jamaicans have. Also, she suggests that Americans be careful in their assumption that the Jamaicans they interact with and seek to connect to, are all people who do not have as much as the American trying to give back.

Come Back to Jamaica: Travel as Escape and Homecoming

When I asked Girlfriends to tell me about their deep connections to Jamaica, most referred to their arrival stories—the first time they stepped off the plane, smelled the Jamaican air, were caressed by the breeze, and saw a country full of Black people they believed looked just like them. They felt a sense of homecoming, a spiritual connection, which some had a hard time putting into words. Jacqueline describes her arrival story here:

> From the moment you landed in Sangster, you looked around and saw just Black people. _Your people._ Mostly. Not to say there are not other races in Jamaica. Everybody knows that. But overwhelmingly, when you see your people, you're no longer in the minority, it's mostly *Black* people that you see [*tone rises in excitement*]. I mean right off the bat that makes you feel like you came home, somewhere. It's like, "Wow! My folks!" It's like a big family reunion. And I immediately felt like somehow part of me belonged here.

This feeling of homecoming was so poignant for some travelers that their trip reports often began with the memorializing of this specific moment.

However, some Jamaicans.com boardites, like Sarah, put this homecoming story into a more explicit diaspora narrative, describing Jamaica as a type of "practice Africa" or a stopover in their pilgrimage to one day get back home to the continent. During my fieldwork, Sarah attended only one annual Girlfriend Tour, but it was clear that she had formed close friendships with multiple women in the group over the years. A veteran traveler and frequent participant in the web community, Sarah was from the North but had lived a significant part of her life in two states in the South. She was in her early fifties and a single mother of a teenage son.

In an interview in the United States, Sarah declared that Jamaicans and Black Americans shared similar life experiences because they "were in the same boat" during the transatlantic slave trade, "but just got off at different stops." She stated that she was thankful she had a few trips to Jamaica under her belt before she went to Kenya, because her sixty-six trips to Jamaica helped her "deal with the same tricks and hustles" present in tourist areas in Kenya. The quick flight from the United States to a country where she felt she could navigate unfamiliar streets on her on and learn the cultural expectations meant she was able to get her feet wet traveling internationally before going to another space that was farther away and even more culturally and linguistically dissimilar to home.

A few Girlfriends echoed Sarah's sentiments, claiming that they liked being in Jamaica because it was nice to be around and observe Black people who did not have to deal with the daily burdens of American racism. One American woman went so far as to state that Jamaicans were better off, because their stop on the transatlantic slave trade meant they did not have to be raised in the "stressful Babylon of the U.S." Finally, some Americans spoke of Jamaica as a transcendental home, a place where they should have been born and where they wanted their spirit to go after death.

These stories of homecoming and spiritual return are similar to, yet slightly different from, the narratives of homecoming present in Saidiya Hartman's and Bayo Holsey's work. Holsey's discussion of heritage tourism in Ghana moves us away from Mary Louise Pratt's concentration on contact between whites and racialized Others to a geographical site where differentials of power are wrapped up in the construction of gendered, classed, and nationalized African diasporic identities. In "Transatlantic Dreaming: Slavery, Tourism, and Diasporic Encounters," Holsey writes about the "sense of personal and collective catharsis" these homeland voyages that are the crux of diaspora tourism provide to African Americans.[15] She reminds us that this "fantasy trope of transatlantic reunion" is not simply desired by African Americans; Ghanaians also participate in and construct these diasporic fantasies, although from a disadvantaged economic position. She writes,

> In [Ghanaians'] eyes, diaspora tourism serves to confirm the success of U.S. capitalism, with African Americans as its agents. But their critique is not primarily a critique of the world capitalist system; rather, it is a critique of their unfavorable position within it. In other words, they seek

access to travel as well as to flows of capital and goods that they see tourists enjoying.[16]

Holsey argues that "both African Americans and Ghanaians participate in simultaneous yet reverse imaginative processes or transatlantic dreamings that converge within sites of painful memories of slavery's past."[17] It is important to note that both Ghanaians and African Americans engage in the construction of diasporic relations based predominately on the recognition of similar phenotypes.

Although Girlfriends certainly kept pleasure and leisure as their first priority, and are less invested than the tourists in Holsey's work in revisiting an "original" moment of dispersal in Africa, or even Jamaica, they do actively seek to connect with others whom they believe are diasporic kin based on this assumed shared history. Their stories describe a different kind of imagined homeland from those previously highlighted in the scholarship on diaspora—one that keeps Africa in sight, and recognizes its significance, but places it in the periphery of the diasporic imaginary. Their focus on "Africa" could be critiqued as a pop culture, fantastical imagining of a homeland without particular attention to the politics and specificity of contemporary life on the continent. Their imagining of Africa is a byproduct of sorts to their primary obsession and desire for Jamaica. At no time during my ethnographic study was I made aware of actual plans to travel to Africa, nor were they realistically discussed. Nor did any of Girlfriends point out the irony in the fact that their frequent trips to Jamaica were at least financially prohibiting their goals of reaching the "original" homeland.

Finally, it seems that most times Girlfriends were not cognizant of, or at least did not explain, how their nationalized and classed perspectives influenced how they imagined Africa. Gina Dent warns about this in her work:

> Black Americans in the United States now have unprecedented access to cultural and economic capital "by fair means or foul" as bell hooks points out. We must, therefore, begin to analyze the relative power derived from our position as citizens, however unsatisfied, of these United States. And this means thinking through the hall of mirrors in which our cultural power gets projected as political power, but also the ways our cultural power allows the project of one national black culture around the world as Coco Fusco calls "prototype of blackness." We must mark the dangers not only of an Afrocentrism that reinvents Africa to satisfy our need to fight our own internal national cultural battles, but of what Paul Gilroy renames it as—Americocentrism. How often, for example, do we think of what it means to have those privileges, like the ability, barring the eco-

nomic contingencies that overwhelmingly plague us yet, to travel where we want? Unlike the Haitians and the Sudanese and other African and diasporic peoples who cannot enter the United States and certainly are not invited to stay, we can visit the Africa we want to reinvent.[18]

Here, Dent wonderfully illustrates the nationalized, classed, and diasporic forces at play as Girlfriends utilize their American class status and citizenship to travel to other countries, but imagine these spaces—Africa *and* Jamaica—in narrow ways that serve their own nationalized conceptions of Blackness. This "prototype of Blackness" they hold on to prescribes certain stereotypes and notions about what Blackness is and hinders one from seeing how privilege influences access to other Black spaces.

As part of a series of public dialogues on diasporic hegemonies at Duke University in 2005, scholar Saidiya Hartman wrestled with some of the complexities of this relationship between African Americans and Africa. She asked the audience, "If we leave the U.S., can we leave the history and results of slavery and racism behind? How can we return home without focusing on Africa? Can the desire to reach the promiseland be satisfied without journeying to Africa?"[19] I would argue that for most of the Girlfriends the answer to the first question would be "no"—while they love Jamaica and travel there frequently to escape American racism, part of what draws them specifically to Jamaica is their perspective that it is a central node in the historical and contemporary imagining of the African diaspora and transatlantic slave trade. But they would probably answer the second and third questions with a "yes"—for some of them, their trips to Jamaica are a returning to an ancestral home, although they understand that it is different from those motherlands and homelands in Africa.

Engaging "Other" Black Peoples in Diasporic Contact Zones

Requesting that we complicate the narrow focus on moments of dispersal, a homeland, or chronology within diasporic imaginings, anthropologist Lena Sawyer encourages researchers to examine the ways diaspora is connected to production and consumption, particularly the reproduction of Black subjectivities in processes of racialization and nationalization. In her article "Racialization, Gender, and the Negotiation of Power in Stockholm's African Dance Courses," Sawyer explores how racialized and gendered power relations are negotiated and reconfigured through interactions between African men who are dance instructors and white Swedish women students in African dance classes in Stockholm. Sawyer takes up the concept of Pratt's contact zones to theorize identity formation and cultural exchange in Stockholm; however, she updates the theoretical utility of this concept by connecting these micro-spaces of identity production and negotiation with larger processes of globalization, including migration and gendered divisions of labor. Her investigation of the ways race, place, and gender are utilized in discourses of belonging and legitimacy by both Swedish women and African men centers on the multiple imaginings of Africa these individuals articulate and enact and the ways these shifting conceptions of Africa are used to reconfigure and disrupt ideologies of power.[20]

While some of the African men Sawyer interviewed thought of Africa as home, as a place where family resided, and as an integral part of their African identities, some of the white Swedes Sawyer interviewed echoed long-held stereotypes of the continent, conceptualizing Africa as a place of rich customs and premodern traditions, where people were close to nature, earthy, sensual, and musical. In fact, African dance instructors (especially Gambian men) drew upon long-standing stereotypes of Africa to create their own economic niche and market their dance classes to these working- and middle-class, white Swedish women. In this way, the African dance classroom becomes a site where different imaginings of Africa may be reconfigured as African men and Swedish women encounter one another. Sawyer explains how various imagined Africas were incorporated into a sensual and sexual Black masculinity that these African immigrant men performed, while simultaneously encouraging and providing space for white Swedish women to access their own sensuality. This access to African musicality and sensuality through African dance gave white Swedish women who "love the culture" a leisurely outlet for escaping the burden of labor inside and outside the household. Through performances of "traditional" African dances, white Swedish women are promised that they will become "real women" through personal transformations and can expect to "reconnect with [their] feminine and womanly sides."[21] In the classroom, white Swedish women can relinquish their cold, rigid body movements and learn how to bend and be flexible in a sexy manner. In these contact zones, Sawyer demonstrates how the interactions between white Swedish women and African men are fraught with struggles over power, including those related to performances of gender roles, claims to racial authenticity, and access to labor opportunities.

Although the Black American women in this research are racialized differently than the white Swedish women in Sawyer's work, there are some similarities. Just as white Swedish women connected with their sensuality in the African dance classrooms, some Girlfriends did express a connection to a sensuality and sexuality in Jamaica that they felt was unavailable to them in the United States. Additionally, some Girlfriends shared similar conceptualizations of a "traditional" African culture and believed it influenced cultural traditions and practices in Jamaica. In this way, Jamaica was viewed as greatly impacted by Africa, as a space that was closer to African culture because of its location in the historical transatlantic slave trade and because it was predominately Black. Jamaicans were seen as holding on to traditional African culture in ways that African Americans could not for numerous reasons: (1) African Americans were one geographical step farther away from Africa in the slave trade; (2) the white majority in the United States desecrated and purposely erased African influences; and (3) African Americans were not able to know, or were not interested in knowing, their connections to Africa in the ways Girlfriends assumed Jamaicans did and could. For some of the women, Jamaica was imagined as an island paradise where the land and people are natural (represented by the Rasta's dreadlocks), earthy (especially the ganja), sensual (heard in the lyrics Jamaican men use to draw in tourist women), and hypersexual (ascribed onto the Black bodies of young men interested in older, foreign women).[22]

While describing how Jamaicans and Black Americans are different, Jacqueline invokes some of the same "traditional" concepts of Africa the white Swedish women in Sawyer's work held on to:

> The difference is that Jamaica is . . . and thank God, this is what I admire about this country so much. I think they have vastly held on to the African-centric parts of this, of our culture *more* than we Americans were able to. I think we were forced to assimilate a lot more, give up a lot more for us to blend in. But because it's basically a Black nation, a Black culture, they were able to hold on to more of the Afro-centric part. . . . So much of it Americans, African Americans have had to make up like that Kwanzaa mess [*disgusted tone*] and all that stuff. We just had to go and make us up some stuff to try and reconnect with our African roots. But Jamaica, they never let go of it. They never let go of the obeah woman, they never let go of the drumming, they never let go of the nine night, they never let go of the yam, of the boiled banana, they never let go of certain foods and everything that is just so earthy, and so African.[23] Even their attire, their hairstyles, you know, that kind of thing. But we, we just totally assimilated with white people and then tried to flip back [*motions with hand*] and find our Black roots afterwards, like [*raises voice*] "Oh! Gee, I'm Black! I need to be doing something." They never let go of it. That's why I admire Jamaican people more. I'm not downing *my* folks. I'm just saying *circumstances* made things happen differently. And when I come here (and my next step is to Africa), but along the way if I could

trace the route through the Caribbean and then back to Africa [*makes imaginary route with her finger*], and you *know* I'm gonna make it there. That's what I admire about the Jamaican culture. It's more Afro-centric than the African American culture.

In this quote, Jacqueline references the different racialized experiences African Americans and Jamaicans may have, which is a discussion I frequently had while in Jamaica. Jacqueline argues that Jamaicans were able to preserve more of their "African" cultural roots, such as the obeah woman and the nine night, better than African Americans because they live in a country populated by a Black majority, while African Americans are a minority in a predominantly white country. In fact, members of both groups repeatedly pointed out that Jamaicans often described themselves as "Jamaican" first and "Black" second, arguing that they do not have to define themselves in opposition to white people. Girlfriends viewed this ability to describe oneself by nationality first and race second as a privilege symbolizing a sense of freedom or racial progress, or as a release from constantly experiencing life within the racialized dichotomy of Black and white.

As I accompanied a multigendered, multiracial group of American tourists on their trip to Negril in 2006, it became quite clear that some Americans had a difficult time with the "Other" Blackness they encountered while in Jamaica. Maya, one of my key interlocutors, organized this trip for eleven of her friends and coworkers (and their significant others). In her late fifties, Maya was a civil servant from the Midwest who lived on her own at home. She was the mother of a grown daughter, who would sometimes travel to Jamaica but not often during an official tour. While Maya was the primary recruiter for this tour, GFT cofounder Angie helped organize the trip and accompanied group members on the tour. The group was composed of fourteen people from the Midwest—one white man, one white women, two Black men, and eleven Black women—ranging in age from twenty-eight years old to late fifties. Initially, I was excited to accompany this group during their travels because for many of them (twelve, to be exact) it was their first trip to Jamaica. I was interested in observing how "newcomers" to the country might have different experiences than the individuals I normally traveled with, who were associated with Girlfriend Tours International and Jamaicans.com. I wanted to compare their new experiences encountering nationalized difference with those of the Girlfriends and board-ites, who seemed to be more knowledgeable about, or at least aware of, the cultural differences Americans might encounter as they interacted with Jamaicans.

The differences were obvious almost immediately. Throughout the trip it was clear that these individuals knew very little about Jamaica or Jamaican culture and that they had not come into contact with many Jamaicans in their hometown or frequented places where Jamaican food or music was available for consumption. Although Maya, a veteran traveler, attempted to prepare them by telling the group about her own experiences in the country, their lack of knowledge about Jamaica, and their unwillingness to "experience Jamaica the right way" (in her opinion), contributed to the fact that this trip differed drastically from our previous trips with Girlfriend Tours and Jamaicans.com. None of the members of the group were boardites in the virtual community, nor did they seem to know much about the website's role in Maya's life. They had simply heard her discuss her trips to Jamaica at work and wanted to experience some of the things she described in her stories of "paradise on earth."

Throughout the trip, there were numerous moments where individuals seemed to be negotiating the varied classed and racialized positions people of African descent living in the United States and Jamaica occupied. In a conversation with other group members about global poverty, Eric, an African American man, said he did not know Jamaica was considered a "Third World" country. Although he stated on two occasions that parts of Jamaica looked like the impoverished areas of his hometown (seeming to make a connection to the similar classed experiences people in these two locations may have), Eric often engaged in discourse that distanced his U.S. home from Jamaica, describing Jamaicans as "those people" and discussing Americans and Jamaicans using an "us vs. them" form of discourse.

Eric went on to inform me during a drive through the hills that he thought my research "experiment" should actually be to take a family from Jamaica to the United States and see how they reacted to the houses, wealth, and technology we had there. "It would blow their minds!" he exclaimed. When I replied that Jamaicans have been traveling to and making homes in the United States for generations, he responded with silence and a look of confusion. It did not seem to register that the Jamaicans living in New York, Florida, or even in Mississippi and Louisiana could have possibly come from the exact same hills we were driving through. Furthermore, he saw no irony in the fact that *his* mind was blown and that he was enthralled by some form of racially charged, class-based cultural shock while he experienced Jamaica, particularly the extreme poverty some lived with. He was often heard stating, "I couldn't do it! I couldn't live like this."

Throughout the trip I noticed Maya getting more and more annoyed with some of Eric's comments about Jamaicans. In her room late at night, or under her breath at meals, she would murmur that Eric and some of the other group members weren't "doing Jamaica right." They were not getting it in the way she and other Girlfriends got it. In a later interview with me in Jamaica, Maya discussed how foreigners and native folks alike always discouraged her from looking for Black communities when she traveled, whether it was in Puerto Rico or Jamaica, warning her that these areas were dangerous. She did not understand this sentiment, declaring, "Black people gonna find Black people! I always wanna go and see me." Maya informed me that one of the main reasons she traveled was to understand how Black people lived in various locations, and she repeatedly traveled to Jamaica because she felt a deep connection to Black communities there. She could see the differences, and wanted to learn more about them, but also saw all Black peoples as part of one diasporic community and a reflection of herself as a Black person. This was different from Eric's perspective.

Eric's comments pronounced that while Jamaicans were Black people, the living conditions of some he encountered and the less industrialized nature of the country led him to conclude they were differently Black in a way that did not draw him closer but instead emphasized the distance and differences from him and his community. While Eric readily admitted that he was not rich in the United States, his declaration that he could not "live like this!" implies that he saw himself as having access to some privilege that Jamaicans did not. In this way, he was not "doing Jamaica right" by the standards of GFT. Whereas Maya and other Girlfriends often prided themselves on releasing their U.S.-based expectations and their sense of privilege, and accepting Jamaica and its people on their own terms, Eric refused to do this, going as far as to rebuke Jamaican cuisine and eat pizza and pasta for the majority of his trip.[24] In many ways, Eric's conclusions that Jamaicans were poor, ate strange foods, and were dangerous reinscribed the stereotypical notions of Blackness Maya was trying to rebel against by seeking Black communities out when she traveled. Here, we see a rupture and fracture in the diasporic imagining that many Girlfriends, especially Maya, sought to hold on to during their trips as they sought diasporic connectivity and belonging. However, Eric was not the only person who saw differences between African Americans and Jamaicans.

Girlfriends did at times note the differences between their lived experiences and that of Jamaicans. They seemed to get particularly frustrated when Jamaicans did not share their sense of racialized consciousness, "see" racist acts, or get angry with white people for racism. In her interview in the United States, Gayle shared,

> For instance, they don't think racism exists in Jamaica. And yeah, you could say it doesn't to some extent, and it's really class. But it's the same thing in the long run. It really is the same thing. It is the method of choice

that keeps a *whole* race of people down. And because it's about one race of people, it's racism. They may say it's about class of people and all that. It's racism. So they don't see it that way. And I think it's because they just have not been exposed to it. People don't talk about it. It's not revealed [to them] in the way it's been revealed to us. They don't have the Martins, the Malcolms, the James Baldwins—they don't have all of our history that has traveled all over the world and has come back and said, "Okay. This is what racism looks like." You know. The Maya Angelous. All of the female authors that say, "This is how you Black women should look at yourselves. You are the queen. This is what you're doing to tear yourself down." They don't have all of that there. And so they just don't see it. But it is the same. I think it's delivered the same way. They just don't see it.

Gayle was frustrated by the argument some Jamaicans made that racism was a burden African Americans brought to Jamaica, and not one indigenous to their country. It was an argument I heard from quite a few Jamaicans after Girlfriends left and I was able to interact with Jamaican interlocutors one-on-one, or once they heard that my family was Jamaican but I lived in the United States. In the middle of a nightclub one evening, an older Jamaican man who had lived in the United States for twenty years cornered me by the bar and, yelling over dancehall music, schooled me on the differences between Jamaicans and African Americans. He thought African Americans were lazy, took free public education for granted, did not work as hard as other Black people (mostly immigrants) in the United States, and then brought all of their "racism issues" with them everywhere they went, including when they came to Jamaica. According to him, Jamaicans were hard workers, valued education because they had to pay for it, were from a small island making a big impact on the world (see reggae music), and understood that if you wanted something you had to go after it or make it yourself. They didn't wait around for white people to hand it to them. While certainly not all Jamaicans I spoke with echoed this man's sentiments, it was surprising to me how many Jamaicans shared pieces of his argument with me as I tried to engage them in discussions about racism.

It was this line of thinking that annoyed Gayle and led her to these passionate statements in her interview. Here, she claims that Jamaicans are ignorant, or at least less informed and educated about the ways racism operates, because they do not have access to the worldwide observations that activists and writers such as Maya Angelou and Malcolm X publicized to the African American people. Seemingly unaware of the activism and writings of Caribbeanists such as Marcus Garvey, Amy Jacques Garvey, Walter Rodney, and C. L. R. James, Gayle perpetuates a strong sense of African American ownership over the experience of racism. She was not able to recognize that racism operates in a variety of ways and may be differently connected to class, gender, and nationality in various locations. Nor was she able to push against "a homogenization of transnational Black [American] identities," as Clarke and Thomas urge.[25] I somewhat understood her frustration, as my conversations with Jamaicans who insisted that racism was over often became heated, and I was sometimes labeled as one of those "ridiculous African Americans that are always focused on race."

Of course, this was not how all Jamaicans I interacted with felt. There were times when I would have the pleasure of traveling outside tourist areas and relaxing in a Jamaican friend's home or neighborhood where folks would play dominoes, do hair, or just relax and engage in reasoning.[26] In these rare and sometimes brief encounters I would hear from those who disagreed with these narrow pronouncements about racism, and I would begin to understand some of the complexities surrounding how race and racism operated in Jamaica. Many of the Rastafarians I spoke with, or those who subscribed to some of the Black nationalist ideologies of the Rastafarian religion and culture, discussed the social and institutional oppression that global Black peoples have experienced and, in some instances, shared. However, the majority of Jamaicans I spoke with, both women and men, felt disconnected from African Americans, particularly in relation to the assumed shared experiences of racial discrimination.

Devan, a Jamaican hotel worker in his early twenties from Ocho Rios, proclaimed unequivocally that Jamaicans and Black Americans had very different experiences when it came to race and racism. Devan did not have much interaction with Girlfriends during their trips, but knew them because he worked at one of the hotels they frequented. In my interview with him, he stated:

> I think Black people in the States think it's safer for them [race-wise] in Jamaica. There are not as many racial restrictions for them in Jamaica, that's why they keep coming back. I believe if you stop talking about racism, it will go away. Black Americans and Jamaicans have different definitions of racism. What Black Americans see as racist, Jamaicans would not see it as that. An Indian Jamaican calling a boy a "Black dutty bwoy."[27] Jamaicans would see that as an insult, but not racist. It's not the "Black" part that would bother them; it's the "dutty." Americans see the "Black" as racist. We don't have that type of chip on our shoulders. Because racism doesn't exist here, Black Americans and white Americans are more comfortable.

Devan echoes Girlfriends' and other Black American tourists' commentary that Jamaica is a place where Black Americans can experience a brief escape from American racism, which is what keeps they coming back. But in direct opposition to Gayle's perspective, Devan feels that racism is not a shared experience for Jamaicans and Black Americans. In fact, he implies that if Black Americans would stop talking about it, it would cease to exist.

I asked Devan how he would explain the differences in Jamaican and Black American understandings of race and racism, especially since the African Americans I interviewed were adamant that racism existed. He responded,

> People [in Jamaica] only began to take offense to "nigga" when they started watching cable and found out it was an insult.[28] "Oh, now it's bad." We've been saying it in Jamaica for a long time. Before it was about money or no money in Jamaica. But now the miseducation of Jamaican people is by American culture through cable. That's how the U.S. controls the world. CNN tells everything from an American perspective. The miseducation of Jamaican people is what causes us to differentiate now and be aware of race.

Several things stick out in Devan's response. Here, and throughout the interview, I noted that Devan's definition of "racism" was centered in the idea that racism was about individualized acts of discrimination and language. This may be why he immediately turns to the use of the word "nigga" as an example of something (Black) Americans would deem racist. This definition of "racism" was different from the one Gayle was operating from in her interview, which included both everyday acts of racist behavior *and* institutional racism and structural forms of oppression, such as discriminatory business practices. Furthermore, Devan at times used the terms "racism" and "race" synonymously, implying that an awareness of race was also an awareness of, or even a claim to, racism. As an African American who sees many things through a racialized lens, Gayle argues that Jamaicans need to be more exposed to racialized analyses so they can better see the shared experiences they have with Black Americans. However, Devan argues that this infusion of racialized lenses into Jamaican culture through an invasion of American media is a form of miseducation. From his perspective, Jamaicans were previously discussing and analyzing the classed and economic inequities in Jamaican society, but now are distracted by the race talk brought in through cable television. Also telling is that Devan does not distinguish between Black Americans and (white) "Americans" in his comments. Subsequently, when he states that the "U.S. controls the world," Black Americans are indicted in this statement alongside Americans of other races.

Sasha, an interviewee who was born in Jamaica but grew up in the southern United States, provided some more texture to this discussion about African American and Jamaican relationships to race and racism. Sasha was a young woman in her mid-twenties who was not a parent. She never joined any of the Girlfriend tours and seemed to be more of an associate of the group through her frequent participation in the web community. During my research with GFT, Sasha only joined the women for dinner once. However, her participation on the website and her close relationship with one of the Girlfriends motivated me to interview her, since I wanted her take on the group as a Jamaican American who knew some of their activities. We met in the United States for her interview after I returned from one of the annual GFT tours.

Partly backing up Gayle's claim that Jamaicans do not "see" racism, Sasha gave me some insight into conversations she had about Black Americans with her family members in Jamaica:

> [Black Americans] focus on being *Black* too much, and focus on the Man too much. Yeah, 'cause I guess in Jamaica you don't really deal with racism too much, you deal more with classism. So, I guess that's the whole big difference, [Jamaicans] just don't see it. The white people that they see there are tourists and they're acting friendly, smoking weed with you, talking with you, giving you money or something, so.

Sasha's, Devan's, and Gayle's comments are especially meaningful because they point to an important disconnect between African Americans and Jamaicans. Shared experiences of racism and Blackness were the linchpin in African American imaginings of the African diaspora and their connection to Black peoples globally. However, Jamaicans hardly ever invoked this same notion of diaspora or spoke about racism in the same terms as the tourists. When Jamaican interviewees did invoke diaspora, it was often a discussion about the "Jamaican diaspora" rather than the "African diaspora," specifically their family members or friends who had moved to the United States or the United Kingdom. In fact, connections with Jamaicans abroad were centered on family members or friends, and seldom about a broader community. Rastafarians, or other Jamaicans I spoke to who held a deep connection to Pan-African ideology, sometimes invoked the notion of a larger African diaspora. However, the concept of diaspora seemed less salient for Jamaicans I spoke with, as these residents rarely used the actual words "diaspora" or "diasporic" to describe Jamaicans living abroad. "Diaspora" as a community concept was often relegated to the academy, newspapers, or political forums, where scholars, politicians, economists, and tourist industry entrepreneurs debated the utility of diaspora as a tool for economic prosperity and political empowerment.

This isn't to say that Jamaicans did not understand that the history of slavery *linked* them to African Americans. But rather, they seldom discussed this connection as a *shared* experience. Although Jamaicans saw similarities in skin color and historical racialized experiences, and were well aware of the assumed diasporic kinship African Americans felt, they themselves rarely claimed these Americans as diasporic kin in explicit terms. While African Americans' diasporic focus was almost always centered on what they saw as an original dispersal moment of transatlantic slave trade, Jamaicans were not focused on this moment in the same way. Instead, Jamaicans often demonstrated Stuart Hall's claim that the Caribbean is the home of hybridity, and in these spaces there are multiple forms of origin moments. While African slave trade came up as an important element in Jamaican history, it was not *the* central node for their understanding of Blackness and Black identities. More often than not, in relation to the concept of "diaspora," African Americans and Jamaicans were speaking past one another and not speaking of the same diasporic community.

I would argue that these different ways of relating to the history of slavery and the historical narratives of racism influenced the contemporary relationships African Americans and Jamaicans had with race and racism.[29] I examine these disjunctures between African American and Jamaican imaginings and experiences of race and diaspora in the next section.

Black Americans with a Master's Complex

Girlfriends traveled to Jamaica because they thought Black people there would feel familiar. At the same time they sought the "strangeness" of a different Black culture and lived experience. Although giving back and traveling with a diasporic heart were essential to GFT's tour experiences, some of the women struggled with holding the idea that Black people in Jamaica had both similar *and* different relationships to Blackness than they did. A key example of this was when Girlfriends stated that they thought all Black people should get along, or at least recognize that they were "in the same boat" in their respective countries. This notion of "the same boat" sometimes gestured toward the literal ships Girlfriends imagined African American and Jamaican ancestors shared during transatlantic slavery. Many times, it referenced the systemic racism African Americans presumed both groups experienced in the United States and Jamaica. Assuming that a shared diasporic history and their American conceptualizations of "Blackness" and racism translated to those in Jamaica, some Girlfriends were troubled by Jamaicans who did not want to unify or rally explicitly around their racial identity as Black peoples. This was particularly stunning when Jamaicans distanced themselves from Girlfriends because it was clear the ladies were "American" first in their view, then Black.

An example of this would be when Jamaicans would ask Girlfriends about the ongoing war in Afghanistan, and how they felt about the actions of *their* President George Bush. Across the board, Girlfriends would respond that Bush was not "their" president, and as Black Americans they had nothing to do with the President's actions or views. They explained that it was a majority of white Americans who voted Bush into office. Jamaicans would retort that since President Bush was the American president, he in fact represented the Girlfriends. For these African American women, traveling outside the United States was the first time they truly considered the fact that to others they were Americans, and signified all that came with that national identity. At home, their experiences with racism and sexism taught them that they were not truly American, and many had embraced the identity of being an outsider inside their country. Leaving the United States necessitated that they come to terms with the fact that as they traveled, they represented Americans as a whole, even if they were not seen as completely American at home.

While there seemed to be some shared understandings about how gender operated in the United States and Jamaica, there were different notions about what Blackness meant, how it was utilized, and what it required of those racialized as Black. Additionally, though Girlfriends were more open to recognizing the ways their American citizenship and economic status gave them access to privileges that Jamaicans did not have, some had a harder time seeing how they contributed to the oppression and exploitation of Jamaicans through tourist practices. These different conceptualizations and experiences of what Blackness is sometimes led to moments of diasporic disconnect and mistranslation between Jamaicans and African Americans. The emphasis placed on race and racism by African Americans, while Jamaicans focused on class, added fuel to these fractures.

In 2004, after the annual Girlfriend Tour in Negril was complete, some of the ladies and I remained in the country for a few days to travel to Ocho Rios. During this trip I met Mark, as he was employed by one of the women to drive her around the island during her two-week stay. Mark became a constant presence in the group; he shared our meals, drove us to many of our outings, and sat on the veranda with the ladies in the early evening to converse about the day's events. Throughout our stay, Mark saw it as his duty to teach us all about the "Jamaican" way of doing things, which included encouraging us to read the *Gleaner* (the Jamaican newspaper) daily and keeping us away from "bad" elements while shopping in the market or dancing in the club. During our conversations, Mark was especially vocal about the power and privilege he saw associated with American citizenship, particularly our easy access to international travel and the exclusiveness of U.S. immigration laws and procedures. As days went by, I wondered what were his impressions of these African American travelers and what conclusions he had formed about American tourists in his years of service.

I interviewed Mark shortly after the ladies left Jamaica, hoping he would give me some insight into what some Jamaicans really thought about American tourists and their impact on the larger economic and social contexts of Jamaica. Since Mark was a regular in the tourist areas because of his job, and we had already spent the better part of two weeks together, it was easier to get him to accept being interviewed than many other Jamaican interlocutors I connected with. Mark used the interview as an opportunity to discuss the differences among Black peoples and comment on the tourist gaze he felt Black Americans placed on him and other Jamaicans. Here, I suggest that Mark's comments are an attempt to return the tourist gaze. In our first interview, Mark introduced me to his concept of the "master's complex."

> MARK: I think one of the main things, especially with Black Americans, I think they think we're [Jamaicans] all about money, hustling. And most times they come off as if they're, even though we are all Black people, as if they are like better than us, you know? We know economically, financially, maybe you guys earn a little more, but most times the Americans come off as if they are like, they want to be your master, even though you know you are providing a service, they want to be your master. I don't accept that.

> BW: So white Americans don't have this whole, "I wanna be your master" complex?

> MARK: No. I don't see that.

> BW: I'm trying to figure out why . . . I mean it's a [racial] issue, because you're telling me that white Americans come open and chill, and Black Americans don't. I'm trying to figure out what it is that the Black Americans have experienced that makes them critical of you guys.

> MARK: This is why. If you really understand the whole Black thing, right, sometimes you don't even blame the Black Americans because it's like, it's like how you just said. I would say it's maybe a little phobia where from long time ago Black people don't want to take chances. It's a mental Black. It's a mental block. So once you come up against your own, you know, it's like you feel like "Oh my God. I want to walk the straight line

because maybe you want to trip me or something like that." Bob Marley and Marcus Garvey say that Black people will never ever know themselves until their back['s] against the wall. And you must free your mind from mental slavery. So a lot of Black Americans, it's like they come here, and their minds are not free. . . . White Americans come, they have an open mind. Black Americans don't do that. They just come, "Oh my God. I'm better and I have my money." They don't understand. It's like a lot of people see Jamaicans, they think Jamaica and they think that everybody lives in a little hut, you know what I'm saying. But I'm all right. I have a beautiful house, own my own home, and stuff like that.

Mark echoes Gayle's notion that African Americans and Jamaicans are "all Black people." But he points to the different relationships each has to their Blackness, notions of freedom, and class status. Mark describes a sense of empathy or pity he has for African Americans, as he understands that their performance as the "master" is a result of the stress and paranoia caused by their historical and nationalized relationship with racism. Citing Bob Marley and Marcus Garvey, Mark turns Gayle's previous comments about Jamaican ignorance of racism on its head, arguing that it is actually African Americans who are mentally enslaved and locked in by a newfound sense of class privilege. For Mark, the Black American tourist is a privileged foreigner whose American citizenship allows him or her almost unlimited access to global mobility and economic prosperity.

In my interview with Jacqueline, she unknowingly supported Mark's argument and attempted to provide an explanation for why African Americans perform class privilege the way they do in Jamaica:

Well, from what I heard from Jamaican people, they say Black Americans don't tip well [*she smiles*]. And that they're very demanding. You know, 'cause the thing with Black Americans is we're just now coming into our own. And we're in the first generation, second maybe, of privilege. And we're just now learning how to get manicures, pedicures, massages and feel like we, we *deserve* something. So we take it a bit overboard, 'cause now we feel like we're just the shit. You got to learn in this country to just chill! Stop rushing people! I may complain back home, but I will not complain here. I just wait. Whenever the hell it comes, that's when it comes. To be honest with you? We probably come off as very obnoxious because we are probably just so damn glad that we can get two steps out the ghetto and can afford to go around the corner. . . . And probably Jamaicans are like "Oh God. Here come these African Americans. They are so obnoxious."

Compare this with Gayle's interview:

GAYLE: I'm sure Black Americans when they go [to Jamaica], whether they want to admit it or not there is on some level, a little appreciation, that *finally*, I am somewhere where I am superior to somebody. And we do feel slightly superior, and it's because of the economic situation, but you do it. So if everybody would really, really search deep and look at the truth there probably really is some truth to that, and [Jamaicans] feel it. White people don't have to look for a place to feel superior because they know wherever you go, you are superior. White people think, "I can play with the natives. I can pretend that I'm down with you because I know I'm really not. I know I'm superior. There's no question about it." So, to me, that's my theory. . . . White Americans don't sweat the small stuff, because the world is theirs. . . . If they don't get it today, they'll certainly have an opportunity to get it tomorrow. So they don't have to sweat everything. . . . Black Americans, we sweat EVERYTHING!

BW: Everything?

GAYLE: Eve-ry-thing. We have to be twice as good, work twice as hard, just to be accepted as average. So when we pluck down our hard-earned money for anything, buddy, you better rise to the occasion. White people are not like that. . . . Now white Europeans and white people will study about the national heroes and . . . they'll converse with you and get your ignorant ass on that boat and bring you over here and put you into slavery. It is a MASK! They are going to pretend to be *down* with you, but you come over here [to the United States], they're not down with you anymore. And if you ever step out of your place, 'cause over [in Jamaica] they're pretending to be down with everything, if you step out of your place (and they have a definite idea of what your place is), they will point it out quickly, and they will put the master thing on you. I don't think that we do that. And I think Jamaicans think that we are doing that because we expect so much. Because [white people] expect so much from us [in the United States], we don't know how to come there and shed this skin. Because we are born with it, we live with it, and you better not step out of that skin in America, because it's actually part of your armor. You have to stay in this mode at all times. So we're still in the same mode. White folks, they can jump in and out of the mode and fool you. But they are the same.

Here, Gayle somewhat agrees with Mark's initial comment that African Americans are locked into a "mental Black" and "mental block." However, she describes it as part of the armor necessary to fight off the burden of racism and the wear and tear that comes with working twice as hard to be seen as average, or as good as a white person, in a racist society like the United States.

For Gayle and the other Girlfriends, the shadow of American racism is never far away, even while on vacation in Jamaica. In fact, it is their awareness of racism that partly fuels their desire to travel with diasporic heart and give back. Although they find comfort and some relaxation in Jamaica (which is why they keep returning), they are always aware that racism may rear its ugly head at any time, particularly if their fellow white American tourists choose to remove their "masks." And they know as they travel as African American tourists through Jamaica, interacting with Jamaican residents in these highly politicized tourist spaces, they are being compared to white Americans who travel with a different sense of freedom and privilege. With a diasporic heart, Gayle feels a responsibility to lift the mask and teach Jamaicans about racism. In other parts of the interview, she describes her fear that her diasporic kin in Jamaica could be hoodwinked, like she imagines her ancestors in Africa were before they were forced into a boat to endure the Middle Passage. Mark wants African Americans to recognize that they are acting like masters and treating those they seek to have kinship with as less than. According to him, they are acting superior, exploiting and thinking lowly of Jamaican workers in the tourist sector, which Mark notes is how they themselves feel as Black people in the United States.

Conclusion

In some ways, the relationship between traveling with a diasporic heart and perpetuating a master's complex highlights the distinction between intent and impact within diasporic relationships. Here, within the tourist sector, the fractures of this diasporic community begin to show as Americans and Jamaicans interrogate the social and economic ramifications of their different racialized and economic positions within global processes.

For some Jamaicans and African Americans in my research, the classed differences associated with the "American" in "African American," and the subsequent access to class and geographic mobility, frequently caused the unity or the sameness of diaspora to become troubled. As Paulla Ebron writes, "Power differences . . . are inscribed in different configurations of mobility," and it was evident in the diasporic contact zones in Jamaica.[30] Although Girlfriends were deeply committed to their imaginings of a shared diasporic identity with Jamaicans and to giving back, their embracing of the master's complex and centering of hegemonic ideas of Blackness made diasporic connectivity difficult.

When Jamaicans held up mirrors to the ways African American tourists were implicated in U.S.-based capitalist endeavors, in the exploitation of Jamaican culture and peoples, or in the mentality that those based in tourist destinations are only there to serve tourists, Girlfriends were frequently taken aback. Instead of simply defining their Blackness in opposition to whiteness, Girlfriends are pushed to redefine their Blackness in conjunction with, and while clashing against, other modes of *being* Black and *doing* Black that are present in Jamaica. Ironically, though these women choose to visit a country where they think they will encounter Black people who are like them, they repeatedly meet (Black) Jamaicans who force them to recognize how different Black peoples, particularly African Americans, are. These moments, when one's way of being is "too" differently "Black," point us to the interesting relationship between race and nationality. In some ways, what this allows us to see is the emotional frenzy that ensues when Blackness is shown in all of its diversity. Here we see that difference is constitutive of, and central to, the construction of diaspora.

Because racialized, classed, gendered, and nationalized power differentials are embedded in the practices of tourism, it begs the question of whether tourism can be an effective site for giving back or empowering those based in tourist destinations. Even when diasporic hearts and desires are present, do the structures and politics of tourism make efforts like those of the Girlfriends futile? The answers to these questions are complicated. Despite tensions and fractures, there were also moments of amazing connection and a strong sense of belonging between the African Americans and Jamaicans present. During late-night conversations in hotel rooms, shared bliss in dancehalls, hugs in the airport, or deep spiritual experiences near the ocean, these individuals and communities connected to one another based on this ambiguous thing many called "Blackness." It was these moments that kept bringing Girlfriends back to Jamaica and fueled their diasporic hearts.

As the plane lowered toward the ground, I took in the crystal-blue waters and lush green hills of Jamaica from my small window in the sky. I said goodbye to the elderly Jamaican woman who sat next to me during the flight from Fort Lauderdale to Montego Bay, and walked onto the steaming hot pavement of Sangster International Airport. I was in Jamaica! The sweet aromas of ocean water, flowers, and citrus fruit tickled my nose as I quickly escaped from the oppressive heat into the cool air-conditioning of the airport. Jamaican celebrities on colorful billboards sponsored by businesses such as Digicel, Sandals, and Margaritaville welcomed my fellow passengers and me as we rushed through the corridors toward the Immigration and Customs area.

When I reached customs, I remembered to walk toward the line on the left where, according to the veteran travelers on Jamaicans.com, the customs line always seems to be the shortest. The female customs officer looked at the forms I filled out during the plane ride, glanced at my passport, and gave me the once-over. After a few moments of interrogating me with her eyes, she asked, "Is this your first time to Jamaica?"

Something about the tone in which she asked this question put me on edge immediately. "Yes, this is my first visit," I replied.

"Is this business or pleasure?" she asked.

"Pleasure. A vacation." I decided on the plane that giving the details of my preliminary research trip probably was not worth the hassle, especially since I was not sure of the details of the research project just yet. I was still in the brainstorming phase of the project. I would worry about this question during my future trips.

She glanced behind me and beside me. "A vacation *alone*?" she inquired. "Yes."

"Do you have any family in Jamaica?"

"No," I replied. At least, I did not know any of them personally.

"Where are you going to stay?" she asked.

Luckily, I had written the address of my hotel in Montego Bay in my notebook, so I happily handed the sheet of paper over to her.

She handed me back the paper and without looking up asked, "How much money did you bring with you?"

"What?!" I said. At this point I was at a loss for words. Why was it any of her business how much money I was bringing into the country? Why was I being interrogated like this? I stood in silence for a moment, weighing whether or not this was a serious question. She glanced up and her eyes stared firmly back at mine. "Five hundred dollars. Why do you ask?" I replied.

"That's not enough to last you for two weeks. Do you have access to credit cards?"

Again, I was silent with shock. After a few moments I resigned to answering her question, realizing that I could not get into the country without doing so. "Yes, but I'm not sure why you're asking."

"Well, five hundred dollars is not enough for you to survive on for two weeks, so we need to make sure you have access to more funds," she stated.

"Ok," I said hesitantly.

"Go downstairs to collect your baggage and enjoy your trip," she said without a smile.

Annoyed yet relieved, I went downstairs to find my bags among the crowd of luggage that now sat around the conveyor belt. I quickly headed outside to get a taxi to go to my hotel, where I spent the next few days exploring Montego Bay and getting acclimated to the city.

I heard multiple versions of a similar story from the women of GFT and other travelers. For first-time African American travelers, in particular, this experience was often a shock, as they expected their Blackness to protect them, or at least connect them, to other Black people in Jamaica. They talked about the surprise of being policed by customs officers who look like you. The feeling as a Black person that you are not to be trusted or that you have some other agenda besides leisure when entering a predominately Black country you naively expect to be a less racist oasis. The invasiveness of questions about your financial situation. These stories became so prevalent in the travel section on Jamaicans.com that many African American women would advise other women traveling to Jamaica for the first time to seek out a line with a Jamaican man customs officer than a Jamaican woman officer, for they argued it would make the experience easier. Other boardites opined that while these experiences in Jamaica were surprising, the often-extensive questioning and force Black Americans experienced as they went through U.S. customs to get back into their home country was much worse. However, the tense energy between Jamaicans and Black Americans, specifically African American women and Jamaican women, was sometimes sparked right here in this early moment of the trip, when racialized, gendered, classed, and nationalized expectations, assumptions, and differences related to travel, leisure, money, and authoritative power came to a head at the airport.

3

Why Jamaica?

Seeking the Fantasy of a Black Paradise

"So you study Stellas going to Jamaica to get their groove back?"

My conversations with people about my research usually begin with some version of this question. Inevitably, whether they are fellow researchers at conferences, folks at parties, or students in the classroom, someone raises this question—with a chuckle, a wink, or an elbow nudge. Sometimes it is a genuine inquiry. Sometimes it is a condemning statement, minimally hiding one's opinion that social science and anthropology are insignificant or useless. And sometimes the fifteen-second overview of my research is met with a broad smile—usually from a sista—who immediately connects it to whichever fantasies Terry McMillan's movie and book *How Stella Got Her Groove Back* invoke in her imaginary. During one of these brief discussions at a conference, a Black woman staff member stated that she knew I wasn't a medical doctor but wanted to know if I could write her a prescription to Jamaica because racism is real (!), and she needed a vacation and a dose of happiness *immediately*. In these types of conversations with Black women, I often return the smile, waiting to hear the story about their first trip to Jamaica, or their hopes and dreams for trips they haven't been able to take yet. There are other times when I sigh, look cynics straight in the eye, and proceed to explain my research, starting with, "Well, it's more complicated than that. I research Black women and happiness, and the group of women I study travel to Jamaica for a variety of reasons, including their pursuits of happiness." After I provide the information for one to contact Girlfriend Tours International, or hear smart comments about fieldwork being easy on beaches and with a Red Stripe in hand, most conversations usually end up in the same place:

"But why Jamaica? Aren't there other places they can visit and have the same experience?"

This chapter delineates multiple answers to this question by laying out the numerous ways Jamaica becomes an object of desire for Girlfriends and what benefits this object provides during their transnational pursuits. To understand "why Jamaica," it is necessary to consider the broader factors related to (emotional) transnationalism and tourism that influence Girlfriends' decision to travel to Jamaica. McMillan's *Stella* and the popular imaginings connected to this story are linked to the racialized, gendered, and nationalized context of these larger forces.

For the women of GFT, feeling "Black" was oftentimes influenced by the transnational and the diasporic. Traveling to Jamaica allowed them to connect with other Black peoples and Blacknesses while they searched for a geographic escape from U.S. racism. They wanted to visit a Black paradise, a place that had a predominately Black population and provided sun and beaches. Jamaica was a central node of their fantastical ideas about paradise because of its landscape, the way that residents are portrayed as "irie" and laid-back in tourism commercials, and the popularity and familiarity of its musical culture.[1] Jamaica's proximity to the United States made it both familiar and foreign to these Americans, as they had easy access to the land and its culture. It is about good food, great music, and seeing Black bodies dancing and relaxing—the escape from urban life that is unique to Jamaica. According to them, Jamaica becomes the center of their Black paradisiacal thinking because they feel less of the burden of American racism there, and it is not as industrialized (or "Americanized" as they would say) as other Caribbean countries, such as the Bahamas or Trinidad. It is a promised paradise; and they hope and believe the promise of happiness rings out as they navigate the landscape and interact with Jamaicans.

(Black) Tourist Women and Transnationalism

In the last forty years, scholars interested in globalization and transnationalism have explored the differences between our contemporary economic, political, and social lives and those of previous eras. These investigations have focused primarily on the links between recent transnational movements of peoples, ideas, and capital, and the reorganization and transformation of time, space, and labor.[2] For the most part, this extensive theorization of the present globalized moment has examined complex, mobile networks and the stimulation of new conceptualizations of citizenship, belonging, and difference.[3] Subsequently, fiery debates about the structural integrity of the nation-state, the relationship(s) between the local and the global, and the shift from production to consumption have been generated in several canons of scholarly literature.[4] With the publication of texts such as Christine Hine's *Virtual Ethnography* and Daniel Miller and Don Slater's *The Internet: An Ethnographic Approach*, researchers have attempted to document ethnographically how people use new technologies to form and maintain relationships across territorial boundaries.[5] However, while scholars have extensively analyzed how processes of globalization and transnationalism transform gender roles, alter class structures, and transcend national boundaries, less work has been done on how other boundaries— especially racial ones—are often maintained and even more fiercely policed.[6] Girlfriends' engagement in emotional transnationalism as they move from the United States and Jamaica and back often highlights the ways that notions of belonging, difference, and community are problematized as border lines are blurred.

The theoretical framework of transnationalism offers a lens for understanding how processes *and* people are changing the world and the ways we live in it. Since the late 1980s, much has been written about the intensification of transnational migration, the feminization of a global labor force, and the commodification of culture, particularly in the field of transnational studies.[7] Given that these broader processes of political economy influence cultural identity formations and the relationships individuals form with one another, tourism is another significant site wherein racialized, classed, nationalized, and gendered identities are formed and reconfigured. That is to say, while much of transnationalism literature focuses on a particular group of mobile people—transmigrants— this field of study provides great insight into the larger effects that result from changing relationships between the nation, culture, and identity. Although researchers rarely integrate the canons of scholarship on transnational migration and tourism, it is increasingly clear that these disciplines address some similar issues. By focusing on the movements of goods and people across virtual and geographic borders, and exploring how spatial and temporal boundaries are troubled in an increasingly mobile and global world, both canons provide analytic tools for understanding the effects various forms of travel and movement have on specific groups, individuals, and their cultures.

In one of the earliest texts to define transnationalism as a field, Glick Schiller, Basch, and Blanc-Szanton write that they called what they were researching "transnationalism" because it "emphasize[d] the emergence of a social process in which migrants establish social fields that cross geographic, cultural, and political borders."[8] Moving away from earlier anthropological scholarship that often conflated physical location with national identity and culture, Basch, Glick Schiller, and Blanc-Szanton suggest that transmigrants create social lives across national boundaries.[9] In these "transnational cultural spaces," which Sutton and Chaney describe, transmigrants are seen as both distant subjects of their country of origin and simultaneously new participants in the "national economy and political processes of their country of settlement."[10] Transnational studies, with its history in borderland and migration studies, pushes anthropologists to look at the specificities of globalization when observing the tools people use to make sense of the world, negotiate their relationship to hegemonic ideologies, and execute a response to oppressive structures.

In contrast to theories of globalization, where people, their desires, and their emotions can get lost in the analysis of large processes and institutions, transnationalism enables us to understand the personal and the public, the individual and the social. Scholars such as Aihwa Ong have emphasized the effects processes of transnationalism and globalization have on people. In her book *Flexible Citizenship,* Ong claims that the ebbs and flows of global capital influence *individuals* as well as governments, with individuals often having to realign political agendas and personal identities in response to them.[11] Bringing together a macro- and micro-analysis of the power differentials involved in transnational processes, Ong shows how different regimes of power (family, state, and economic enterprises) structure cultural meanings, ideas, and norms, and how these cultural logics subsequently inform and structure border crossings and transnational relationships at the individual level.[12] Here, I use Ong's work to suggest that an anthropological approach to transnationalism and the ways it affects people would help us better understand tourism as a racialized, gendered phenomenon in which identities are formed and reconfigured, including the emotional aspects of these experiences. With this approach, people do not get lost in the abstract theorization of mobility, power, and difference.

It is clear that pioneering transnational studies scholars intended for transnationalism literature to focus on transmigrants. However, in the past twenty-five years the study of transnationalism has expanded to a variety of populations, including tourists, social networks, and political groups. In this expanded definition, the African American women of GFT are provocative and active participants in transnationalism. If transnationalism was created to draw attention to a particular set of politics related to migrants' crossing of borders, some might ask what the political implications are of using the term for these African American tourists. How might the various forms of movement and mobility Girlfriends are participating in be different or similar to those of transmigrants? What is useful about analyzing these women tourists under the rubric of transnationalism?

The African American tourists of GFT are both like and unlike the transnational migrants in traditional studies of transnationalism. Their transnational mobility differs because it is not forced, as they travel willingly to Jamaica. In general, they are not under extreme political distress, nor are they usually traveling to Jamaica to move there and seek better opportunities for housing, employment, or education. Girlfriends are not migrants, refugees, or a group of people who have been forced to leave their homes for explicitly political or economic reasons. However, their everyday experiences with racism, sexism, and even ageism in the United States, and the effects this has on their sense of self, make them feel as though they must leave home to travel to another (virtual or national) space in search of happiness. They imagine themselves as diasporic subjects who are connected to Jamaica and its peoples through a notion of "home." The conditions in the United States, their experiences with racism and sexism, push them to leave one home to pursue happiness and comfort in Jamaica. Although their travel is driven by a search for leisure, and they can avoid some of the hardship that nation-states often place on migrants through strict citizenship requirements and travel regulations, they still experience some aspects of state surveillance as they move through airports and across national borders as mobile Black people.[13] Additionally, in similar ways to transmigrants, Girlfriends use travel and technology to create and maintain ties with those they imagine as diasporic kin. Their movements across national borders, and the new networks of friends and family that this mobility enables, change how these women think of themselves as racialized *and* diasporic subjects.

Black people have always been mobile, whether it was through movement of their choosing or forced movement. Of course, the leisure travel of these African American tourist women is very different from those of enslaved Africans who were forcibly removed from their homes and made to endure the Middle Passage and unimaginable violent acts afterward, if they survived. This global market of enslaved Africans required movement deeply entrenched in death, pain, agony, and suffering, and those who survived had a longing for home that most of us today could probably never fathom. However, if we understand that for the ladies of GFT, transatlantic slave trade is a significant history haunting their vision of this imagined diasporic community, then it is useful to think of their movement in relation to that of their ancestors. For some of the Girlfriends, their longing to connect with Jamaicans is influenced by what they see as a shared history of slavery and a moment of origin for the creation of diasporic community. They want to belong in this community and believe that

Jamaica and Jamaicans somehow fulfill this. Girlfriend Tours' movement is connected to a desire to create diaspora with pleasure and leisure at the forefront; however, there is a longing and recognition of previous traumas in the diaspora that is acknowledged in this contemporary movement.

The physical and social mobility made possible in Jamaica is essential to their happiness. The ability to move back and forth, to not have to stay in one place, to not be confined but to spread one's body out, to experiment with dance, intimacy, and sexuality, to be seen and made visible but in a different light than in the United States—these are integral to their pursuit of happiness. Whereas before, the movement of their ancestors was indicative of powerlessness, the mobility of the women of GFT is an attempt to experience empowerment and privilege. However, the diasporic longing, and the need to escape racialized and gendered oppressions, is a reminder that this previous history of violence and disenfranchisement is never too far away or behind.

Emotional transnationalism is useful in this analysis because it is best for exploring the dynamism of the human experience, particularly the ambiguities and contradictions embedded in the pursuit of happiness and wellness while living within the context of global capital, racisms, and patriarchies. Girlfriends' choices about whom to love, how to relax, and where to find personal acceptance and community tie together countries and cultures using technologies different from those in the past, resulting in new forms of connectivity and belonging. Exercises in power and privilege, practices of reciprocity and solidarity, the transfer of cultural meanings, and the modification of identity formations both construct and problematize the creation of their transnational network and community. Their access to class and geographic mobility—their movements in virtual and physical spaces—challenges notions of happiness and wellness that mistakenly bound these pursuits to one's home or nation-state. And the fact that they are African American women, descendants of Africans whose mobility changed the world in a different way, and women who have been told they should not prioritize leisure or engage in too much travel, is significant. While their story starts with the trauma of the transatlantic slave trade and the yearning for diasporic connectivity is a significant aspect in their pursuit of happiness, their story also involves the realm of transnational spaces and fields. The Jamaican cultural forms and events accessed through travel expand their understandings of what their Blackness and womanhood can feel and look like. Additionally, their travel to Jamaica helps them better understand the salience of their national identities. Therefore, I place their pursuits of happiness within the context of emotional transnationalism because I understand that transnational forces and diasporic imaginings influence their notions of self, community, and belonging.

Tourism as a Lens into the Politics of Transnationalism

Much has been made of the recent intensification of transnational labor migration, the proliferation and distribution of cultural commodities, the feminization of a global labor force, the deterritorialization of capital, and how these processes have transformed time, space, and social realities. Although the movement of capital, goods, and people through migration and tourism has been a global phenomenon for centuries (particularly in the Caribbean), the anthropological examination of these circulations and networks during this recent period of globalization has focused particularly on the cultural economy of globalization. However, a lack of analysis around race and gender in these contexts continues to plague the scholarly literature in the globalization canon, especially in the context of tourism. Tourism, as representative of the larger processes of globalization, is a rich site for understanding how consumption practices and processes of identity formation (such as racialization) are being reshaped. Unfortunately, leisure, recreation, and tourism remain under-researched and undervalued subjects, especially in the discipline of anthropology.

In some of the scholarship on tourism, "hosts" is a term used to describe the people who are native to or live in the country travelers are visiting. John Urry, one of the most prominent scholars of tourism, offers the concept of the "tourist gaze" as a tool for examining how culture is presented and received within tourist settings. Urry argues that one's gaze is socially constructed, and it affects not only *what* a tourist sees but also the *way* the tourist sees. He offers several forms of the gaze, including the "collective gaze," which is constructed as travelers tour in a group, where the presence of other tourists adds to the excitement of the spectacle and cultural displays of "Otherness." According to Urry, many times these groups are mostly working-class tourists. Another gaze is the "romantic form of the gaze," which mostly upper-class tourists engage in, emphasizing solitude and privacy.[14] As demonstrated in previous chapters, the women of GFT engage in both forms of this gaze, particularly on the annual Girlfriend Tour. The "tourist gaze" has been critiqued by some for its privileging of the visual experience.[15] At the same time, anthropologists have found it useful for examining the power relationships involved in performances of culture and identity, including the ways that hosts might use their knowledge of the tourist gaze, and their ability to return the gaze, to modify how they are seen and perceived by tourists.[16] While the tourist gaze has been used as a framework for thinking through the (sexualized, gendered, and classed) power relations involved in "First World/Third World" host/guest interactions and transactions, it would also be useful for examining how racial inequities are integral to the expansion of capitalism, especially in the contemporary moment of globalization when old racial hierarchies are reinscribed and racial differences are fiercely policed.[17] In this vein, the study of tourism is perfect for the analysis that Thomas and Clarke call for: a "macro-level analysis of racialization that combines 'local responses, translations and innovations,'" while also considering the ways "globalization has both reproduced essentialist racialized structures of citizenship and community, *and* provided new technologies through which these structures are potentially transcended and/or subverted."[18]

For countries like Jamaica that rely on tourism for economic development, the tourist gaze and the social meanings and understandings constructed through it have real economic, political, and social effects. Although most tourists do not remain in these tourist destinations for long periods of time, their interactions with hosts during their visits, and the economic capital that accompanies them, do have a profound impact on the economic mobility of those living in the country and the representation of national identities in the global market. In contrast to the high hopes of economists, anthropologists have rarely theorized tourism as resulting in positive effects for the host country, instead pointing to increases in poverty, drug markets, sex tourism, AIDS rates, and environmental pollution, as well as a widening in the gap between the rich and the poor, with this wealth stratification leading to social and political conflicts. The host countries are said to become dependent on tourist dollars and are under pressure to sustain an inflowing tourist population, subsequently taking away attention from the creation of alternative development strategies. Subsequently, when tourists stop coming, there are less economic alternatives for people to sustain themselves. As Girlfriends travel to Jamaica, some are aware of the important ways their American dollars impact Jamaica and Jamaicans, and others attempt to become informed about the economic, social, and cultural impact they have on the places they visit. In fact, part of the reason these African American tourists are dedicated to "giving back" to Jamaica is because they see it as an integral part of their African diasporic imaginary: by helping Jamaicans, they believe they are helping their diasporic kin.[19]

Scholars interested in questions related to gender equality and the contemporary period of globalization and capitalism have begun to analyze women's increasing participation in these processes, including women traveling solo across the globe, engaging in sex and hospitality tourism, and prioritizing leisure, recreation, and various experiences of pleasure. Researchers Susan Frohlick and Jessica Jacobs write, "These relatively new phenomena present fundamental challenges for thinking critically about female agency and desire and women's negotiation of power through modern modalities of travel and consumption."[20] As women become more situated as middle-class consumers with their own disposable income in the global market, there is a push to call these women "liberated" because they have access to modes of mobility and privileges that are traditionally gendered as male. Pushing against this conclusion, Frohlick and Jacobs argue that "these actions are hardly free of deep gender ideologies and inequalities, nor are such actions entirely without meaningfulness, pleasure, and the gainful negotiation of gender identities and personal transformation."[21] In their edited volume, *Feminist Genealogies, Colonial Legacies, Democratic Futures*, M. Jacqui Alexander and Chandra Talpade Mohanty note that a gendered analysis of globalization and capitalism is important because capitalism is "a set of processes mediated through the simultaneous operation of gendered, sexualized, and racialized hierarchies."[22] Within these systems, "women's bodies are disciplined in different ways: within discourses of profit maximization, as global workers and sexual laborers; within religious fundamentalisms, as repositories of sin and transgression; within specifically nationalist discourses, as guardians of culture and respectability or criminalized as prostitutes and lesbians; and within state discourses of the originary nuclear family, as wives and mothers."[23]

In contrast to some investigations of gender equality, capitalism, and travel, Alexander and Mohanty demonstrate the importance of analyzing race, gender, and sexuality. The authors argue that these intersectional analyses enable scholars to analyze aspects that are not often included in examinations of capital, goods, and the nation-state, such as women's sexual agency. I suggest that African American women have played important roles in tourism and transnationalism as mobile consumers, specifically in the realms of sex and romance tourism, which have traditionally been constructed as male-dominated arenas of consumption.[24] For Girlfriends in particular, sexual agency, and the ability to experience themselves as sexual and desirable beings, is part of why they travel to Jamaica. In the context of sex and romance tourism, Black women are often narrowly viewed as sex workers, hotel staff, entertainers in tourist areas, or the left-behind partners of men of various races who travel for fun. While mobility and global movements may be a way for some women to experience what it feels like to be a powerful man, for other women, particularly African American women, travel and virtual mobility are methods used to escape American sexism and racism. By highlighting Girlfriends' experiences in Jamaica, I expand the population of women included in studies of tourism and transnationalism to gain a more accurate and refined understanding of women's positionalities in globalizing processes that can both oppress and empower individuals. Their narratives are important because they illuminate the ways that race and gender influence our conceptualizations of who is a tourist, what is leisure, and who has access to the privileges (and status) of consumption.

In 1899, Thorstein Veblen offered a theory of the leisure class that pushed against the conspicuous consumption elite classes used to demonstrate their economic power and social status. Veblen argued that the elite's acquisition of luxury goods and participation in leisure pursuits contributed to social and economic stratification in U.S. society. For the purposes of this book, most important is his claim that leisure during the nineteenth century and in earlier periods was very much connected to those who were rich and had access to usually exorbitant amounts of wealth. His theory directly connects leisure and recreation practices to those who have the most power and privilege in society. As economics have transformed and studies of leisure and recreation have expanded since Veblen's time, researchers suggest that those in the other classes, particularly the middle class, have their own leisure practices. Currently, it is common for those in the American middle class to discuss their ability to travel inside and outside of the country, particularly with the easy access the Internet provides for booking hotel accommodations or airfare on the web. However, Black Americans in the upper or middle classes, particularly Black women, are not often included in analyses of leisure and recreation. Much of the discussion about Black women's travel, leisure, and recreational practices is relegated to blogs, newsletters, or travel companies often created by Black women. The absence of Black women in theorizations of leisure and recreation encouraged me to study the Girlfriends' emotional journeys in order to know how these women define leisure and to figure out what they do in their leisure practices.

But Why Jamaica?

This conceptual discussion about race, gender, transnationalism, and tourism hints at one of the answers to the question of why the GFT women travel to Jamaica: these women's tourism is about establishing relationships and belonging in the context of the changing and unchanging gender and race boundaries in the contemporary moment. As a key site in the history of colonialism, migration, and tourism, the Caribbean has always been an important location for the study of global processes such as transnationalism and diaspora formation.[25] Diasporic subjects create their understandings of diasporic community within the context of social, economic, and geopolitical histories. Therefore, it is important to mention that the relationship between the United States and the Caribbean, and Jamaica specifically, has continuously been one of economic and cultural exchange and labor extraction.

In his book *To Hell with Paradise*, Frank Fonda Taylor provides an overview of the formation of tourism in Jamaica, emphasizing the tenuous relationship Jamaica has had with its nearby neighbors in the United States. Since the infancy of Jamaica's tourist industry, the relationship has been so complicated that one of Taylor's Jamaican interviewees described the United States as a "social enemy but commercial friend."[26] Although Jamaica was a British colony until 1962, American tourists and business investors played a prominent role in the formation of Jamaica's tourist industry, particularly in the transition from the banana trade to tourism. Initially, developers of Jamaica's tourist industry focused primarily on luring potential foreign investors to the island to fall in love with the climate and geography and become residents or invest capital in the country. For the developers, the actual income-producing benefits of the industry were a secondary venture.[27] The United Fruit Company, formed in 1899 in Boston, became the chief propagator and fund-raiser for the tourist industry in Jamaica, building hotels and transporting American vacationers to Jamaica by banana boat. The social relationship between the two countries certainly was antagonistic: Jamaicans attempted to resist the racist attitudes white American travelers brought with them, while white Americans tried to enforce a system of racial superiority similar to what they were accustomed to in the United States. Nonetheless, the economic relationship between the countries produced significant profit for commercial enterprises in both places, although some would say disproportionately.

The cultural and musical exchanges between Jamaica and the United States in the realm of Black music and popular culture are probably the most publicized form of exchange. As a result of the global popularity and interconnectivity of Black musics such as hip-hop, reggae, and dancehall, American and Jamaican consumers and producers of these musical cultures are constantly in dialogue with one another, shaping and co-producing the many manifestations of "global Blacknesses" through songs, films, theater, poetry, e-mail conversations, MP3s, and Internet blogs. Norman Stolzoff describes a particular period of musical exchange between the United States and Jamaica when he writes,

> Contact with the church music of Black American missionaries as well as the prestigious big bands in the 1930s attuned the Jamaican ear to Black American creations. However, without the dominating U.S. economic, cultural, and political infrastructure, Jamaicans may never have embraced Black American music more emphatically than the other musics in the African Diaspora. Differences of size and power between Jamaican and U.S. societies account for the fact that Jamaican music did not catch on

among American Blacks, although shared experiences help explain their shared musical appreciation.[28]

Although Stolzoff argues that Jamaica's music might not have caught on in the United States because of Jamaica's small size, Carolyn Cooper has emphasized in her research the dedication of Jamaican artists to speak to Jamaicans on the island first, and then concern themselves with global appeal afterward.[29] This approach to musical performance and production echoes the sentiments of Jamaicans in my research who described themselves as "Jamaican first, and Black second." Additionally, for the past few decades, Jamaica has figured prominently in the global music scene, acting as a major force in the production of hip-hop, reggae, dancehall, and reggaeton, having a reach much larger than its small size might imply. Deborah A. Thomas points to the borrowing, reinterpreting, and resisting Jamaicans do with the American-based concepts of Blackness that accompany these musical forms and cultures: "Caribbean people have always engaged 'America' critically, negotiating its power and promise while actively building new notions of national belonging and racial mapping."[30]

As a result of the transatlantic slave trade; the marketing of important exports such as bananas and sugar to the United States; the massive advertising of Jamaica as a tourist destination nearby; the increased access to the Internet, which enables one to book her own travel quickly and spontaneously; and the popularization of reggae and dancehall music, Jamaica has sat prominently on the social radar of the United States, and of Girlfriends specifically. These factors work together to make Jamaica the ideal location for the Girlfriends' pursuit of happiness and imagined diasporic community. Bob Marley's (and the Jamaica Tourist Board's) promise—that "Every little thing is gonna be alright"—rings in the ears of Girlfriends as they travel, and it is a promise they believe can be fulfilled. When people ask me why GFT members travel to Jamaica, they are often familiar with the Jamaica presented in Jamaica Tourist Board commercials—that of pristine beaches, colorful food, and reggae music ready for consumption by international tourists. They believe these are the answers to their question. However, what most people are really asking is why GFT members decide to make *repeated* trips to the country, which some see as simply one vacation option among many others in the Caribbean. The answer to this question is the Girlfriends' fantasy that they have found a Black paradise.

Seeking Black Paradise and Winston

Since the early 1990s, scholars and tourism agencies alike have noticed the elevating numbers of women from various racial and national backgrounds traveling to the Caribbean. As Terry McMillan's book *Stella* and the film adaptation increased in popularity, the narrative of the African American woman looking for love and sex with a younger (Black) Caribbean man became part of international popular discourse. Like millions of readers and moviegoers, Girlfriends connected with McMillan's fictional story of the rendezvous between Stella, a middle-age African American woman who travels to Jamaica and falls in love, and Winston, a young Jamaican man. However, the film and book were important to Girlfriends because it influenced their imagining of what Jamaica would look like and how Jamaicans would interact with them. It provided comfort to them in a foreign space because things already felt familiar thanks to the storyline and descriptions of places. It influenced their imaginings of whom they thought they would meet, how they believed paradise would look, how Jamaicans would perceive them, and what they would do once they got there. And *Stella* was written by a Black American woman, so it implied that Jamaica was not only a welcoming space but a safe, exciting, loving space for Black people, particularly African American women. Moreover, it gave them permission as older Black women to travel and pursue leisure (and possibly love), which they felt was not encouraged by their families and communities at home in the United States. Similar to the ways Europeans and white Americans have built an entire fantasy industry comprising books, films, and experiential sites focused on women searching for Jane Austen's Mr. Darcy, Winston was the African American women's version of this fantasy. The search for Winston—or at least the desire to temporarily experience the love, attraction, intimacy, or attention of someone like Winston—is part of the fantasy that propels some of these women's trips to Jamaica. Knowing that the book was loosely based on the author's own real-life love affair during a trip to Jamaica only added fuel to the fire. Apparently, many Black women caught Jamaica fever after the release of *Stella*, as Jamaicans repeatedly told me that from their perspective, the number of Black American women traveling to Jamaica had increased exponentially.

Although many of the ladies of GFT claimed that love or sex with a Caribbean man was *not* the primary reason they traveled to Jamaica, none of them could deny the influence of *Stella* on their imaginings of what they would experience in Jamaica. Each person mentioned that praise from Jamaican men made them feel appreciated and valued in ways they did not feel at home in the United States. Furthermore, some of the women talked about the strong sisterhood and girlfriendship displayed between Angela Bassett's and Whoopi Goldberg's characters in the film (Stella and Delilah, respectively), stating that they were looking for fun that could act as a catalyst for their own girlfriendships. In this way, the representations of Jamaica, Jamaican men and women, and leisure in McMillan's work become interwoven with these women's hopes for pleasure, happiness, and belonging in a Jamaican paradise. This made the geographic locale a site full of affective promises.

Interestingly, these African American tourist women were not the only ones taking *How Stella Got Her Groove Back* into consideration. I witnessed Girlfriends frequently being "hailed" as Stella during their trips, particularly in Negril, a beach-centered tourist environment.[31] Men, frequently merchants, well-known drug dealers, or water sports operators, would call out to the women, "Stella! Stella! I'm here. It's me, your Winston," in an attempt to get the women's attention to make a sale or some other connection. Most of the time this attempt to build a connection based off Stella's narrative would be laughed off or ignored, but sometimes it was a conversation starter. Girlfriends might take a look at what was being sold and answer questions about where they were from and how long they were staying.

These moments when Stella was invoked were often done with humor; however, some of the women did not always desire this type of visibility. At times, the hailing felt like a critique or an intrusive question, asking why these African American women were present in Jamaica. It was used to draw attention to their assumed desire to partner with or "borrow" a Jamaican man, particularly a younger man, for love, sex, or intimacy. For Jamaicans to draw attention to the fantasy in this way wasn't necessarily welcomed by some of the ladies, especially if they were adamant that they did not want to get a Jamaican man. This calling out of the narrative of sex and romance tourism implied that the only reason the women had come to Jamaica was for these intimacies and that their trip was focused on a man. Girlfriends did not want to be seen as sexual consumers, even if it was the case for some of them. Furthermore, they were uncomfortable with being seen as having a particular level of economic or national privilege. They did not want to be perceived as like the white American and European women who engaged in romance or hospitality travel, and would frequently argue that what they were doing in Jamaica was different. According to them, they were there to enjoy the diasporic connections, to be in a Black paradise, and to build girlfriendships with one another, and the gaze, lyrics, or romance of a Jamaican man was an added bonus, if it happened. This desire to find diasporic belonging and connect with other Black peoples was different from the other (white) women tourists who were stereotyped as only coming for sex. While Girlfriends did embrace the fantastical love narrative of *Stella*, many did not appreciate when Jamaicans drew attention to the narrative or the limitations of Stella and Winston's romance, because it seemed to expose or burst the fantasy bubble of the Jamaican paradise.

For some Jamaicans, hailing these women as Stella seemed to be a method of pushing back against or speaking back to the ways they understood their country was being commodified and utilized as a site for romance and sex tourism. Calling a Black American woman "Stella" said, "Yes, I've seen the movie and know why you're here on the beach taking up this space." At the same time, because it was useful for establishing customer connections, familiarity with the book and film was profitable. It was a joke that could both open up conversation and draw a woman in, while simultaneously being a bit subversive. I witnessed Jamaican men calling Girlfriends "Stella" quite a few times to their faces. However, I did not hear Jamaican women use this term with them so openly—it was said behind their backs in patois, in low whispers, or in conversations with me after Girlfriends left the space and I was read as Jamaican or Jamaican American. More often than not, the invoking of *Stella* from Jamaican women was a calling-out tinged with critique, a way to exert power over the nature of these tourism-based relationships. This use of *Stella*—stated with humor, judgment, or both—pointed to the interesting ways that Girlfriends could be made visible and invisible, be recognized and misrecognized within the diasporic community they envisioned themselves as members of. *Stella* both enables and constrains Girlfriends' relationships with Jamaica and Jamaicans. It is a narrative, a fantasy, a promising of an experience laced with racialized, gendered, classed, sexualized, and nationalized meanings that travel transnationally.

In addition to the fantastical influences of *Stella*, many of the Girlfriends stated that they traveled to Jamaica because it was a predominately Black space where they could lay down the burdens and stress of U.S. racism. Their American dollars and citizenship provided them access to a country, a Black majority space, that gave them better opportunities to experience emotional wellness, increased class status, and privilege. Whereas the United States is usually described as the land of opportunity in migration narratives, in some ways Jamaica held promises of affective opportunity, such as happiness, affirmation, and belonging, for these Black women. As Girlfriends travel to and from Jamaica, they felt this mobility across American and Jamaican national borders initiated an affective and seemingly physical transformation from burdened Black American bag lady to stress-free, visible, and appreciated Black American woman. In the United States they were constantly in conversation with historical images of the asexual Mammie, the hypersexual Jezebel, the angry Sapphire, and the super-independent Strong Black Woman. In Jamaica, they felt appreciated for their curves, stylish hairstyles, aged wisdom, racialized kinship, and (assumed) economic capital and status. While none stated they were completely free from racism in Jamaica, the burden they felt while traveling there definitely felt lighter.

Jamaica, for the women of GFT, is "an object of desire," which Lauren Berlant writes in *Cruel Optimism* is a "cluster of promises we want someone or something to make to us and make possible for us. This cluster of promises could be embedded in a person, a thing, an institution, a text, a norm, a bunch of cells, smells, a good idea—whatever."[32] For them, traveling to Jamaica physically, and virtually on Jamaicans.com, not only holds the promise of happiness and escape from their homes, but these spaces are also where they feel free to express themselves as Black American women. Some Girlfriends travel there four times a year, some once a year, and some only make the trip once in their lifetime. While some are simply looking for a vacation, for others, this escape from home, and the promise of another trip to Jamaica in the future, is exactly what they need to keep going, to survive and thrive at home in the United States. Their solo trips to Jamaica, and the group tours, need to be repeated again and again for this reason. The possibilities—the fantasies about what Jamaica holds, the adventure and/or romance that you did not get to experience this time but may the next, the people you will meet—and the process of pursuing their fantasies in a Black paradise are what grants them fleeting, temporary happiness. Happiness is profoundly felt and therefore "real," even if it is never fully achieved.

Fading of the Fantasy

A number of Girlfriends who physically visited Jamaica frequently found themselves in the precarious position of trying to stay in Jamaica as long as they possibly could without ruining the sense of fantasy, freedom, and enjoyment Jamaica gave them. Although many would cancel their return flights and extend their departure for a day or two later, almost every woman expressed a concern about staying in Jamaica "too long." Too many trips to the bank and grocery store or receiving inadequate customer service were often incidents that immediately sparked conversation about the fact that the visit no longer felt like a vacation. At times, running errands, getting wrapped up in neighborhood politics, or running out of money brought an undesired feeling of "everydayness" to Jamaica. Jacqueline describes this feeling as she recounts her conversation with a Jamaican taxi driver about her desire to avoid getting involved in local politics:

There was this one driver that asked me, "Why don't [you] just get a place and live here?" And I said, "Well you know I just don't think I can live here." And he said, "Why? You visit so much. This is trip number seventeen." And I said, "Well, if I was to live here, I would get immersed in the politics of the area and it would taint my enjoyment." And he said, "Oh I don't mix in politics!" And I said, "Okaaaaaayyy" [*she stretches the word out with sarcasm, as if she does not believe him*]. Then he immediately started talking about how all the rich people dem are making all the money and how if Dolphin Cove would just fold, everybody would start making money again. Because Dolphin Cove had paired with Dunns River Falls, and they were offering a package.[33] And how the little man couldn't make any money, and I said, "You know what? What you're just talking to me about now is politics! You said you don't mix in politics! You see this is what I would get upset about. The fact that you can't make any money. And the fact that those dolphins are not happy. And the fact that those dolphin fins are standing straight up instead of curved over because they are made to tote 350 pound tourists around a small circle twelve hours a day, which is not what they were designed for by nature."

Jacqueline is clear that understanding local politics would taint the enjoyment of her time in Jamaica and ruin her fantasy. However, what is interesting, or even ironic, here is the way she purposefully brackets her own political concerns in order to sustain the fantasy of Jamaica as an object of desire. She was a committed boycotter of Dolphin Cove because she felt the dolphins were mistreated and imprisoned. However, in the conversation with the driver, she states that she does not want to get involved in local politics, but she does not see her stance related to the animals' welfare or her boycott as an embracing of a politics. Even after seventeen trips to Jamaica, she takes precautions to keep her time in Jamaica leisurely and fantastical. While she was open to engaging in conversations about the differences Jamaicans and Americans experienced in their lives, once these conversations veered into a discussion of policy, civic participation, or something she deemed explicitly "political," she no longer seemed to enjoy the discussion.

The significance of Jamaica as fantasy is essential in the ways Girlfriends negotiate this space. Because diasporic connectivity and a Black paradise are fundamental to their desires being fulfilled in Jamaica, I would frequently observe them giving back to those they viewed as less privileged in Jamaica, by bringing donated goods and money from the United States to people's homes and schools. Girlfriends were often particular about where they spent their money and were dedicated to making a positive impact on the Jamaican economy. And while women like Jacqueline were committed to their politics, some did not seem to view these actions as necessarily political, or kept explicit politics at bay, as they attempted to keep their noses out of Jamaica's politics in order to maintain the fantasy. This complex web of pursuing happiness, desiring escape, being politically aware, and showing diasporic loyalty became even more apparent to me as Jacqueline spoke about her desire to see Jamaican tourism prosper in one breath but stated the following in the next:

> JACQUELINE: Things are booming here! I don't want to see them boom to the point where Jamaica loses her culture. I hope that never happens. I hope it never becomes like the Bahamas.

> BW: That's how it is in the Bahamas?

> JACQUELINE: Bahamas is America with palm trees. It's sad.

Here, Jacqueline gestures toward the ways that industrialization, and what she sees as a loss of Black culture, makes the Bahamas a Caribbean space that feels like the United States. As the country experienced booms in its tourism and catered to the wants and needs of the increased tourist population, Jacqueline believes it lost its soul and consequently its ability to be an escape for Black peoples. What she can get there, she can get at home in the United States, and she hopes Jamaica never becomes like that as the tourism industry grows ever more profitable.

Several times I heard different Girlfriends say they wanted to return to Jamaica consistently, so their American dollars could contribute to the economy's growth. However, when new stores geared toward tourists opened or "too many" new roads were paved, Girlfriends often complained that Jamaica might become too urbanized to still feel like Jamaica. This fear that Jamaica would somehow change so drastically that it would feel like the United States, and that their American racialized and gendered realities would follow them, was frequently spoken. During a longer stay of a few weeks, Maya describes this concern in her interview:

> And the thing about that is, even coming here, or any island, after a period of time, reality sets in here too. Your reality follows you. Yeah, because reality is setting in for me. You know, I'm no longer looking at it through rose-colored glasses. I know that's a beautiful ass ocean out there, but I can't swim, and that sucker will kill me! I know that walking on the sand next to the ocean, those waves could come and knock me down.

I'm saying all that to say the beauty is still there, but the reality is here too. For me.

Although determined to experience the "real" Jamaica and get something more than the tourist view of the country they love, Girlfriends simultaneously desire to keep certain parts of Jamaica a mystery, in order to perpetuate their fantasies and feelings of happiness. If one stays too long, or engages in too many real-life, everyday discussions, then the fantasy begins to fade away, like sand running quickly to the other side of the hourglass. The realities of Jamaica begin to bleed through the fantasies, and Girlfriends become more aware of the ways they don't belong, or at least of their foreignness in these spaces.

As part of the fantasy of a Black paradise, Girlfriends often discussed Jamaica as a "commodity-free" space where they were not imprisoned by things that mattered in the United States, such as name-brand clothing or jewelry. Their true essences, the expressions of their authentic selves, were the only things that mattered here. However, their relationships with Jamaica and Jamaicans were often facilitated by a desire or need to consume. Their encounters with Jamaican men and women were often primarily initiated through transactions at merchants' booths or service encounters in the hospitality industry. It was pretty rare for a Girlfriend to meet a Jamaican person in a tourist area and begin a friendship or casual connection with the individual without money, service, or a commodity facilitating the interaction. In order for them to engage the Jamaican middle-class women who would be their counterparts or Jamaican men who were not interested in a business or romance interaction, they would have had to venture out and spend a significant amount of time in non-tourist areas. Some veteran travelers were eventually able to do so, building friendships, and sometimes intimate relationships, with women and men who lived in surrounding cities or towns from tourist areas. But the longer Girlfriends stayed, and the more class- and gender-diverse their networks became, the easier it was for the fantasy of escape and political ignorance to erode.

Conclusion

In the end, staying in Jamaica for too long disrupts the fantasy of *Stella* and the Black paradise. At times, the desire for deep engagement with Jamaican people and culture repeatedly marks these African American women's privilege, obstructing the fantasy of happiness these trips promise. However, each new trip has a new promise for happiness and connectivity. Some might say that the connection to diasporic kin during their trips to Jamaica is an illusion. If they are, these illusions and fantasies that are fulfilled fleetingly are still powerful and productive. Illusions can provide hope and sustain one's soul. The promise of something that may never come to be can still provide pleasure and joy. In fact, many scholars of happiness argue that the expectation, the imagining of something that may happen, is more powerful and gratifying than actually obtaining it. So while these women may never actually get the type of diasporic relationships they desire, or the happiness they envision as ever-present in Jamaica, their practices, their "do-something" actions, and their imaginings of diaspora are productive in their lives.

While the economic and political aspects of transnationalism and tourism are often what people focus on when thinking about these global processes, Girlfriends' two-nation pursuit of happiness shows us that the fantasies, imaginings, and emotional aspects of mobility, border crossings, and boundary-blurring are just as significant. The affective dimensions of transnationalism, or emotional transnationalism, are important for understanding why particular forms of community are sought after and how individuals actually practice community-building. As Girlfriends experience racism and sexism at home, their desire to escape these burdens and connect with other Black people motivates them to go back and forth between the United States and Jamaica. When tourism is the mechanism used to seek diasporic belonging, emotions are mixed with the business of culture, and the contradictions and fissures that always ride the waves of capital are embedded in these diasporic relationships. Examinations of racism, sexism, and difference emphasize the fractures within their diasporic fantasies, even as some use economic capital to access better opportunities for emotional wellness, belonging, desire, the possibility of love, and escape in Jamaica. The fantasy of a Black paradise is always haunted by racism, even if leaving this behind is the goal of their movement. However, Jamaica's close relationship to the United States, as not too familiar or too strange, provides a necessary comfort throughout their emotional journey. In this way, Girlfriends are able to imagine "the possibility of living with two hearts rather than one divided heart."[34] They are able to keep their lives in the United States and the comforts their families and communities provide, while also living a full life, even temporarily, in Jamaica.

At the end of each interview I would ask the interviewee if they had anything they wanted to add that they had not already stated. Jacqueline surprised me by pulling herself up off the couch and moving to speak directly into the recorder:

I hope that nothing I've said, nor opinions I've made have been offensive, but I want to say that there's something about this country that makes me feel welcome. And there's something about this country that makes me feel comfortable. I feel like I can come here and it's another home that I've never known. Why I never found it before I'll never know. Jamaica doesn't have to tap dance for me. Jamaica doesn't have to do anything for me. Jamaica doesn't have to perform for me. If Jamaica would just let me come and sit in for a little while, and have a little peace, like right now I'm looking at a beautiful view, and I'm with a people person, and I know for a fact if somebody came along with a blood pressure cuff right now it would be 110 over 70. That's valuable to me. That's valuable to me to feel relaxed. And it's valuable to me to feel comfortable. And it's valuable to me to feel at peace for a while in my life. Even if it's only on vacation. And so to Jamaica I say "thank you" for that. I hope I haven't misrepresented any of your people and if my observations have been off base, remember that it's just my impression, and I'm no expert.

While riding in a taxi during one of my rare stays in Montego Bay, I got the opportunity to listen in on a "private" conversation between two Jamaican women passengers who looked to be in their forties and our thirty-something male taxi driver. As we drove through the Hip Strip, the area's main tourist section, we passed by a group of thick-bodied, older women who looked like African American tourists. They seemed to be traveling to the local beach (Doctor's Cave Beach) and were wearing the "traditional" tourist gear of mesh bathing suit cover-ups, T-shirts over bathing suits, and wide sun hats.

PASSENGER #1: "Cooyah, watch dem two yah a come out dem hotel with no bra, like dem no av no respek fi demself (kisses teeth).[1] U tink dem woulda know better still. Eh driver?

[Look at those two coming out of their hotel with no bras, like they don't have any respect for themselves (kisses teeth). You would think they would know better. Right, driver?]

DRIVER: [*Nods in agreement and groans.*]

PASSENGER #2: "Y dem tink is awright to walk street inna dem bath suit? Like dem nah no common sense."

[Why do they think it's ok to walk the streets in their bathing suit? Like they don't have any sense.]

PASSENGER #1: "Yow, is wha inna di food inna farrin? Wha dem a nyam so in the U.S.? Dem ooman ya big, eeh?"

[What's in the food over there in the U.S.? Why they eat like that? Those women are big, right?]

PASSENGER #2: "Listen mi nuh, u nah go fine no ooman in Jamaica dat big and mampi. Dem too busy a walk up and dung an' av too much tings doing."

[Listen to me, you won't find women in Jamaica that big. They walk too much and have too much work to do.]

I am not sure if the women read me as Jamaican (which was regularly the case in Montego Bay), or if they figured I was a foreigner who would not understand their patois. Either way, I appreciated this precious opportunity to hear how these Jamaican women felt about African American tourist women in their country and how they read these women's bodies. They clearly did not appreciate how these particular tourist women walked the sidewalks in their bathing suits, deeming this inappropriate for the streets. There is also the sense that the African American women are flaunting their privilege and leisure, as their thick bodies are connected to eating too much or being lazy, and not working hard like Jamaican women.

Like the ladies of GFT, I had few opportunities to interact with Jamaican women who were not hotel staff, waitresses at local restaurants, or women with some other participation in the service industry. I have to admit that the conversation in the taxi made me chuckle, as the women were obviously very disappointed in the standards of respectability and fashion their American counterparts displayed. However, this conversation also made me realize that Gayle, the other tourist women I studied, and I were missing a vital piece of our Jamaican experience because of the disconnect between Jamaican women and American women. For if Gayle had heard the commentary I eavesdropped on in that taxi, she may have revisited her frequent statement that Jamaicans loved her for her "true essence." This led me to want to better understand the role gender played in creating and maintaining diasporic connectivity and belonging.

4

Breaking (It) Down
Gender, Emotional Entanglements, and the Realities of Romance Tourism

In 2005, the ladies of Girlfriend Tours International decided they would bring an "American Thanksgiving" to Jamaica. The idea began during the summer GFT tour, when the ladies and I discussed the different foods we could rarely find in grocery stores in Jamaica. We began a short list, starting with watermelon and macaroni and cheese, and after several responses, someone brought up turkey. We joked about the various ways we could successfully get a large turkey through customs and the trouble one would be in if they were caught trying to sneak the bird into the country. Finally someone (Maya, I believe) asked, "How about we all come to Jamaica and have Thanksgiving dinner here this year?" There was a brief silence. "Oh, I don't know how my children would feel about that," said one woman. "Yeah, my family wouldn't be too happy," said another. Others seemed to silently weigh the consequences of the criticism they might receive from friends and family for missing such an important U.S. holiday. But after a few moments, excitement about the possibility grew and everyone enthusiastically agreed that it was a great idea. They were going to turn their "American Thanksgiving" into a Jamaican one this year.

In the following months, they discussed the details of their Jamaican Thanksgiving extravaganza over the phone and online through e-mail and posts on Jamaicans.com, deciding who would bring which dish and finalizing the list of invitees. Though I participated in the virtual planning, unfortunately I was not able to make it to this fabulous event to observe the occasion with my own eyes. However, several individuals passed on their versions of what took place, helping me fill in some of the gaps from the online trip reports I read about the event. In fact, the trip—particularly the dinner I will describe—was such a highly discussed topic by so many GFT members who attended that I found myself asking Girlfriends for their perspectives on the dinner during interviews a few months later. The following is a combination of several individuals' interpretations of what happened during that trip.

Although several people initially agreed to participate in the Jamaican Thanksgiving, in the end the party was smaller than expected. Some of the initial participants did not have the funds to make the trip, while others could not get the vacation time off from work. Gayle, Jacqueline, Keisha, Lauren, and Maya, the women who were able to make it, invited several of their Jamaican friends to the dinner in Ocho Rios, including staff from the apartment complex where they stayed, fishermen from the beach they frequented, and various male friends they met during previous visits. Pulling off this international, cross-class event was no small feat, and there was tension among the guests. Some of the administrative and housekeeping staff from the hotel (mostly women) felt it was below them to break bread with the fishermen, as many lived on the beach and were popularly viewed as vagabonds or local criminals. A few offended staff members actually refused to eat the food prepared by fishermen's hands, which supplemented the cooking done by GFT members. The staff tried to explain to the women of GFT that this type of shared class space was not a customary practice in Jamaica.

As longtime friends with GFT members, many of the fishermen found the high-mindedness of the hotel staff and the resulting tension humorous and entertaining, aware that their relationship with the Girlfriends was secure. Some of the fishermen, such as Stretch and Lion, had been friends with GFT members since the ladies' early trips to Jamaica years ago, supplying seafood, local gossip, friendship, and, at times, cooking skills. One or two had engaged in sexual or intimate relationships with a couple of the women, although I only know of one long-term relationship between a woman of GFT and a fisherman. These friendships or other forms of connection to fishermen were not surprises to the hotel staff, as they would frequently see GFT ladies and these men travel up and down the hill to get to their rental apartments and Fisherman's Beach. What was different about this particular moment was that hotel staff members, fishermen, and Girlfriends had never simultaneously shared a space for a long period of time, especially to share a meal together. The Jamaicans in the room were not present specifically to work (as many were regularly expected to do in the tourist sector). And the American tourists were not treating the dinner as an opportunity to learn more about Jamaican culture or do anything "authentically Jamaican," as they often did. In fact, Girlfriends saw it as an opportunity to bring something from home to another place where they felt at home. However, it became apparent that the politics of tourists and residents and the different roles, positionalities, and responsibilities that tourism frequently reinforces could not be left behind. With complex classed, nationalized, and gendered boundaries and relations of power present, some did not know how to deal with the shifting expectations around behaviors and norms.

Jamaican businessmen and other male friends viewed as middle class in the city joined the dinner later in the evening and seemed to navigate the inter-classed space quite well. Days after the holiday event, I spoke with a couple of these men, who had only good things to say about the music, food, and atmosphere of the event. It seems that their classed and gendered status may have eased their experience in this space, or at least kept them from feeling like they had to participate in the cross-class tensions. As members of the middle class, they were viewed as men with "respectable" jobs (or at least not criminals) by the mostly women hotel staff (some of whom were also viewed as middle class) and were not expected by GFT members, fishermen, or the staff to participate in the cooking or dinner planning, hence their late arrival. In this way, these men embodied American and Jamaican traditional norms in terms of a gendered division of labor, where their jobs and economic status fulfilled expectations of them being breadwinners and primary money earners, a status that earned them the right to be served and catered to by women. While the fishermen's well-being was also asked after, and GFT ladies served them food and drinks when dinner was ready, the men's labor as cooks and their assumed criminality troubled the expectations of what "respectable masculinity" looked like for some of the hotel staff members. What is interesting to note here is that Jamaican men of both classes appeared comfortable in this multiclass, multigendered space, noticing the tension but seeming not to be particularly troubled by it. From the stories I heard on- and offline, and my conversations with some of the Americans and Jamaicans present at the Thanksgiving dinner, it was mostly the American and Jamaican women in the room who felt the burden of this classed and gendered tension.

Attendees who chose to eat dinner ate well, while some of the women on the hotel staff dashed out of the event early, providing various reasons for not staying longer. When I discussed the tensions and controversy with Gayle she said, "We're all Black people and we should be able to share a meal together, especially a holiday dinner. I just didn't get it." This idea that all Black people should get along was a prominent sentiment expressed among the African American ladies of GFT during my years of ethnographic fieldwork with them.

Assuming their American understanding of "Blackness" and a shared diasporic history translated to those in Jamaica, many of the Girlfriends could not understand why Jamaicans would not want to rally or unify around their racial identity. Although there seemed to be some shared understandings around how gender operated in the United States and Jamaica, there were different notions about what Blackness meant, how it was utilized, and what it required of those racialized as Black. These different conceptualizations about what Blackness is frequently led to moments of diasporic disconnect and mistranslation.

Here, however, I want to focus on the ways gender, even shared understandings of gendered responsibilities and performances, troubled GFT members' search for diasporic connectivity and a sense of belonging. As Girlfriends seek personal relationships with Jamaican people, various social cleavages and power imbalances, particularly those related to romance tourism, complicate these efforts. This chapter explores how emotional entanglements between African American women and Jamaican men frequently led to a diasporic triangle of tensions between African American women and Jamaican women. Through this examination, one is able to observe how personal relationships and various forms of service and emotional labor are linked to transnational flows of capital, culture, and privilege.

Oftentimes there were three agendas at play in the relationships between African American women, Jamaican women, and Jamaican men, all of them taking place in the context of Jamaica's informal romance tourism industries. African American women were searching for *Stella*'s Winston and sisterhood from Jamaican women. Some of the Jamaican men GFT members encountered were workers in the romance tourism industry, looking for American women to provide economic support and resources. Because romance tourism is so widespread in Jamaica tourist areas, there is a thin distinction between men identified as part of the informal romance industry and those who interacted with Girlfriends without any connection to the industry. In fact, I would argue that it is difficult for most Jamaican men, particularly those who are young and of lower class status than U.S. Girlfriends, to separate themselves from this industry. Consequently, there were always questions of (dis)trust, genuineness, and authenticity underlining the encounters between Girlfriends and young Jamaican men, even as GFT members sought diasporic connectivity.

Most of the Jamaican women engaged by GFT members served at hotels and restaurants, or they were the partners or family members of the Jamaican men providing hospitality and romance services or in a relationship with Girlfriends. Subsequently, even if money was not explicitly discussed in these gendered interactions, much of the implicit engagement was around service provisions and affective and/or economic transactions. Gender influenced this complicated diasporic relationship and the contours of imagined community, particularly as these different agendas played out. While Jamaican peoples were frequently negotiating economic and gendered realities, these African American tourist women were often navigating their own fantasies of diasporic belonging and happiness. As a part of these complex tourism-based and diasporic relationships, Jamaican men and women were constantly explicitly or implicitly requested to supply multiple forms of emotional labor to African American women as they pursued their desired diasporic fantasy.

In discussing these African American tourist women's interactions with Jamaican men, I concentrate on the gendered ramifications these affective transactions have for the women personally and the African diaspora more broadly. This contrasts with some other studies of the sex, hospitality, and romance tourism industries that focus primarily on the sexual and economic details of tourist women's liaisons with "sex workers." Differently, I investigate how these intimate relationships make the women feel, while exploring how their encounters and participation within the Jamaican tourist industry help them reflect on their racialized, gendered, aged, and diasporic positionalities. Scholars have analyzed the power dynamics embedded in the economic and sexual relationships between white European and American women tourists and their Black male lovers and companions in the Caribbean. However, fewer researchers have focused on the interesting racialized and gendered aspects of the relationships between Black women tourists and Black Caribbean men, particularly in the context of diaspora. This chapter describes the interactions between the Black American women of GFT and the Jamaican men they became involved with, providing some insight on the gendered dimensions of these ladies' journeys toward happiness and diasporic connectivity. I explore the gendered dimensions of diasporic subjectivity and girlfriendship by examining the relationships these tourist women seek and engage in while they are in Jamaica.

Friends or Lovers? Politics of Authenticity and Respectability

Before I move on, I feel I must clarify what I mean by the term "relationship" when I use it to describe the types of interactions Girlfriends have with Jamaican men. Contrary to the common notion that American tourist women travel to the Caribbean looking for Black men to sexually experiment with, control, and conquer, I discovered that the relationships were much more complex than this narrow characterization. Some of the women I studied established long-term, long-distance partnerships with their Jamaican boyfriends. They initially traveled to Jamaica for a vacation, fell in love, and returned numerous times in order to continue the relationship. During my study, there were four women with this type of relationship. Two of these Girlfriends had the longest long-distance relationships with Jamaican men of all the tourists I interacted with: one for eight years, the other for six years. Although a few of the newcomers and first-time visitors went to Jamaica with the intention of starting short-term liaisons or "hooking up" with Jamaican men, this was not the intention for the majority of Girlfriends. For those who did engage in a liaison, it usually did not last for more than one or two trips, as the fantasy began to fade. However, the lines between liaison, hook up, and partnerships were often in flux and difficult to determine. At times there were inconsistencies among what Girlfriends stated, what their actions demonstrated, and how they interpreted the intentions and actions of Jamaican men.

Jennifer, an African American woman who was a friend of some of the Girlfriends, shared:

> I know the first time I said something to Maya about having sex with Jamaican men, she said, "You've had sex with a Jamaican man?!?" I said, "Yeah." She said, "Well, you said you hadn't been in any relationships." I said, "I haven't. I found someone attractive, and I wasn't dating anyone back home, I was in-between relationships, and so . . . " And she said, "Well, damn! I never pictured you like that." And I said, "Pictured me like what, though?" I don't know any woman that's been [to Jamaica] more than once and hasn't had a relationship or sex on the island. Honestly. Maybe they haven't done the whole relationship thing, but they have at least had sex. I don't know any. I'm sure there are some. But . . .

Jennifer highlights here some of the respectability politics surrounding Black women's sexuality that haunted some of the conversations I had with Girlfriends about their interactions and relationships with Jamaican men.[1] Most Girlfriends subscribed to the notion that each woman was grown and able to participate in whatever type of relationship she desired. I did not hear or observe blatant policing around how women should engage sexually with Jamaican men within the group. However, I did note that Girlfriends were concerned they might be judged, criticized, or policed for their sexual and intimate behaviors. Although some frequently pointed to the gazes of Jamaican women as the culprit for this type of policing, Jennifer's description of the conversation between her and Maya points to some of the potential judgments that showed up periodically among American women tourists.

Jennifer explains, "I think a lot of women, especially Black women—because of the way most of us were brought up—you don't go around having sex with men you don't know. And I think that most women get sex and love mixed up all the time. Because they go from having a sexual relationship to thinking, "Ok, it's love, after two days." In this part of our conversation, Jennifer connects the dots between how Black women are socialized to think about their sexual agency and respectable interactions with potential male partners, and the ways tourist women interpret and label their relationships with Jamaican men. Since Black women are taught to be conservative in both whom they partner with, and what should take place in those partnerships, Jennifer suggests that different types of relationships may be labeled as "love," since there is an authentic and respectable connotation to this form of intimacy.

As mentioned in a previous chapter, almost all Girlfriends hoped and desired to be the subject of a Jamaican man's appreciative gaze and seductive lyrics, even if they did not take them up on the proposition. The performance of the chase and the experience of being desired were central to the fantasy of Jamaica. While the women were aware they could engage in numerous sexual acts with multiple willing men, those going to Jamaica that were open to finding a relationship stated they were looking for a lover or a companion for a committed partnership. Jamaican men and women repeatedly told these women that it was unrealistic to expect their Jamaican lovers to remain faithful and monogamous when Girlfriends returned home to the United States. Yet those interested continued to desire Jamaican men who were willing to be monogamous and believed in their vows of commitment when they were made. Jacqueline discusses this situation while comparing American men to Jamaican men in an interview in Jamaica:

Jamaican men have perfected the art of finding out what it is you want to hear and giving it to you. American men feel like they don't need to because they're the prize. They will quote you all kind of statistics about how few good men are out there, and how it's eighteen to one in Atlanta, and it's fifteen to one in Savannah, and how lucky you are to get them, you know. Not to say that when a tourist lady comes here she really quote has a Jamaican man because be aware that he probably has two baby mamas, three, four, five, a current girlfriend, and, uh, seven Canadian, Jamaican, English, Australian, and German girls who come in circuit. But, it's just like, ok. Let's say one is selling hot dogs on the street of New York City. You gotta convince everybody your hot dog is the best. That's called entrepreneurship. So, just because a Jamaican man might have perfected the art, should you hate on him? No! They got it down to an art form.

For the women I observed, sexual exploration and satisfaction were definitely important; however, their relationships seemed to be less about sex and more about their desires for committed relationships comprising intimacy, companionship, mutual appreciation, and sensuality.

Girlfriends described the men they interacted with as "boyfriends" and "friends." Categorizing their Jamaican male companions or lovers as "sex workers" is problematic, as the connections with these men were more complicated than that indicated in a simple transaction with what many describe as "gigolos" or "rent-a-dreads."[2] Some of these men were merchants, hospitality industry workers, fishermen, taxi drivers, bartenders, or restaurant managers who did not engage in any formal sense of sex tourism. In fact, a formal sex tourism industry in Jamaica seems nonexistent when it comes to Jamaican men, as who is "selling" their body, companionship, and love for money is not always clear. The difference between a man who is a romance/sex worker (seemingly engaged in relationships for money) and a man who prefers dating several tourist women who sometimes pay for his leisure activities is difficult to judge, particularly since almost all of these men are also engaged in domestic relationships with Jamaican women. This worked differently for the few Jamaican women I observed at clubs, beach parties, and at hotels who were involved in sex work. There appeared to be a more formal sex tourism economy composed of Jamaican women and white foreign men, where the interactions were sex for pay. One could often observe this at night during beach parties, where these couples would enter rooms upstairs from the performance space and appear again later on during the evening. There wasn't a prerequisite narrative of romance or intimacy required, and one could observe the same white tourist man engaging multiple Jamaican women workers during one trip. The seduction, intimacy, and connection that was essential to the *Stella* narrative, or even the narrative of romance in Jamaica, did not seem to be present in these relationships. I imagine the gendered differences of this context—and the power differentials associated with privileged and powerful white tourist men and less privileged Jamaican women—account for some of these differences.

This chapter focuses on the relationships Girlfriends had with Jamaican men who were lovers, friends, and potentially sex workers. While Jamaicans may have identified some of the men present in these relationships as "sex workers," in the eyes of the ladies this was sometimes difficult to distinguish. Gayle speaks on the affective and economic complexities of these transactional relationships between Jamaican men and American tourist women, stating:

I say to women that fall in love with Jamaican men on their trips, "I would never tell you that he doesn't mean what he says. I don't know him! I don't know his heart. I can tell you what I think based on my experiences. There's a good chance he's lying. But do I know that for sure? No. I'll never say that. I think that he likes you. And I think he enjoys being with you for whatever reason. It could be that he is getting nice, crisp, clean sheets every night you're here, and then dined and wined, and having great sex, and that's what he likes. But when he says he liked being with you, yes, the answer is 'yes.' Whether or not it's *just* you, I don't know! But it may be the whole package, including your money. I don't know."

Examining the politics of affective authenticity in the context of sex and romance tourism is an exercise that I found Girlfriends, their Jamaican interlocutors, and myself engaging in all the time during our travels.

In addition to Jamaican men who were boyfriends and sexual partners, there were also young Jamaican men who hung out with Girlfriends, enjoying the various activities they participated in without having a romantic or sexual relationship with any of them. From my observation and conversations with the ladies, these men were platonic friends. However, everyone's awareness of the romance tourism industry, and its central role in narratives about women and travel in Jamaica, oftentimes brought the platonic nature of these relationships into question for many, American and Jamaican alike. For example, Jamaican American, Sasha passionately argued that many of the Jamaican men that American tourist men called "friends" were not true friends if money was being exchanged. She said,

When [tourist women] say "Oh, I met this person and they're my friend." I mean, you're paying them. If it's your friend, you're gonna say, "Pick me up at the airport" and they would say, "You don't have to pay. You're my friend." That's a friend! They're not a friend if you're paying them. If you carry them a little gift, and say 'thank you', and that's your friend, that's different. But I don't see how they're your friend if you're paying them. If I go to Jamaica and I have a friend and I say I need to go from point A to B, they're not going to say, "Well, give me gas money" or you know, "I'll charge you $500 Jamaican dollars for that trip." The man that drove you around the whole one week is not your best friend.

The complexity of these emotionally complicated relationships with Jamaican men was demonstrated during the Jamaican Thanksgiving trip.

Breaking Down the Romance Fantasy

For most of the trip, GFT members Jacqueline, Keisha, and Lauren stayed up at the Columbus Heights apartment complex, while Maya and Gayle stayed at a rented villa in a town a short distance from Ocho Rios.[3] Maya was dating a guy she met while staying at a hotel the year before, and Gayle had a boyfriend whom she had been in a long-distance relationship with for about five years. The ladies explained that the lure of the beautiful villa, and the fact that both boyfriends lived outside the tourist area and closer to the small town, were the reasons they were staying outside of Ocho Rios and distancing themselves from the rest of the crew for this trip.

Maya had been dating her boyfriend, Sam, for a few months. Sam was almost thirty years younger than she was and presented himself as a responsible single father, taking care of the grounds at a local hotel to provide for his son. Most of us had met Sam during our previous trip to Ocho Rios in July 2004, when Maya introduced him as a friend who worked at the hotel at which we were staying. At the time, I thought nothing of it. I had met several of the women's male friends before, and a number of them appeared to be simply platonic relationships. Not until several people conveyed the following story to me after I missed Thanksgiving did I become aware Maya was dating Sam.

According to Jamaican and American observers of the holiday trip, the fun-filled, light feeling of the visit came to a screeching halt one morning. As she did every morning during her trips to Jamaica, Jacqueline set out for her daily run down the main road of Ocho Rios around six o'clock. This particular day she came out of her apartment at Columbus Heights to find a Jamaican woman she had never seen before sitting on the stone wall that bordered the mountainous hills one had to walk down to get to the road. The woman caught her attention because she was sitting perfectly still, upright, and silent, as if she was concentrating hard on something. Jacqueline said "Good morning," and the woman nodded her acknowledgment of the greeting but did not say anything back. Not giving it another thought, Jacqueline headed down the hills to begin her morning routine, saying hello to the merchants and fishermen setting up for the day's work.

When she returned from her run an hour later, the woman was still there basking in the morning sun, but the look of concentration she previously wore had turned to one that looked like concern. Jacqueline passed by without saying a word but returned the woman's look of concern, itching to ask her if she was all right. Hours later, as Jacqueline, Keisha, and Lauren headed into town to look for lunch, the woman was still perched on the wall as if she had not moved a muscle since earlier that morning. More than two hours later, when the women returned from eating and shopping, the mysterious woman had moved from her spot on the wall and was now sitting directly in front of Jacqueline's apartment door, with her head hanging down. Hesitantly, Jacqueline quietly said "Hello?" to get the woman's attention. The young woman raised her head slowly, her face full of distress and determination.

"How can I help you?" Jacqueline asked.

"Where's my baby?" the woman demanded.

Shocked at the question, Jacqueline asked in turn, "Well, baby, who's your baby?"

"I know who you are and I know the American woman is your friend. I'm Sam's baby's mama. I know what he tells you all, but I'm that baby's mama and I want my baby back," said the young woman.

At a loss for words, Jacqueline took a breath to gather her thoughts. Keisha and Lauren went inside the apartment to give them some privacy. After a few minutes of conversation, Jacqueline finally understood why the young Jamaican woman had been waiting all day long perched on the wall by her apartment—she was there to get her baby, who Sam had apparently left with a couple of days ago.

According to the mother, she had not heard from Sam or the child. Jacqueline called Maya at the villa to fill her in on the situation and was surprised when Maya got upset with her for disturbing her vacation with her boyfriend. Jacqueline requested that Maya and Sam come to the apartment complex immediately to at least provide the baby's mother with an explanation or give her back her child. Maya refused, saying that she did not want to get involved. After Jacqueline relayed the conversation to the Jamaican mother, the young woman threatened to call the police, stating that she did not care what Sam was doing or if he wanted to remain with the American woman; she just wanted her baby back. Apparently they still lived together, though Sam had not informed Maya of this. Eventually, after several phone calls, it became clear that neither Maya nor Sam was coming to handle the situation. The young woman left upset but did not call the police. This event caused a huge rift in Maya and Jacqueline's relationship, and although they eventually reconciled, tensions between them ran high during the next couple of trips on which I accompanied them.

Out of all the women I studied during my fieldwork, Maya and Gayle were certainly the most private about their relationships with men in Jamaica. Subsequently, I should make it clear that although several individuals' perspectives are compiled here to provide a version of this story, Maya has never discussed this event with me. I did not get her perspective on the events that took place, as it was difficult throughout my research to get Maya and Gayle to openly discuss their romantic and intimate relationships (as evidenced in the Interlude following this chapter). It was frequently expressed that they saw me as a "daughter-figure" and we were engaged in a mother-daughter type of relationship. In their eyes, I was too young and "innocent" to hear, or be provided with, the details of their relationships with Jamaican men. They deemed this inappropriate. Maya specifically did not want me to know that she was engaging in sexual and intimate activities with Jamaican men in the first place. And while they would never say they were ashamed of their activities—as they were clear that they were grown women with sexual autonomy who could do whatever they wanted with their bodies—I always wondered if politics of respectability were at play, and if they thought I would judge them in some of the ways their families and friends did at home in the United States. It is possible they felt I was one of the judging, critiquing gazes that Jennifer references in her narrative. I was constantly negotiating my positionality as an African American, Jamaican, young woman researcher, who was sometimes mediator, confidant, "play niece," or "play daughter" for the ladies of GFT. Consequently, I felt that asking for Maya's side of the aforementioned story would make our personal and research relationships quite difficult to navigate for the remainder of my project. Instead I did my best to compare multiple versions of the story for clarity and verification, taking out parts that narrators described differently.[4]

None of the Girlfriends would have described Sam as a worker in the sex or romance tourism industry. Because he had formal employment at the hotel where they resided, and served them in that capacity, his relationship with Maya was seen as what happens when two adults flirt, spend time together, like each other, and decide to embark on a relationship. It was similar to the beginning of any intimate relationship. However, it was evident from interaction with the mother of his child that something was awry. While it was not clear that Sam and this Jamaican woman were married, it was clear (at least from her narrative) that they lived together, that they co-parented the child, and that she knew he had an American girlfriend who did not know about her. As shocking as it was to some of the Girlfriends, this situation was not too uncommon in Jamaica. I heard numerous stories of Jamaican men who were married or living with Jamaican women and who had foreign girlfriends whose gifts of money and other material things helped contribute to the household. Through the grapevine I heard that, while cautious at first, during their relationship Maya had paid Sam's son's school fees and was thinking about contributing funds to a future business endeavor. I know, from conversations with Maya about love relationships, she believed that those in intimate relationships should actually partner with one another, and I imagine these gifts were a demonstration of her commitment to this partnership. This is what those in a committed, monogamous relationship did for one another. However, I am not sure what Sam's commitment or participation in this relationship was, and I never had the opportunity to ask him.

Sometimes in these relationships taking place in the context of romance tourism, a Jamaican girlfriend, wife, or baby mama was aware of the relationships with foreign women and either left the home, embraced the foreign relationship, or resigned herself to deal with the situation, no matter how much she did not like it. The economic benefits of the arrangement and the ability to address the family's financial needs were sometimes too much to pass on. This was a common narrative surrounding Jamaican men who dabbled in the informal romance tourism market. But this story demonstrates why it is difficult to identify and pin down who is involved in romance tourism and what the parameters of the industry are. Questions about genuineness, truth, intent, economic interests, and general emotional matters of the heart make analyzing the costs and benefits of an industry based on romance difficult, especially when the lines between love, romance, and money are so blurred.

Trying to gain some insight into how Jamaicans viewed the complex relationships between Jamaican men and tourist women, I interviewed Michael, a British Jamaican tour guide in his early fifties. Michael was born in Jamaica, but had lived for over two decades in London, where he had been a deejay and party promoter in his early years. In our discussion of race, class, and tourism, Michael drew on his experiences traveling in Germany, Spain, and France, and provided some insight on how love, sex, money, and friendship become interwoven in these relationships. After getting some background on how he saw race and class politics operating in Jamaica, I asked his perspective on what he thought brought tourist women to Jamaica. In the following interview excerpt, Michael broke down the particulars of the romance fantasy:

MICHAEL: The rent-a-dread thing is a new phenomenon for the African American women. But it is an old phenomenon for Europe, the white world. I would say this thing has been going or building since the 1950s when the Jamaicans hit Europe, through England. It didn't take [Jamaicans] long to establish our selves from the Africans or other Blacks, because we are different.

BW: How?

M: With the carrying on, the loudness, the love of dancing, the love of women, the love of showing off, just the love of everything. The first women that really started to take notice was the middle class white women, because nine times out of ten, they frightened the white man. With the women's movement, they quietly became independent. And it wasn't nothing publicized, but between themselves, women who chat among women spread the word that if you want to have a nice time, be flattered and spoiled, then Jamaican men were it.

BW: It was a status thing?

M: No, the same way here in Jamaica. The [tourist women] that come to Negril for that, if they were to walk along the beach or road and didn't hear that "pssss pssss" or "hey baby" they would be disappointed. Cause that's what they came for. We would walk somewhere [in England] and not know a soul. See a woman that we don't know, walk up to her and say, "Hey darling, I really love you."

BW [*chuckles*]: And it would work?

M: And it worked! Because nobody else is going to do it. English men would go down to the pub and drink with their friends, and they will take their women. But the women would stay in the corner and music would be playing and they wouldn't pay any attention to the music or the women. Now, the Jamaican man, as soon as the music gets to him, he's moving and that looseness and the moves usually grabs most women. A nice set of music comes on and you just want to dance. And that one move itself gave us fifty percent of our women. The better you dance, the more girls you get. It's the out and out feistiness of a Jamaican man! Even if her date is beside her. He'll stand there and say, "Darling, I really think you're attractive. If you ever finish with this guy, I'm your man, yeah?" And she'll say, "You're cheeky. And I love it!" If you had that ability, the story would spread and before you know it, you were a busy boy. At first it's like "I'll buy him this" and "I'll buy him a car," and he keeps coming back for more and everyone is happy. Before you know it, it's what the guy expects the woman to do, cause if I wait long enough, I'm going to find a woman who is going to come along and buy me a car. Supply and demand.

BW: Is this what's happening now? In Jamaica? Is it the same thing?

M: In Negril, the women come with their dollar or their pound and they want some connection or a good time. And when they find him they will spend their money just the same. In their heart they are not renting anybody. But the Jamaican's mentality is that he's getting money out of it . . . A lot of it is mental. The physical is there, but it's a mental thing. A woman who is forty or fifty years old is flattered that this twenty year old is finding her attractive and paying for her attention. And in some ways she can be more controlling and forceful, more aggressive in the way she maneuvers in the situation.

BW: Because she has the money or why?

M: One, because she has the money. Two, because she might be more experienced than the candidate. He might be one of the biggest dogs, workers, whatever you want to call it in the pack, but he probably hasn't got the experience or the know how to deal with the more sophisticated woman he is dealing with. The ones that are not young and innocent may play the innocent game well. So they're like "I have four kids, and I have to send them all to school." He is not asking her for any money, but he is showing her what kind of pressure he is under. So indirectly she's going to say "Well, he didn't ask me for anything, but I know I can help." So you see, it's how you play the game, and about the skill and class of the prey against the predator sometimes. Most times the predator, in this case the woman, has got far more experience than the prey, like in this case, the dread.

In this excerpt, Michael lays out the context in which Jamaican men and women—whether it be white British women or Black American women—are often creating relationships within. From his perspective, Jamaican men known for their dance moves, lyrics, and confidence, provide affective services to the women they have set their eyes on. The women are flattered, attended to, and get to experience the seduction of a man with game, while exercising sexual agency and aggression they may not be able to experience in other relationships. The men gain access to economic benefits and the pleasures of sex and companionship, without directly asking for money. This leads to a mutually beneficial relationship for both people, which is predicated on each performing their gendered, classed, and nationalized roles. The affective and economic transactions that fuel the romantic fantasy are simultaneously real and performative.

Jamaica Is (Not) for Sex!

During one oppressively hot summer day in Negril, eight ladies of Girlfriend Tours International and I packed into our tour guides' vans to travel to a nearby waterfall. This excursion was one of the main events on the annual tour's itinerary, as the drive through the bush and the waterfall tour itself served as a good introduction to the nature and beauty of Jamaica outside of the regular beach scene. Dressed in bathing suits, swimsuit cover-ups, T-shirts, and shorts, the ladies and I spent the forty-five-minute drive calming the fears of those terrified to swim in the falls and engaging in a boisterous discussion about the sights and people we saw through our dusty windows.

As we passed by a restaurant along the road, one woman remarked that it reminded her of a scene from *How Stella Got Her Groove Back*. The comment generated a conversation about each person's favorite scenes, complete with quotes from the film and reenactments from their seats. In the middle of a reenactment, Marilyn turned to me and asked, "Are you taking notes on this for your book?" I blushed and laughed as I normally did when they directly referred to my research and outed me as an observer among them. Vera, a fifty-something Southern woman who was in a long-term relationship with a fisherman in another city, shared some of her sexual escapades with her boyfriend and a few details about her man's victories in bed. Suddenly she turned to me and shouted, "Bianca, here's a quote for your book. Write this down! Jamaica is for fucking!" Some of the ladies burst into laughter, while others' mouths hung open in complete shock at her straightforwardness.

A couple of months after Vera's sex declaration in the van, most of the attendees from the GFT tour reconvened for a U.S. reunion at a Girlfriend's house. Women traveled by car and plane from St. Louis, Atlanta, and Memphis, while I traveled from Fort Lauderdale to meet them and their friends. The first night we looked at pictures from our summer trip, cracked jokes about the best lyrics we had heard from men, and gossiped about the events taking place in new trip reports on Jamaicans.com.

The following morning, the vibe was calmer and quieter as we sat outside drinking tea and coffee and shared what we missed about Jamaica. Shooting up from her chair, Vera ran to get her cell phone from the kitchen, deciding to call her boyfriend in Jamaica so he could make fun of us for moaning, groaning, and being nostalgic for his home. She called him on his cell phone and loudly, excitedly filled him in on what took place the night before. After a couple of minutes of conversation, Vera excused herself from the group and took the phone into another room. When she returned, her face was stricken with sadness. She looked absolutely distraught. A silence fell across the room. Jacqueline asked her what was wrong as the rest of us waited patiently for her to answer. In a quiet voice, completely inconsistent with her regularly loud and syncopated tone, she replied that her boyfriend had just broken up with her. We exchanged looks of shock and sympathy as she sat quietly trying to wrap her ahead around what had just taken place.

We spent the rest of the day trying to comfort her and cheer her up. There were hours and hours of discussion about what could have prompted this sudden breakup, which included a review of their relationship by different women who had been present to witness it. As her shock slowly morphed into quiet anger, Vera told us about how she had sent him money that she did not have, how she gave him good loving, how she selflessly allowed his friends to spend time with them during their vacation time when she wanted her boyfriend to herself.[5] As tears streamed down her face, Vera admitted that she felt like she was never going to have love like that again in her life. She explained that there was something special about him and the loving they shared, and that it was not only about getting "some young Jamaican dick."

I share these two snapshots of Vera's relationship to demonstrate how extremely blurred the lines are between sex, intimacy, and love in the context of what scholars have described as "sex tourism" or "romance tourism." In fact, the debates about what to call these relationships where love, sex, and money intermingle, and how to categorize the agents taking part in these affairs, point to the complexity of these affective and transactional relations. It was quite clear to me from the emotions stirred up at the U.S. reunion that these trips to Jamaica, and the relationships created during these trips, were about more than sex, despite Vera's shocking claim in the van. Contrary to the popular notion in many studies of sex and hospitality tourism that "First World" women are simply traveling to the Caribbean to exchange food, hotel accommodations, money, and other gifts for fun with hypersexualized Black men, I argue that these emotional relationships are based on complex forms of affective labor and investment for both the men and women involved. Moreover, in these intimate interactions, African Americans and Jamaicans are examining national difference while attempting to understand how gendered and nationalized privilege may highlight the different processes of transnationalism and tourism in which these groups are implicated.

I do not mean to paint the relationships between Girlfriends and Jamaica men as free from the stress of power differentials and moments of exploitation. Ironically, these Black women, who are often stereotyped as hypersexual and promiscuous in the United States, actively engage in conversations in which they designate Black Jamaican men as "Other" because of their class status, religious beliefs, and most significantly, their assumed "inherent" sexual abilities. An example of this emerged in an interview with Gayle, when she discussed whether she believed sex tourism was new in Jamaica. She said,

I think that American white women have always gone to Jamaica. American white women have always known about the Jamaican man and his sexuality. They always find out the good stuff before we do. Always! I was saying to Jacqueline, these white women get all the best toys EARLY! Right when they come off the shelf. [White women] were doing it way back when. But it's Stella, it's a big draw for Black women. For the past six or seven years. Terry McMillan did more for the economy of Jamaica, I think, more than any single person outside of Butch Stewart. I think so.

Gayle points to the historical, colonizing practices of white women in tourist spaces and their objectification of (Black) Jamaican men, while also commodifying Jamaican men's sexuality herself. Though much of this was said in jest, her remarks support the analysis that scholars such as Jacqueline Sanchez Taylor have about national privilege, race, gender, and class. In her research on sex tourism in the Caribbean, Taylor argues, "Notions of 'racial' otherness and difference play a key role in allowing tourists, as much as their male counterparts, to ignore imbalances of age and economic power between themselves and their local sexual partners."[6] She continues, "Being able to command 'fit' and sexually desirable bodies which would otherwise be denied to them reaffirms female tourists' sense of their own privilege as 'First World' citizens."[7]

Although Girlfriends frequently discussed the differences in economic status (not necessarily power) in their relationships with their Jamaican male lovers and companions, serious reflection about the gaps in age were less frequent. Most Girlfriends subscribed to the idea coined by one Girlfriend that "as long as there is a '2' in the front of his age, it is okay with me." This statement implied that as long as the man is at least twenty years old, he is old enough to engage in a consensual relationship with these women. This consent is supposed to release the older Girlfriend from any guilt that may arise from others' perception that she is robbing the cradle, or engaging in an age-inappropriate relationship.

In general, when someone would point out the age differences between one of the women and her Jamaican boyfriend/companion, or the fact that she would probably not date or flirt with a man half her age in the United States, most of these comments were met with nonchalance or a shrug. Although the women tourists in Taylor's study were mostly white, her statements apply to the sexualized and nationalized Othering these Black American Girlfriends construct with Jamaican men. However, I propose that this group of African American women seeking male companionship within the context of diasporic community complicates the one-dimensional story scholars of sex tourism often tell. Their interactions illuminate the interplay of (race, nation, class, and gender) factors that influence how power plays out in these relationships.

Sexual Commerce and Diasporic Differences

While a colonialist paradigm certainly applies to other situations of sex tourism, the dynamic between the Girlfriends and the Jamaican men is differently complex and layered, with opportunities for each party to use hegemonic power over the other. Much of the work on tourism that examines racial difference confines the discussion to the emergence and intensification of sex tourism, where Black and Brown bodies (in the Caribbean especially) are desired and exoticized through the lens of traditional colonizing representations of hypersexualized Blackness. These ethnographic studies of sex tourism in the Caribbean connect analyses of global capital networks and gender formations in order to document how women in various locations and multiple social positions experience globalization differently and unevenly, especially in sites, such as tourist destinations, where economic forces intersect with institutionalized gendered ideologies.

Kamala Kempadoo's work provides examples of this "difference" and "unevenness" while arguing that the experiences of Black and Brown women sex workers disrupt feminist theories of prostitution as violence against women.[8] She highlights their resistance to discourses of victimhood, arguing that these women are agents who are able (to the best of their ability) to turn the erotic desires of tourists into capital gains for themselves and their families through sex work. Kempadoo moves away from feminist arguments that the global sex trade is simply a form of violence against women all over the globe, offering instead a transnational feminist framework that studies women of color's sex work to "explore and theorize differences and commonalities in meanings and experiences in the sex trade."[9]

Recognizing the racialized and gendered power dynamics in these relationships between tourists and Caribbean men in their article, "Fantasy Islands: Exploring the Demand for Sex Tourism," O'Connell Davidson and Sanchez Taylor argue that many of the sex tourists in the Caribbean want racialized "Others" because of a "desire for an extraordinarily high degree of control over the management of self and others as sexual, racialized, and engendered beings."[10] While it may be true that some tourists, particularly the white European and American tourists O'Connell Davidson and Taylor study, are able to realize their desires for control in part or in whole, I argue that the control the Girlfriends desire or believe they have is in some ways a bit more difficult to obtain and maintain because of their race and gender.

Girlfriends were often engaged in relationships with younger Jamaican men where the economic and social power dynamics involved in "stereotypical" male-female relationships were inverted. Here, American women were economically better off and of a higher social status than the Jamaican men they were partnered with, and had access to privilege and power associated with their American money and citizenship. Additionally, as Michael explained in his narrative, the older women in these relationships are sometimes more experienced and knowledgeable about sex, love, and intimacy, and may be able to navigate the relationship in a more confident way than women are traditionally expected to act. Despite these advantages in generational, economic, and social capital, oftentimes the ladies still had very little control over the Jamaican men they were with. The women had little sway over when they saw the men they were dating, when they had sex, the duration of the relationship, and if the man remained loyal and monogamous. A surprise breakup, the discovery of another girlfriend or wife (Jamaican or foreign), or a refusal of sex were all incidents that quickly showed the ladies that the control their economic and social power mediated was a fantasy, or at least unreliable and erratic, and that men could draw from their own reserves of gendered power. Although they sometimes exploited and objectified the person their affection was directed toward, both individuals in the relationship felt the effects of disempowerment and exploitation.

A story told often to warn Girlfriends of the risks of falling in love with a Jamaican man and giving him their all was that of "Half House Sue." The legend is that there was a white American woman named Sue who fell in love with a Jamaican man in Negril. They had an exciting, romantic love affair, and after a year or so of traveling back and forth from the United States, Sue decided to move to Jamaica. She sold her business and all of her belongings. Her children and family members thought she was losing her mind and actively tried to dissuade her from moving to Jamaica for her lover. She did it anyway, and they got married in Jamaica. In the first few weeks after she moved, she enjoyed making her new home, getting to know his family better, and making friends in the community. The home was a simple wood structure near water, but it had the view she always wanted. However, after a short time she realized that her man had another lover—a Jamaican woman not too far away. After trying to get him to stop seeing this other woman to no avail, she filed for divorce and took him to court. The judge eventually ruled in her favor and concluded that their belongings be split in half. A few days later, when Sue returned to her house, she found that the structure had been cut in half, and the other half was nowhere to be seen. Apparently her husband had come for his half of their home. From there on out she became known as "Half House Sue." Of course, none of the Girlfriends knew if this story actually took place or if the details are true. But repeatedly I would hear veteran travelers share this legendary story when they saw a first-time Girlfriend or newcomer too quickly falling for the lyrics of a Jamaican man. At the end they would be told that the Jamaican proverb that one "stands in love" but does not "fall in love" had wisdom and power in it. They were encouraged to take love slow, enjoy the romance, but keep their eyes and ears open.

Girlfriends were quite aware of the inversion of power present in their relationships and often discussed how it affected their understandings of gender roles in heterosexual relationships. Maya and Jennifer, a woman in her early forties from the South, provided their thoughts in an interview:

MAYA: "This motherfucker don't even have a job! How's he supposed to run the [relationship]?" I say that a lot.

JENNIFER: You do say that a lot.

M: You know. And I equate, it's not that I equate money with power—

J: But it is power.

M: It's that I equate *job* with power.

J: But almost everybody equates money with power. You would be way outside the norm if you didn't equate it with power.

M: Ok.

J: I mean I think, to me, that's why people want it, that's why people kill for it, that's why people flaunt it.

A few minutes later in the conversation, they returned to this point:

MAYA: I don't mind taking care of . . . I'm a bossy person anyway. But I prefer not to be when it comes to the male in my life. And ironically, I'm not even used to that because my son is dominating and my grandson. And he's six. And I respect, I love that, and admire that in both of them because they're men! Even if you don't have but five cent[s], you still supposed to be in charge. To me. And I'm so used to, fifty-four years of being in charge, and you don't know how *tired* I am of [it], and I don't wanna, but it's too late now, for me, to change.

BW: What do you mean?

M: [It is too late for me to] not be a dominating person.

Maya expresses her feelings of exhaustion with the idea that she will have to be in charge of her children, grandchildren, *and* her potential mate, stating her desire for the man to "run things," even if he has less money than her. Maya represents many of the Girlfriends who find their burdens of responsibility too great and seek a male partner to lighten the load or take it over completely. In some ways, more privilege and power in a relationship meant more responsibility they did not want. Maya's comments echo those of some of the other women I interviewed, who often reinscribed patriarchal understandings of heterosexual relationships, desiring a relationship where the man runs things while the woman is taken care of. In this way, the control that O'Connell Davidson and Taylor discuss and the fantasy of control that I describe are powers that women such as Maya would like to relinquish. Instead, she expresses a desire to have her man take care of her, provide for her, and in some ways dominate the relationship. At the same time Girlfriends recognized that this domination, or at least lightening of the burden, would require them to trust their partners as they took on responsibilities, which was tough for some used to doing the work in their families for a long time.

In conversations, Girlfriends stated that they appreciated Jamaican men for their confidence, machismo, and sense of empowerment in the bed and in other areas of life. During her interview Gayle said, "[Jamaican men] have that confidence because they have so little to lose. They're one step from the bottom. Versus, for us to leave our $70,000 a year to go after our dream, we've got a lot to lose." In Gayle's opinion, because Jamaican men are often in a less privileged economic position than the African American women they are dating and have less to lose, they are able to have a certain sense of confidence that these women cannot afford. According to this line of thought, for all of her economic and social empowerment in Jamaica, an African American woman must still maintain control and walk carefully, because she can fail and lose everything. In this way, Gayle suggests that while African American women are assumed to have more privilege because of their American class status, their race and gender (Blackness and womanness) work to disempower them.

As the discussion turned to comparing Jamaican men and African American men, Gayle's commentary on nationalized gender roles becomes even more complex:

> GAYLE: It is the confidence we [American women] see, their machoness is what we see when we're in Jamaica. Do they have that same confidence in their everyday life, when they're not in the presence of an American woman, when they're dealing with their Jamaican counterpart? Do they

still have that confidence? Or is just that they show that confidence because they know that [American women] are a market that they are comfortable with. Because they're thinking, "I *know* they want ME."

BW: Well, what do you think when you compare Jamaican men to American men?

G: I think Black American men are so sissified in so many ways.

BW: Sissified?

G: Yeah, they are able to deal with strong American, strong women easier than the Jamaican man that's not on any level sissified. *At all.* I mean, you have the people that are intelligent like a Stedman Graham. Intelligent man. He can still be with Oprah Winfrey because he's on some level very sissified [*she laughs*]. You gotta be! In order to be Oprah *Winfrey's* man. American men have to be sissified. Now, you have a Jamaican man that come up off that beach, can come over here and whip that butt into shape. And he'll run the whole thing. And would have no problem working in a corporation, at the head of a corporation. In fact, Gayle [King] would have to go [*she laughs*]. Because a Jamaican man would be taking her place. She would have to go. She would *have* to *go!*[11]

Here, Gayle reinscribes normalized, heterosexist understandings of Black masculinity and power. Jamaican men are viewed as confident, which seems to correlate with strength, whereas African American men are seen as weak, soft, less masculine. Her opinion is that an African American man is "sissified" or somehow less of a man because he is able to "deal with" a strong Black American woman. Throughout the span of my fieldwork with Gayle, she expressed some of the same sentiments Maya had about being tired of upholding the "Strong Black Woman" stereotype and wanting a man to take care of her, and yet, here it seems that she would deem her male caretaker less of a man, at least if he was American. The argument seems to be that a Jamaican man could come from a lower-class background, move to the United States, and take charge of the woman's entire life, including running her business and replacing her best friend. In a sense, a Jamaican man does not "take any mess." This line of thinking is very similar to the explanation that some interviewees gave about why African American men did not date or engage in sexual commerce with Jamaican women. According to the interviewees, Jamaican women would not put up with African American men's mess, and African American men were intimidated by and feared Jamaican women because of their strong sense of self. In these discussions, old-school heteronormative and patriarchal notions of intimate and sexual interactions between Black women and men are upheld and combined with nationalized generalizations.

Sisterhood and Making Jamaican Women (In)visible

After a while in the field, I realized that the imagining of the diasporic community by Black American Girlfriends was gendered, in that Jamaican women were often left out of conversations about sameness and similarity. Jamaican women were almost always spoken of as different, aloof, and sometimes they were completely absent from the discussion of diasporic community. In fact, Jamaican women were usually only made discursively visible in stories about antagonistic interactions with female passersby, irate customs officers, or young dancehall queens; or physically present in roles as excellent service industry workers and nurturing, elderly impoverished matriarchs. Similar to Jacqueline Nassy Brown's discussion of exclusionary racial practices within the sexual triangle between Black Liverpudlians and American GIs during World War II, the boundaries of diasporic inclusion are troubled by the movement of hypersexualized Jamaican men's bodies from the homes of their Jamaican spouses/baby mamas to the beds of these African American women.[12]

In Jamaica, many referred to the tensions between Black American women and Jamaican women, especially in connection to their relationships with Jamaican men. For the women of GFT, this was a pretty big dilemma because, according to them, one of the reasons they visited Jamaica was to connect to the women there and create bonds with their diasporic sisters. They wanted sisterhood as part of this diasporic belonging and imagined Jamaican women as part of their imagined community. In the context of the *Stella* narrative, they not only wanted the love, desire, and romance of Winston. They wanted the sisterly bond, affirmation, and emotional connection with his mother too!

However, most of the Jamaican women they were able to interact with, and who seemed to respond kindly to their invitations of friendship, were women "employed" by them, including hotel staff, waitresses at the restaurants they frequented, or the singing ladies at the airport. There seemed to be an underlining cost-benefit to these relationships embedded in a disproportionate power dynamic. The younger women the ladies of GFT most often made friends with were frequently a part of Jamaica's lower classes, as they were women Jamaicans would identify as sex workers, or women who worked on Fisherman's Beach (as jewelry sellers, beverage sellers, waitresses, or fisherwomen).[13] The differences in age, class, nationality, and other social experiences between these older African

American tourists and their young Jamaican women friends sometimes made diasporic connections difficult to maintain. Jamaican women with similar life experiences and of the same age and class status, whom the ladies would consider "girlfriends" like those in the United States, rarely entered the tourist sectors or were not interested in mingling with tourists outside of work. The younger Jamaican women still worked in the service industry, although informally, and therefore were readily accessible in tourist areas where their older counterparts were not. Oftentimes these African American women were unaware or did not completely understand how powerful and enforced the classed distinctions in Jamaican society were, including these classed and gendered rules around space and location. In general, there were not many social spaces for these homosocial bonds to be created.

Jamaican men Girlfriends encountered were also (at least initially) introduced to the group through the (formal and informal) service industry, however, their access to male privilege troubled this service power dynamic. These men also desired the potential profits GFT ladies could provide, but there was more lenience for the muddiness of business and personal relationship because of the overarching impact of romance tourism in Jamaica. Jamaican women, on the other hand, generally seemed less interested in the crossing or blurring of these boundaries, particularly if it required them risking their reputations.

Girlfriends frequently wanted to be authentic friends in a situation that automatically placed them in a higher economic status than the women they were trying to befriend, and often, they wanted to ignore or at least not highlight this aspect of the relationship. Jamaican women, on the other hand, were conscious of this dynamic, constantly aware that the basis for their interaction with these American women was the fact that they worked for them. While speaking with some of the staff at the apartment complex where GFT members often took up residence, I heard versions of the following statements: "It is difficult to forget or ignore the fact that we are differently positioned when I just finished cleaning your toilet, making your bed, or cooking your food. It might be difficult for us to be friends, because you are paying me for my services. And I'm often getting paid wages less than I believe I should get." In the end, it becomes difficult to enter a relationship of sisterhood when the person you see as exploiting you, or at least with more privilege than you, is someone who is not fully aware of the different power dynamics. The assumption of sisterhood here is complicated.

Girlfriends would frequently lament the fact that Jamaican women did not seem to like them and that they could not find any Jamaican women to begin friendships with. They seemed completely at a loss when Jamaican women at restaurants or on the street would "ice grill" them, kiss their teeth, give them bad service while mumbling under their breath, or completely ignore them as if they did not exist.[14] Every once in a while a Girlfriend would get back into the van after one of these incidents and state something like, "I don't know why she has so much attitude. It's not like I'm here to come after her man. I'm not like those other women." Believing they were receiving such attitudes because Jamaican women thought they were after Jamaican men, these women would try to separate themselves from the "other" white and Black American and European women they perceived engaging in sex tourism.

Because of my family heritage, and my significant amount of time in Jamaica completing fieldwork, members of GFT saw me as their Jamaican insider. Oftentimes they would ask me to fulfill this capacity by providing some insight into why Jamaican women disliked them so much. Pulling on my fieldwork with American Girlfriends and informal conversations with Jamaican women, I would explain the cycle as something like this: American women come to Jamaica to enjoy the island and sometimes engage in a romantic relationship with a Jamaican man. They often come thinking that Jamaican women are not going to like them, because they have heard from others in the United States that Jamaican women have a bad attitude and are upset that these "Stellas" are taking all of their men. They reach Jamaica, and often encounter a moment of miscommunication, have a bad service experience, or have a difficult interaction with a Jamaican woman. These moments could be anything: interpreting an innocent look as mean, having a different idea of good customer service than Jamaicans do, displacing their own feelings of guilt or apprehension about looking for sex/love in the Caribbean, or truly engaging with a woman who does not like them. Even if they have pleasant experiences with a few Jamaican women, it is still the one negative experience (which they were already anticipating) that they often paid the most attention to, and from this they extrapolate that all Jamaican women are as mean and unfriendly as they have heard.

From the Jamaican woman's perspective, these African American women traveled to Jamaica to treat another group of Black people badly, walk around half-naked, show off the expensive things they own, date men already committed or half their age, and engage in other activities a respectable women should never participate in (especially in their forties and fifties).[15] As these two explosive sets of stereotypes, competitive vibes, hurt feelings, and bad attitudes continually clash, African American women and Jamaican women remain disconnected from one another.

In some ways, this discussion about the potentiality of friendship and sisterhood across power differentials may run parallel to those relationships described in the work of Judith Rollins on Black domestics and the white women who employ them. In Rollins's book, white women request emotional labor from Black domestics who are already poorly paid (and badly treated) for the physical labor they are performing.[16] Like these white women employers, by requesting friendship from Jamaican women servicing them, African American tourist women are requesting additional labor on top of the physical work these Jamaican women are already providing. The sisterhood they desire, this deep sense of friendship and "care-labor," is something many of the Jamaican women I encountered either were not interested in or did not have the time to fully invest in. They had families and other areas of their life to take care of, including the work demands required for them to earn their wages.

Unlike the white women in Rollins's work, GFT members made the assumption that there was a shared racialized and diasporic connection between them and the Jamaican women servicing them. They saw these Black women as diasporic kin with a shared history and assumed that this meant these Jamaican women would want to engage in a sisterhood based on their perceived shared experiences. However, because Girlfriends were tourists in vacation mode, not usually focused on the different dynamics between their class status in the United States and that of women in Jamaica, they were not always aware of the ways these power differentials played out. This is not to stay that Girlfriends did not know of the financial hardships Jamaican women often encountered or were in denial about the fact that their access to mobility was not shared by many Jamaican women. However, there did not seem to be a deep awareness that the care-labor these African American women were requesting from Jamaican women was similar to the care-labor they were expected to perform for their own family members and friends at home. Girlfriends took trips to Jamaica to escape the burdens of this emotional labor without realizing that their requests and expectations of sisterhood and friendship from Jamaican women added to those women's emotional labor burdens also. In some ways, Girlfriends assumed Jamaican women wanted and would benefit from girlfriendships with them in the same way they assumed other Black American women would want friendship. The notion that classed differences would trump shared racialized and gendered identities did not seem to come up for the majority of Girlfriends.

Another way the women of GFT differed from the white women employers in Rollins's book was that many of these African American women were lower middle class in the United States. Most were not returning home to households where they had their own domestic help. Having a maid, a cook, or some other form of service laborer while on vacation was an extravagance and a privilege, not their regular everyday experience. For many, the first time they were able to employ another person, particularly another Black woman to perform a service, was in Jamaica, and most felt uncomfortable with this new sense of privilege. There were awkward moments regarding how much they should tip those providing services, and whether their tips were sufficient for these women (and men) for whom they felt a diasporic connection. They spent a good amount of time deciding how to get around the rules of places that would not allow tipping, by buying children's clothes, perfumes, makeup, and other toiletries or accessories, which could be left in the room as a gift in lieu of money. While most understood these items did not equalize the classed (and nationalized) differences, they did see these gifts as efforts to contribute to diasporic kin and possibly personalize the relationship between tourist and service worker.

The moments in which I did observe African American and Jamaican women bonding over something, and engaging in friendship that could have been a catalyst to sisterhood, surrounded the sometimes shared emotional labor of mothering. That is to say, while Girlfriends and Jamaican women did not necessarily bond over their assumed shared racialized or diasporic experiences, they did have some powerful conversations and moments of deep connection about being mothers and the responsibilities of mothering. They discussed the responsibility of feeding and clothing their children; the multiple informal and formal streams of income to ensure they could afford to take care of their kids; the significance of family; and the presence (or lack thereof) of fathers in their kids' lives. There was a recognition of emotional labor on both sides of these conversations, even while there was also an awareness of how the national contexts (i.e., the different economic possibilities while living in the United States and living in Jamaica) contributed to the different experiences these women had.

However, when Girlfriends engaged in these conversations, many times the assumption was that their shared experiences outweighed the differences in their experiences of mothering. Again, the African American women were approaching this relationship and the discussion from the notion that these were other "Black" mothers, who experienced some of the hardships they experienced because of their assumed shared intersectional identity of being Black, a woman, and a mother. Jamaican women did not necessarily come from this same starting point, bonding around the motherhood part of the discussion but seeing African American women as a very privileged type of woman and mother. However, both of these groups of Black women are responsible for huge amounts of unpaid emotional labor, in their homes and in their communities, and this was a strong point of connection.

In addition to the tense, sometimes awkward navigation of power differentials around economic status, there was also the exchange of information that could potentially disrupt the inner workings of romance tourism. Because the Jamaican women who were hotel staff, restaurant owners, and informal commercial workers were residents who were present for the tourist industry's workings all year, they had access to more information, more knowledge of what was going on in the community, especially the relationships and movement of Jamaican men. They knew the local and international girlfriends of the Jamaican men whom some of these women befriended, flirted with, or had relations with. The staff at the local apartment complex I frequently stayed at could place on a calendar the times of the month when the international girlfriends of one Jamaican man visited like clockwork, clearly understanding the different "shifts" this man had in providing intimacy, companionship, and sex to American and European women. While everyone in the community observed daily events and who was spending time with whom, these Jamaican women had an inside track on the gossip. It was in the best interests of Jamaican men (workers and beneficiaries of the romance industry and men who were already in relationships with Jamaican women) for African American women and Jamaican women not to become friends or diasporic sisters.

Ironically, although the Jamaican men Girlfriends were in relationships with were often of the same age and classed groups as those of the Jamaican women they had the most access to, the "success" of diasporic connectivity was vastly different. Whereas the women described long, intense, deeply reflective conversations about personal beliefs, race, and diaspora with young men they were intimately connected with, they hardly ever seemed to be victorious in creating these times of connections with Jamaican women of any age or class. It seemed that as Girlfriends traveled to Jamaica to be appreciated and made visible by Jamaican men, their pursuits of love and intimacy while on the island frequently kept the struggles of Jamaican women invisible, particularly the wives, girlfriends, and baby mamas of the sought-after Jamaican man. Additionally, the exchange of money from these tourists to Jamaican men through a variety of methods (including buying clothing and cell phones, paying children's school fees, and providing seed money for businesses) affects gender roles and relations between Jamaican men and women long after the African American women leave the country.

Clearly, sisterhood in tourist spaces and service relationships complicated diasporic belonging and the Girlfriends' pursuit of happiness. On the Girlfriends' side of the relationship, there was an interest in creating safe spaces for Black women and enjoying the benefits of shared experiences. As they traveled to Jamaica to create girlfriendships and safe spaces with one another, they also wanted to include Jamaican women in this process. Patricia Hill Collins writes,

"This shared recognition often operates among African-American women who do not know one another but who see the need to value Black womanhood."[17] However, the safe spaces and shared recognitions did not translate well between Jamaican women and African American women. Some of the difficulties were because of classed differences and cultural narratives around *Stella* and romance tourism. Girlfriends' activities and interactions with Jamaican men often worked to silence or invisibilize Jamaican women, even as African American women stated their desire to establish connections. And some Jamaican and Jamaican American women, like Sasha (below), felt as though Girlfriends did not take enough action or put enough effort into trying to establish these girlfriendships with Jamaican women. For Jamaican women, there seemed to be some economic benefit to connecting with American women, particularly in the service industry. But it was also an emotional threat or risk, especially if Jamaican men they loved were involved.

Not truly convinced of these American women's desires to connect with their Jamaican sistren, Jamaicans.com boardite and Jamaican American Sasha argued that Girlfriends were not trying hard enough. Citing their membership in a web community full of Jamaican women, Sasha claimed that the Americans were not utilizing all of their resources to engage in these friendships. In her interview in the United States, she said,

> My biggest thing is you're on a Jamaican board, why don't you go over to General Discussion if you want to make some female Jamaican friends, and start out there? When you go to Jamaica, [Jamaican women are] living their regular lives. They're going to work. They're not sitting here. When you're [in the United States] at work, you're not stopping and saying, "Well, let me go visit that tourist that's looking at the Washington Monument or something," you know? You're not stopping and saying, "Take a picture of me. I want to stop and talk to you. Spend some time with me or whatever." So, [Jamaican women are] living everyday life. They're not trying to holla at you, so it's not going to be like the Jamaican men, or not trying to get any money from you or whatever.[18] So, that just ticks me off. 'Cause there's other Jamaican people there on the board you can go and talk to, ask them questions or whatever.

As one of the top three board members on Jamaicans.com with the most posts, and one of the few Jamaicans who frequented the tourist forums without lurking, Sasha did her part in reaching out to befriend American tourist women. She was disappointed that the efforts did not seem to be reciprocated by American women, particularly African Americans, who claimed to desperately want to create these bonds. I observed several conversations in Jamaica where Sasha would mediate, navigate, and speak back to American tourists, particularly American women, who tried to form friendships with Jamaicans. At times, she would also do some of this work online in the web community. As someone knowledgeable about the United States and Jamaica, she understood both sides of the experiences and tried to shed light on what Americans and Jamaicans were experiencing. However, she was younger than most of the Girlfriends and boardites she engaged with online, could sometimes be a bit crisp and blunt in her responses, and had little patience for ignorance, so some Girlfriends and boardites did not take to her personality. Sasha called people out on the contradictions between their stated desires and their actions (or lack thereof), and it seemed hard for some to deal with.

Despite all of the "bad blood" between Jamaican women and American women, throughout my conversations with Girlfriends there seemed to be a deep sense of admiration for Jamaican women and an appreciation for the strength it took to overcome the economic obstacles with which they were faced. Jacqueline described how American women and Jamaican women are different:

JACQUELINE: Jamaican women are from a very distinct culture that has its mores, and its own societal innuendoes, and American Black women can't even possibly *begin* to comprehend. Jamaican Black women to *me* are the most self-possessed, sassy, together sistas I know. They broach no nonsense. They cut to the chase. They get it done, whatever *it* is. And they don't have time for nonsense. They are hard when they need to be hard, and they are probably soft when they need to be soft. I don't know for a fact, I'm just assuming. I think that, you know how we, African American women try to tout the fact that we need to be strong sistas, yang, yang, I would think that it's nothing compared to what Jamaican women have to do. I would think they got us beat times twenty. I think they would like to like us, but they can't afford to like us.

BW: And what do you mean by that?

JACQUELINE: Well, I think that given the behavior of some of the sistas that come over here, and some of the behavior they engage in, I'ma be honest, [my]self included. I would have a problem with me. Coming over here treating my country as your own personal little recreational playground. You know. And interfering in some established relationships here. Because you know, I have a friend named Michael that always says,

"If you find a Jamaican man that says he doesn't have anybody, he's lying. Or there's something wrong with him." So you're interfering with *some-body's* boyfriend, baby father, *husband*, etc. when you come over here. It's no such thing as a good Jamaican man that's not taken. Even the bad ones are taken [*we both laugh*]. You know so, he's just on leave. There's no just like single guys running around here all viable and employed and stuff like that. You know you can fool yourself to think that's the truth, but that's not the truth. 'Cause it's a small country with a high male-to-female ratio, just like [in the United States]. And heaven forbid the brotha be about something and have a job, No! He's occupied. You know, he just took a break to be with you for the week or two weeks you've been here, or whatever. So, to answer your question, my sistas here, to be honest with you, are twenty times stronger than I am, because of the economy they have to deal with. Because of the world they have to deal with. Because of the issues they have to deal with. They've got small salaries. The same high prices. Out the wazoo gas and utilities. And children they gotta put through school with no free public education. And no healthcare, no benefits.

Here, Jacqueline points to the similarities and differences she sees in Jamaican and American women's struggle with the experiences and gendered expectations that make up the life of the "Strong Black Woman." Jacqueline recognizes that her national and economic privilege may make her life as a Black woman slightly easier than that of her Jamaican counterpart and that this, in addition to the competition over men, may be the reason Jamaican women do not initiate friendships with Black American women. She states, "I think they would like to like us, but they can't afford to like us."

Among the discussions that took place about why Jamaican women and American women did not get along, I never heard a Girlfriend suggest that part of the reason Jamaican women did not want to connect with them was because they did not feel a diasporic link to Black Americans. I am not sure this statement would have made sense to them. Nevertheless, several Jamaican women mentioned this to me in my informal conversations with them, pushing me to understand that much of the desire for diasporic connectivity came from the Americans. This sense of "diasporic sisterhood" or girlfriendship the Americans yearned for seemed irrelevant to the Jamaicans. In fact, many Jamaican women saw American women as competition in their own pursuits of happiness, as these foreigners were "stealing" their potential partners and mates. In the same way African Americans described white American women as using their white privilege to attract Black men from the pool of potential mates, Jamaican women viewed these American tourists as using their national and economic privilege to draw the attention of Jamaican men.

Frequently, the economic and affective relationships between American tourist women and Jamaican men transformed gendered expectations and power dynamics within some of the relationships these men had with their wives, baby mamas, girlfriends, and potential mates. Although Jamaican men were often the individuals engaged in relationships that put money into their pockets, it became more commonplace throughout my research for me to hear Jamaican women presented as money-obsessed gold diggers. In my informal conversations with Jamaican women, they often mentioned that Jamaican men not only saw them as gold diggers but also viewed them as financially irrelevant since they could not provide for Jamaican men as American women could. I paraphrase Petagaye, a young Jamaican woman I interviewed who was a merchant on the beach: "American women come and spoil Jamaican men, paying them to have sex, tell them lyrics, and make them feel good. That's not work! We need them to provide for our families, but when we ask them for money or to take care of the kids, they call us gold diggers. American women mess it up for the rest of us."

According to some of the Jamaican women interviewees, Jamaican men claimed they did not like to date Jamaican women because these women only wanted them for the things they could buy them, the name-brand clothing they wore, or the cars they drove. In fact, when asked about how she understood American women to be different from Jamaican women, Sasha compared her life to that of her commodity-conscious Jamaican women cousins.

SASHA: They'll be with somebody else's man, or married men, or they'll be with one man and know that he has five other women, and it might be two of their best friends or whatever. That type of thing, as far as the culture, and what they think is acceptable, I just can't get with it. I can't do it. I don't really, like those things don't impress me, like the F150. I've been with somebody that drove the F150 or the Escalade or something. I don't really go, "Oh my God! Look at his car!" Or if he gives me the equivalent of $10,000 Jamaican or whatever, I'm not going to drop my pants. Because I have a job. I make my own money. I make good money. I don't need a man to come pay my bills. So I don't need to depend on him. If I don't have him, I'm not done or anything. . . . I can't bother with it! And I feel uncomfortable, 'cause they ask me something and I'm saying how I think or how I feel, and they're like, "Are you stupid? What are you going to do when you want these clothes or this outfit? When you want to go to Negril?" I don't know. It's uncomfortable.

BW: Are these personality differences or cultural differences?

SASHA: I think that it is. Because if I grew up there [in Jamaica], I would probably be like that. Then again, maybe I wouldn't. I'm just saying, 'cause my mother would still be American and my dad would still be British, and I'd still be able to travel or whatever, so probably not.

Sasha suggests here that because her family heritage and national citizenship provide her with access to international mobility and privilege, she would not have to make the same choices or succumb to the "gold-digging" she sees her cousins engaging in. However, like Jacqueline, Sasha also seems to recognize the economic predicament many Jamaican women find themselves in when she mentions that her cousins are in relationships with already committed Jamaican men in order to get new clothes or travel to other parts of the country. Stating that she has a job, makes her own money, and can buy her own things, Sasha acknowledges that her cousins do not have access to the same opportunities she has living in the United States, while admitting that this makes her uncomfortable.

Throughout my fieldwork, the diasporic triangle composed of sexual, economic, and intimate relations between Jamaican women, Jamaican men, and African American women intrigued me; by following the links of these various relationships I could observe how affective labor within the tourist industry had real implications for all parties involved. The rift in women's solidarity was extremely prevalent as Jamaican women and African American women found themselves sharing the same space, particularly in hospitality and service spaces. Ironically, in pursuit of their own happiness, intimacy, and girlfriendship, Girlfriends were causing their Jamaican counterparts to experience a sense of loneliness, hopelessness, and economic hardship similar to that which repeatedly made them escape to Jamaica. Although they experienced a sense of class and national privilege, Girlfriends were sometimes duped into relationships where Jamaican men were not faithful or monogamous. Some Jamaican women dealt with the difficulties of also being in relationships with disloyal men, frequently not having access to opportunities that would empower them financially, and could not visit another country to "escape" these obstacles. Jamaican men seemed to be stressed about fulfilling their duties as family breadwinner, intimate partner, and sexual pleaser, claiming that there were no "good" Jamaican women to partner up with. In the end, each party labored to make the best of whichever situation they found themselves in, trying to attain happiness, economic empowerment, and intimacy in the relationships they engaged.

Conclusion

My time with the ladies of Girlfriend Tours taught me that the possibility of finding love, sex, intimacy, and companionship in the arms of a man was only part of the reason some consistently returned to Jamaica. Although the moments of romance and disappointment involved in their emotional relationship roller coasters were important to them, more often than not they were searching for something else—a sense of racialized belonging that was missing within the national borders of the United States. Sometimes this sense of belonging could be found in the arms of a Jamaican man, but sometimes this diasporic embrace could simply be found in the crowded streets of Black people in the town center.

The ladies withstand deep criticism and isolation from friends and family to become more extroverted, well-connected social beings in Jamaica. Although the women of GFT often reinscribe heteronormative ideologies, uphold stereotypes of the hypersexualized Black man, objectify their partners, engage in patriarchal heterosexual relationships, and desire significant amounts of emotional labor from Jamaican women they oftentimes help make invisible, they also embody a sense of agentive Black woman's feminism through international mobility and sexual autonomy that is not usually ascribed to African American women of their generation. Their efforts to wade through their tears and reach toward Jamaica as family and friends criticize and isolate them are important for our understanding of emotional transnationalism and of the aspects of love, desire, intimacy, fantasy, and hope that fuel Black women's passion (some would even say "need") to travel and leave the United States for their emotional wellness. Their ability to counteract their loneliness caused by racism, sexism, and ageism in the United States by seeking leisure and pleasure is exciting and challenging. Their struggle to make themselves and other African American women visible is both commendable and problematic, as they engage in exploitative practices. Their pursuits of happiness in the search for sexual freedom, love, and companionship are thrilling and sometimes disappointing. The contradictions in their pursuits of happiness demonstrate the complexities of the emotional entanglements as capital moves between people and across national boundaries.

I sat in Keisha's living room listening to her tell me about her wedding in Jamaica. Keisha and her husband, Rob, were often referred to by Girlfriends and other boardites as the "Jamaicans.com Couple," and their son, the "Jamaicans com Baby," as his parents were matched together by determined Jamaicans .com members acting as virtual cupids. Keisha met Rob on the website after he posted a trip report about a visit home to Jamaica to see his mother. Rob had been a fan of Keisha's trip reports for a while but did not have the nerve to begin a virtual correspondence with her, so he continued to lurk. After Jacqueline read both Keisha's and Rob's reports and decided they would be perfect together, Jacqueline PM'd (private-messaged) Keisha and requested that she read Rob's report, and then she did the same with Rob. Eventually, with some prodding from several board members, the two connected through posts, trip reports, and PMs, set up a face-to-face meeting, and began traveling between their two states to date. In her late twenties, Keisha was the youngest Girlfriend I had come across.

Throughout our interview, Keisha often emphasized the national and cultural differences she was continually made aware of as an African American woman becoming accustomed to being a part of a Jamaican family. Although Rob had moved from Jamaica when he was fourteen, lived in Brooklyn for years, went to college in the South, and currently resided on the East Coast, to Midwestern Keisha, he and his family were very "Jamaican." For example, Keisha reported that her dad thought Rob was a Republican when he first met him because he was a JAG officer and a card-carrying member of the NRA. Her father kept asking, "What type of Black man is he?!" Like many other couples composed of African American and Caribbean partners, Keisha and Rob frequently engaged in passionate discussions about the African diaspora and their varied racialized experiences as they navigated and came up against their national differences.

A particularly dynamic conversation began during our interview in their home in the United States. Rob walked into the living room just as Keisha was stating her sentiment that African Americans have a "lock on our brains," referring to the mental slavery she felt they had endured throughout the history of slavery and institutionalized racism.

Rob kissed his teeth and shot her a look.

"And that's one of the reasons why we cannot just stand up and say we're not going to take it anymore like my husband says we should," Keisha said.

"You need to take what's yours. You all built this country," replied Rob.

"We don't own shit! We're dealing with four hundred years of oppression," Keisha exclaimed as her voice rose.

"Well, how long is it going to take to free yourselves?"

"Probably another four hundred years."

"No, that's way too long," Rob said as he shook his head rapidly. "My son can't grow up in that."

Keisha shot me a look of exasperation, then lifted her hand to make the sign that Rob was ridiculous.

Rob turned to me, looking a little frustrated. "Some Jamaicans think that African Americans don't take advantages of the opportunities available to them."

Keisha turned to him and asked, "Why does the world hate African Americans?"

"This is my Jamaican elitist comment of the night— 'The whole world hates African Americans,'" he replied with sarcasm.

Keisha continued speaking as if she did not hear his answer. "Chinese, Japanese, Cubans, I don't know. Even Australians. We are the lowest on the [hierarchy]."

Rob replied, "Foreigners from anywhere are always going to think they can do better in a place than those that live there. Americans think they could make it better in Jamaica, right? Jamaicans think they can come to the U.S. with all these opportunities and do better than Americans. There are two groups of Jamaicans—those that think living in the U.S. is too hard, so they don't want to move here. And those that think if they just got over here, they could make more money in a month than they would make in a whole year in Jamaica.

Those people initially think, 'What are African Americans complaining about?' But then they begin to send money back home and work tons of hours to keep up, and they end up returning to Jamaica where life is harder and easier at the same time. If I ever experienced racism, it was when I came here to the U.S., and it was from African Americans who treated me like I was lower than them."

Keisha took a moment to take this all in. Then she said, "I think all racism is economic. They weren't hating on you because you are Jamaican. They were hating on you because you are taking their jobs. Jamaicans often come over here and work for a lower price for the same jobs. Do you understand that that has to do with racism also?

Rob nodded.

"No, really. Do you?" Keisha asked.

Rob nodded again.

"Well, why do Jamaicans hate Haitians?" Keisha asked Rob.

"Now *that's* racism!" he answered excitedly. "Because Jamaicans think they are the highest group in the Caribbean, and Haitians are the lowest. They are seen as backwards. I don't understand that."

"I thought you were all Caribbean. I didn't see the difference. I thought you were all on your little islands together," Keisha explained. She turned to look at me, as if she wanted me to note that I was included in this statement. And with that, the conversation ended, the baby cried, and we readied to eat dinner.

5

Navigating (Virtual) Jamaica
Online Diasporic Contact Zones

In chapter 2, I discussed how the women of Girlfriend Tours International became aware of their diasporic differences while physically visiting Jamaica. This chapter focuses on how Girlfriends and members of the Jamaicans.com community experienced their diasporic and nationalized differences online. Diasporic relations are always formed and influenced by broader processes and dynamics of power globally, such as transnationalism. Here, I suggest that an anthropological emphasis on *people* as mediators of experiences, instead of conceptualizing media technologies as neutral objects, gives scholars the opportunity to investigate how agency, power, and pleasure drive the circulation of both media technologies and the racialized ideologies that circulate with them. Arguing that race *still* matters, I focus on people and the technologies they use to pursue happiness while creating and participating in diasporic contact zones. Although some of the newcomers and one-time visitors to the website may not engage it as a diasporic space (preferring to get quick answers to their questions about hotel accommodations and concerts in Jamaica), many of the active African American and Jamaican community members participate in conversations which suggest that they imagine this site as a diasporic space and as a community.

With this in mind, here I focus on the ways boardites interrogate and police the boundaries of both their virtual community, and the broader community of the African diaspora, through activities and discussions related to three themes: (1) the relationship between their virtual lives and "real" lives; (2) their experiences with nationalized cultural differences and various forms of cultural policing; and (3) how Jamaicans.com makes Jamaica accessible for those who cannot travel to Jamaica and prolongs happiness and connection for travelers when they are not physically in Jamaica. By investigating how Girlfriends use travel and the Internet to find temporary refuge from the burdens of American racism, while simultaneously engaging in their own methods of racialized and cultural policing on- and offline, I document how these women both transcend and reinforce racialized and nationalized boundaries. Although their use of electronic media is important, I place more analytical emphasis on the emotional connections this media allows them to create and maintain, as it is the sense of diasporic belonging and emotional satisfaction they receive that keeps them returning to the website and the country.

In the following sections, I contribute to the current theorizing of virtual media, particularly the Internet and its role in the construction of racialized subjectivities, moving away from previous literature that reinforces a dichotomy between cyberspace and real life. The theorization of race continues to be significant and controversial because of how it has been used to explain (or explain away) the disproportionate distribution of goods, rights, and political power that results from racialized social classifications. Some analyses of the contemporary period of globalization have argued that race has become less salient as national boundaries become porous; however, other scholars suggest that older racial hierarchies are still operating and are often solidified as new technologies are utilized. Here I examine how tools such as the Internet can provide individuals with mechanisms to appropriate, transform, and resist the racialized labels attached to their life experiences.

Internet users have ignited cyberspace with conversations contemplating the social and political meanings associated with Blackness in the wake of several current events, including the creation of the Movement for Black Lives, Barack Obama's successful campaign for the U.S. presidency in 2008 and 2012, and the debate over whether African and Caribbean university students disproportionately benefit from affirmative action policies. Using web tools such as e-mail, instant messaging, videoconferencing, and blogging to engage in these public interrogations of Blackness, Internet users discuss the ancestry and experiences that enable one to claim membership within Black communities, while recounting their shared and divergent experiences with racism. Although not all of these discussions take place with the goal of creating a diasporic consciousness, it is undeniable that some individuals are using these tools to construct, maintain, and modify their diasporic subjectivities. While scholars are beginning to document and explore the broad ways in which Internet users are innovatively using web media to create new social networks and communities of belonging, engage in cultural exchange, and transform their understandings of self, only a few scholars have done research on how utilizing this technology affects the ways users modify or reconstitute their racialized subjectivities.[1] By ethnographically investigating the relationships between geographic and virtual communities, I shed light on moments when technology enables people to see particular aspects of race clearly and other moments when technology obscures the racial realities individuals claim to know.

Additionally, by interrogating how Girlfriends and boardites construct their subjectivities in virtual contexts, I also highlight the ways nationality or "Americanness" is conceptualized and the effects various racialized and nationalized ideologies have on the construction or deconstruction of diasporic communities. I investigate how the Internet may affect the construction of racial subjectivities, the extent to which these understandings of race lead to diasporic and other group formations, and how, through technologies, these formations might be subverted and reformulated, sometimes in surprising ways.

The Anthropology of Virtual Media

As anthropologists continue to explore how identities, community formations, and lived practices are affected by processes of transnationalism and globalization, an analysis of the role media technologies play in today's cultural politics has become crucial for understanding how people construct meaning, maintain (transnational) relationships, forge networks of cultural exchange, and transcend temporal and spatial boundaries. Anthropologists have examined the roles of both cultural producers and cultural consumers by analyzing how groups and individuals experience media and (re)interpret media texts. Most significantly, anthropologists document the ways cultural producers (especially those of marginalized groups) use media forms to work against pervasive racist, classist, sexist, and heteronormative ideologies prevalent in dominant media perspectives, while also using these technologies to complicate the one-dimensional representations of their communities in popular culture.[2] Furthermore, we continue to explore the ways in which cultural production *and* consumption are sites where people simultaneously contest, contradict, transform, and reinscribe dominant ideologies.[3]

An examination of media, and its close relationship to cultural production, is important for exploring the ideological frameworks within which processes of community and subject formations take place. The introduction of the Internet into some people's everyday lives has prompted multiple examinations of "cyberspace as culture and as cultural artifact."[4] In the past, much of the literature on media assumed that individuals were consuming media individually, not socially. The ever-increasing use of these new technologies in private and public spheres has pushed researchers to generate multiple textual and ethnographic-based analyses of these technologies and engage in interdisciplinary debates about their effects on community and identity formations. One of the major debates focuses on whether Internet technologies undermine the formation of community, or if the formation of virtual communities actually enables new possibilities for communal expression.[5] Although many scholars have celebrated the Internet's ability to provide new possibilities for social and communal experiences, researchers such as Caren Kaplan have encouraged scholars to recognize how Internet technologies are "as embedded in material relations as any other practices," meaning that just like political, social, and economic factors influence our understandings and use of televisions, radios, and cars, they do the same for the Internet.[6] In contrast to David Harvey's account of the flexibility of labor in the current era of globalization, Kaplan argues that the mobility of labor required for the production of machinery and materials of cyberspace is, in fact, "more strictly bounded" in this contemporary moment of globalization.[7]

How individuals construct their identities in cyberspace and through cyberculture is also important as we attempt to understand how Girlfriends, other American boardites, and Jamaican boardites are constructing virtual selves through the mediums available on Jamaicans.com. Debates around gender and cyberspace have focused on women's access to, and relationship with, technology; the masculinist language of technology; the construction of masculinity in cyberspace; and the exclusion of women from "technoculture"; and they have even prompted the formulation of "cyberfeminist" scholarship.[8] Whereas the scholarship on gender and sexuality in cyberspace is diverse, scholars have spent less time studying race and the Internet.[9] Standing out from this silence is the work of Lisa Nakamura, who investigates how "playing" with identities on the Internet, or engaging in what she calls "identity tourism," may be used as a tool for doing subversive or resistive work in cyberspace.[10] Nakamura's research on racial identity tourism and fantasies of racial otherness in video games and cybercommunities is one of the few texts that takes an in-depth look at race in cyberspace, particularly the construction of Asian identities in this space. Other scholarship on race in cyberspace has examined issues related to the proliferation of white supremacist rhetoric and communities in the virtual world, how individuals construct racially mixed bodies for their avatars by choosing assemblages of multiple races, and the construction of white masculinities.[11]

Although some anthropologists have addressed how individuals use and experience the Internet through ethnographic research, and critically analyzed its role in the construction and transformation of racialized, classed, gendered, sexualized, and nationalized identities, the scholarship on Black identities (particularly those outside of the United States) is lacking.[12] The literature on other media and popular culture forms, such as music, and its relation to Black community and identity formations is plentiful, but little work has been done on the ways in which race and "Blackness" may be mobilized differently in virtual and territorial sites of cultural production and consumption.[13] However, Miller and Slater's ethnographic study of the Internet in Trinidad emphasizes the ways that Trinidadians represent Trinidad in cyberspace, strengthen their ideas of nationalism, and maintain Trinidadian diasporic relationships with Trinidadians in countries around the globe.[14] This is one of the few ethnographic studies of the Internet in the Caribbean and Latin America, with very little research completed on African diasporic peoples in the United States or throughout the continent of Africa.[15] Also Miller and Slater's research illustrates the influences offline social lives and identities have on one's participation in cyberspace, gesturing toward one of the largest debates in cyberstudies literatures.

Finally, Shaka McGlotten provides "virtual intimacies" as an excellent framework for theorizing the ways Internet users create connections and deep senses of belonging in a space some deem as fake, superficial, or not real. He troubles the real/virtual binary by analyzing virtual and technological spaces as implicitly powerful, affective spaces. McGlotten writes, "As an immanent power, the virtual is often deferred, sometimes materialized, but always charged with the capacity to help us feel like we belong. Intimacy describes: a feeling of connection or a sense of belonging. . . . Intimacy is also a vast assemblage of ideologies, institutional sites, and diverse sets of material and semiotic practices that exert normative pressures on large and small bodies, lives, and worlds."[16] McGlotten clearly explains the draw of the virtual, the promise of connection and belonging that it can provide. Moreover, he significantly suggests that this space is not outside the parameters of various forms of hegemonic and institutional power, but in fact, these forces are still in operation, working on the bodies of those accessing the virtual. However, McGlotten wants us to understand that while some may view virtual intimacies as "failed intimacies" because these connections take place online, it is more complex than that. Writing about heteronormative and heterosexist understandings of intimacy and sex and their view of queer intimacies as "pale imitations or ugly corruptions of the real deal," McGlotten argues that for some critics, "virtual intimacies approach normative ideals about intimacy but can never arrive at them; they might index some forms of connection or belonging, but not the ones that really count; they are fantastic or simulated, imaginative, incorporeal, unreal."[17]

This is important for this analysis of American Girlfriends' and Jamaican boardites' interactions and encounters in the virtual diasporic contact zone of Jamaicans.com. It points not only to the complexities of their affective experiences, their intentions and desires, but also to the larger processes that influence the possibilities of who they can or cannot be online and how they feel as they engage in constructing these (diasporic and racialized) identities. McGlotten offers that "personhood is not necessarily constituted by what one does, but by how one feels, and by the ways one names those feelings (or doesn't) and puts them into relationship (or doesn't) with larger social histories of difference or national belonging."[18]

Connecting the Virtual and the Real

In the past, scholars studying cyberspace, cybercommunities, and cybercultures who were intrigued by the relationship between the virtual and the "real" concentrated on some form of the following questions: Are virtual identities and Internet social actions ultimately relegated to virtual reality and "life on the screen"?[19] Or do these online communities and cybercultures have real-life political, social, and economic effects?[20] While the two camps debating the distinction between virtual reality and "real time" have been intellectually productive in creating knowledge about cyberspace, ethnographic studies and other methodologies that combine an analysis of both "realities" must document and provide empirical evidence of users' thinking about these "realities." With these questions in mind, I examine the ways virtual media, and this website specifically, shape how Girlfriends and boardites construct their identities, create community, and engage one another as diasporic kin.

In contrast to the literature on virtual communities that emphasizes the appeal of anonymity or "identity tourism" in virtual spaces, many of the boardites on Jamaicans.com claimed they presented as much of their "real" selves as possible within the online community. This aspiration to represent "the real" was because some members had a desire to meet their virtual neighbors at a bashment either in the United States or Jamaica, while others recognized there was a great possibility they might run into other "Jamaicaholics" while visiting Jamaica. The general feeling on the board seemed to be that remaining anonymous, having multiple cyber-personalities, or being dishonest about oneself went against the feeling of camaraderie within the community. In response to my inquiry about her popularity on the board, Marilyn, cofounder of Girlfriend Tours and one of the most prominent members in the virtual community, speculated about why other members were attracted to her postings and trip reports:

> You know, people used to think that the only reason I was on there was to tout my business. But see Girlfriend Tours, Jamaica, and the other things I talk about there are just part of the fiber what makes me. What makes *me*. I just talk about the stuff I do. And so, I think it's because I'm so open, and because I'm willing to open up my *whole* life. And you know it's not the most fascinating and interesting life. But I'm just so honest about my life, and talk about what I really feel and what I really do and see.

In this passage, Marilyn describes her desire to open up her "whole" life to her virtual neighbors, implying that she does not keep her "real" life offline. In fact, when other members thought she was only on the website to publicize her business, some felt she was being disingenuous or did not share the same investment in the community as they had. She received private messages and postings questioning her character and the authenticity of her Jamaica obsession. Eventually, as Marilyn began to share details about events and experiences from her offline life, members embraced her and made her discussion threads some of the most long-lived and popular on the website. Consequently, one can conclude that opening up and being "truthful" about an individual's real life online may actually be a tool for creating a type of social capital, or at least credibility, in this virtual space.

Although some boardites may have embellished the events that took place at home, or used creative license to keep readers interested in their post-vacation trip reports, most felt that being dishonest in the virtual realm could have potentially negative consequences. Very little identity tourism or identity "play" seemed to take place within the tourist forums I studied because members feared that these dishonest words or actions might have real repercussions when they physically met each other. Furthermore, boardites were aware that numerous individuals might access the web to "correct" their embellishments or provide another perspective, including peer travelers who were on the same trip, Jamaicans on the island whom they had interacted with, or someone on the board who had visited the same city in the past. To be dishonest or insincere on the web, and get caught, led to a discrediting of one's character, as other members questioned their authority on Jamaica or their desire to be a "good citizen" in the community.

Interestingly, I observed that it was actually when boardites were physically in Jamaica that some attempted to transform themselves into more social and extroverted beings, or engage in a somewhat basic form of identity modification by wearing different clothes than they would in the United States, or being open to trying new foods, hairstyles, accents, or sexual experiences while in Jamaica. Many individuals engage in this form of experimentation while on vacation, but if it is a form of "identity tourism," it is different from the sense in which Lisa Nakamura uses the term in her book *Cybertypes*. For these board members, the social costs of using the anonymity of the Internet to engage in dishonest or disingenuous forms of communication was not worth losing potential social connections or friendships.

During my fieldwork research I observed that in this virtual community, most members primarily use the Internet to facilitate "face-to-face" relationships, engage in conversations with people they eventually plan on physically meeting, and maintain transnational relationships with friends and associates they have already met. Therefore, I conclude that members view the Internet as another form of communication, like the telephone, which acts as a catalyst for making new connections and maintaining old relationships. This is not to say that board members overlooked the significant temporal and spatial advantages the Internet as a medium for communication provided. Boardites appreciated the benefits of receiving a quicker response from friends through e-mail or private messaging, or having a less expensive tool for keeping in contact with lovers and friends in Jamaica than flying or using numerous calling cards. In these virtual contact zones, American tourists and Jamaicans engage in conversations about everyday life and significant historical and political events, with the intention (or at least the possibility) that they might one day meet face-to-face. For these Internet users, the virtual is an extension of their everyday life, for virtual and real worlds are not entirely distinct or separate but often overlap.[21]

One of the most prominent examples of the virtual overlapping with the real during my field research was when a rift between some boardites online almost cost Marilyn her job as a school guidance counselor. I had been off the boards for a little while, as I was traveling around Jamaica for a few months and did not have regular access to the Internet. Upon my arrival back in the United States, I spent a few days on Jamaicans.com catching up on the postings and trip reports I had missed. Marilyn's absence on the board was hard to miss, particularly since she was one of the moderators of the "Jamaicaholics" forum. I sent her a private message to see how she was doing, fill her in on the events that took place while I was in Jamaica, and get an update on what I had missed on the boards. When Marilyn returned my message, she announced that she had decided to participate less in the discussion forums and was thinking about giving up her position as moderator because of some drama that had taken place in the past few weeks. Not wanting to write all the details down, she requested that I call her so she could give me the scoop.

In a fascinating story of her virtual and real words colliding, Marilyn informed me that someone from the board, another Jamaicaholic, had tracked down where she worked and e-mailed her boss and the school's superintendent. Evidently, the fellow board member wanted Marilyn's superiors to know that they thought that it was inappropriate for Marilyn to be on the website at work, spending hours talking to friends online instead of attending to the kids for which she was responsible. The boardite complained that they paid taxes and thought Marilyn's actions were clear evidence this money was not being put to good use. On the phone, in a voice brimming with hurt, Marilyn claimed that this was not at all true, that she was only online during breaks in her day and when students were not in the office. To avoid any further drama with her boss, or the school system, Marilyn decided to give up her position as one of the forum's moderators and limit her posting to evening hours, even on the days she was off work, in order to avoid further accusations of neglect at her job. This greatly saddened her and other members on the board, as she was one of the people who kept the community alive during the daytime with her interesting stories, words of encouragement, and information about Jamaica.

As a dedicated school counselor and teacher for over thirty years, Marilyn could not understand how someone from the board she loved could believe that she would put her students' well-being in jeopardy. She was saddened even more by the prospect that someone would dislike her enough to go through the trouble of contacting her superintendent to try and get her fired. After an investigation, which included calling and private-messaging virtual neighbors to see if they had information on the identity of the complainer, Marilyn was convinced that a white woman from the board was the culprit and blamed for the fiasco a clique of white veteran board members who repeatedly hated on her trip reports and postings. Apparently, for weeks before the incident, Marilyn and members of this clique had engaged in a heated discussion over the sexual nature of some of her trip reports and her need to talk about her experiences as a Black woman in other forum postings. Some members of this web clique stated that they were tired of hearing about race, and they claimed Marilyn's reports were too sexually explicit. The controversy surrounding Marilyn's trip reports was so large that in an interview months later Jennifer brought it up. As a member of the group defending Marilyn's right to post whatever she deemed appropriate, Jennifer argued:

Here's the thing. I hear women on Jamaicans.com say that they are tired of reading trip reports by Black women because it's all about men. Whereas white women, white people on the board, have trip reports that are more about Jamaica. But here's the thing though. White women are used to being the object of beauty, even here [in the United States] at five hundred pounds and pimply, they know there's going to be some man somewhere that wants them. You know, maybe even some Black man. Whereas for Black women... Everywhere white women go, there's going to be somebody that's gonna be attracted to them because they're *white*.

Even in this virtual space, Marilyn felt that her "Black woman's sassiness" made people uncomfortable and pushed them to do things to make her life difficult. Although this event did make her reduce her time online, it only convinced her that less time spent in the United States and *more* time in Jamaica was what she needed to be happy. In a way, this tainting of her experiences in the virtual Jamaica, and the realization that virtual neighbors could have a profoundly negative impact on her real life, made Marilyn feel as though the geographic Jamaica was the safest space to be the Black woman she was.

Staying Connected with Jamaicans.com

For Girlfriends, and many of the boardites on Jamaicans.com, the website not only provided them with the opportunity to find out more about the country they wanted to visit but also allowed them to connect with others who shared their love for Jamaica. Most of the tourists I interviewed said they discovered the website through an Internet search engine while preparing for an upcoming trip, or right after a trip, as they were feeling nostalgic for the people or the country they had to leave behind. Keisha, a twenty-seven year-old boardite, wrote me an e-mail describing her experience of finding the website:

Upon returning from my first trip to JA, I drove home from the airport, got in the house, and immediately went online to find more info on the country I was falling in love with. I stumbled upon Ja.com and became a member. I enjoyed meeting people that had experienced what I was experiencing as a new Jamaicaholic.

Many of the women shared Keisha's sentiments, describing their participation in the website as something they did to "get" to Jamaica virtually when they could not get there physically, as a result of economic or time constraints. In this way, Jamaicans.com prolongs the happiness they find while in Jamaica by giving them a medium to revel in the nostalgia of previous trips, stay updated on things happening on the island, and communicate with others who have shared similar experiences.

Maya and Gayle claimed that their interactions on the website decreased in the past few years, as the postings and trip reports became more focused on the sexual and intimate liaisons of male and female tourists on vacation. Although they did not mention the controversy surrounding Marilyn's trip reports, their comments echoed other boardites' requests that trip reports focus less on romantic encounters. Maya said,

> Initially, it was a wonderful place to go for information about the country. To get off the beaten path that everyone had gone and done. It provided so much information in the early days. And then it went from that to a bunch of mess. And initially I would look at it, but it was short lived for me. 'Cause I can't tolerate but so much of it, so I just sort of push back from it. Really, it doesn't provide anything for me now, other than the pictures. I love to go on and look at the pictures. And I often don't read a trip report, unless I know, I get a sense of it's going to be something real. But I always go in and look at the pictures. It's my escape back to Jamaica. I don't want to hear about relationships. I don't want to hear about the men. The nightlife. I know. I mean I've seen it and I know it's there.

Gayle, who shared Maya's sentiments, said she believed that people who are on Jamaicans.com all the time did not have much going on in their lives. However, Jacqueline, a boardite in her early fifties and a close friend of Gayle and Maya, describes a different relationship with the website. Jacqueline calls her "Jamaica-holism" an "unhealthy obsession":

> JACQUELINE: I spend way too much time on [the website]. There are people who honestly have concerns about me because of how seriously I take it.

> BW: Really? Like friends and family? Or like people that are on the board?

> JACQUELINE: Like Maya and Gayle, they worry about me. Like when somebody hurts my feelings on there I talk about it outside of there. And they're sorta like, "Girlfriend, it's just a bulletin board." I take the battles seriously, I take the hurt seriously, I take the insults seriously, it's just as though it happened in my real life. And they have concerns about me and I have concerns about myself. Soooo, it's a different kind of website.

I belong to some other websites and I can barely muster up the energy to post and stuff, but Jamaicans.com is different. It's like I got to do it, got to be there. Quite a bit! All during the day. At the risk of losing my job.

Although Maya and Gayle gave Jacqueline a hard time about her connection to the board, asserting that the things she experienced in the virtual were somehow not real or were at least different from her "physical" life, during my research I noticed that Maya and Gayle lurked quite frequently on the board. They were almost always up-to-date on the latest events taking place on the website, particularly the current stories in the Trip Reports section. Furthermore, the people whom Maya and Gayle spoke to on a daily basis (other than their family members) were almost always individuals they had met on Jamaicans.com. Through e-mail, private messages, and telephone calls, these ladies kept in touch with what was happening in the web community and in the lives of their friends, despite their claims that the website was somehow compartmentalized as separate from their "real" lives.

Insider/Outsider Status Online

Although Xavier Murphy, the creator of Jamaicans.com, initially created the website as a way for Jamaicans on the island and throughout the Jamaican diaspora to keep in contact, as the site's popularity grew, he began to see it as a tool for educating non-Jamaicans about Jamaican people and culture. Even though many boardites were aware Murphy did not intend for the site to become as popular among non-Jamaicans as it had, the board members interviewed felt like over the years he had made the website more inclusive. Members cited its motto—"Out of Many, One People Online"—as proof that Murphy wanted non-Jamaicans to feel welcome. However, some of these same boardites pointed to the segregation within discussion boards as evidence that, for some community members, the website's commitment to inclusion was different from its practice. Gayle noted, "Xavier said he wanted to start a board where Jamaicans all over the world could have access to a forum where they could talk. But I think the more and more Americans that started frequenting the board, the more Jamaicans pulled out. You still have a lot, but not that many. And they don't come in the 'Trip Report' and 'Jamaicaholics' forums. They don't. They stay over in General Discussion." Maya echoed Gayle's sentiment, stating, "Another thing I notice, a lot of them Jamaica-borns, I mean it's like, they don't really want us on that board."

Most members of the board recognized that the three tourists forums on the website were divided: (1) "Discover Jamaica" was the space for tourists to ask other members questions about an upcoming trip or a fact about Jamaican history or culture; (2) "Jamaicaholics" was the section mostly composed of self-proclaimed Jamaica addicts. In my experience this was the second most active virtual battlefield for clashes between (mostly American) tourists and Jamaicans; (3) "Trip Reports" was reserved for authors to publish their reflective essays, poems, pictures, and other forms of reports about their trips to Jamaica. During my first visit to this forum I was amazed at how ethnographic and self-reflexive many of the authors were about the politics of their presence in Jamaica. Tourists from all over the world dominated this forum; however, some Jamaican diasporic peoples would often lurk, read the reports, and head over to "General Discussion" to comment and critique the authors, their photos, and the comments of their reading audience. The General Discussion forum was the largest on the board and the most explosive, with clashes arising between tourists and Jamaicans; Jamaicans and Jamaican diasporic peoples; Black boardites and white boardites; and various cliques of virtual friends. Oftentimes the African American tourists I interviewed said they felt unwelcome in this forum and stayed out of it, or simply lurked, out of fear of being flamed or critiqued by Jamaicans.

Sasha, a Jamaican American living in Florida, addressed the nationalized segregation on the board in her interview.[22]

BW: Why don't more Jamaicans go to the tourist forums, you think?

SASHA: I think they do, they just don't post. They lurk, and find stuff to pick at, and then go back to General Discussion and talk about it, or PM and talk about it. But they just don't post. A lot of them don't go like some of the tourists. [Tourists are] going to Jamaica and staying for three months, you know, every other month they're going. Some of [the Jamaicans] don't have that opportunity, so they might feel you know, strange person's coming to my country, telling me about stuff, posting about stuff, taking pictures of this and that, so they don't really have nothing good to say.

In this passage, Sasha points to the various forms of "insider" and "outsider" status people hold on the website. Some view Jamaican diasporic peoples as holding more of an "insider" status than tourists, based on the fact that they were born in Jamaica or have Jamaican family members, and this access to heritage lends authenticity to their views on the website. For some on the website, Jamaican diasporic peoples are viewed as outsiders because they are no longer residents of the country and are seen to be out of touch with the realities of Jamaican life, particularly when it comes to conversations about crime and proposals for government policy. To complicate matters further, tourists, who are often assumed to be on the outside of Jamaica and its cultural knowledge, sometimes know more about what is currently taking place on the ground than the Jamaican diasporic peoples living in places such as the United Kingdom or United States. They have a more inside type of knowledge about Jamaica than those who have Jamaican heritage but are no longer present, since these foreigners travel more frequently to Jamaica than diasporic peoples who left years or even decades ago. By suggesting places to go, activities to do, and merchants and services to patronize in their postings and trip reports, these tourists not only have an effect on how other tourists and visitors experience and consume Jamaica, but also influence the economic and social lives of certain Jamaican businesspersons, workers in the Jamaican tourist industry, and networks of Jamaican friends. Despite the profound impact remittances have on the lives of Jamaicans on the island, in some ways, these tourists who are dedicated to, and actively participate in, Jamaica's tourism economy have more of an impact on the lives of Jamaica's residents than the Jamaican diasporic peoples they communicate with on the web.[23]

The Cultural Police

As a moderator on the board and tour company co-owner, Marilyn often found herself in the middle of numerous controversies related to insider/outsider status. Frequently, tourists from the United States saw her as the resident African American ambassador to Jamaica on the web and on the island. In a sense, Marilyn acted as a cultural broker in these virtual and geographic spaces. A broker is usually defined as a person who mediates transactions between a buyer and a seller; however, in this case, Marilyn acted as the go-between for tourists wanting to vacation and consume everything Jamaican within virtual and physical spaces, and those individuals or businesses in the tourist sectors willing to sell it. She was an educator of sorts, an expert in the field of Jamaicaholic studies.

Marilyn's genuine desire to make sure everyone had a good experience in Jamaica, combined with her valuable contacts in the Jamaican tourist industry, made her famous on the board as a true Jamaica addict and expert trip advisor. In an interview in Jamaica, she argued that she did not want anyone visiting Jamaica to "fall into the wrong hands." She expressed her concern, stating,

> And I *hate* when people get the wrong impression of my country [Jamaica] and don't like it because of some mess they ran into. And I just

beg them, just please, let me set you up, from the moment you are at the airport to the time you leave. I *promise* you'll have a great experience. And I feel capable of doing that. I feel personally, personally responsible for people having a nice time in Jamaica. And I know I can make that happen. I know *how* to make that happen. I know who to hook them up with, what exactly to tell them to do every single day, that they will have a beautiful experience. Because I love this country, and this country is a beautiful country. And it should never have a bad reputation. Never!

Newcomers on the website flocked to Marilyn, feeling her enthusiasm and love for the country she called her own (although she was from the United States), asking her every possible question about the best hotels, restaurants, drivers, food, and beaches. Although the creator of the website prohibits advertisements for any boardite's business outside of the classifieds section, past attendees of GFT's tours provided rave reviews of the tour group in self-authored trip reports, encouraging women from all walks of life to take advantage of Marilyn's and Angie's expert services. Additionally, Marilyn published her own trip reports on the website, often providing the background stories of the new contacts she made during each trip and taking fantastic photos of the places her next group of Girlfriends would enjoy during future tours. For some of the women who wanted to travel solo but had never been out of the United States, Marilyn made traveling alone less terrifying, often providing a step-by-step guide of how to get through customs or how to find some hard-to-reach site in Jamaica. In numerous postings, women claimed that Marilyn made Jamaica feel accessible and enjoyable, even for the solo female traveler. Tourists from all over the globe, including American visitors of various races, would frequently post in the forums looking for Marilyn to answer questions like where locals in Jamaica went to eat and party. These interactions were sometimes tinged with tension as the "locals" present on the web (Jamaicans living on the island who were boardites) were not necessarily the experts the newcomers looked to for answers.

In Jamaica, Marilyn was known as the light-skinned lady with blond hair. Her platinum-blond hair, which grew after she received chemotherapy and survived a battle with breast cancer, was unforgettable. Many times, as we would walk around Negril or Ocho Rios, boardites and lurkers from the website would come up to her and ask, "Are you Marilyn from Jamaicans.com? I recognized you from your picture. Your last trip report was fabulous. We stayed at X hotel because of your suggestion." Marilyn commented on these interesting moments of the "virtual" meeting the "physical":

I really hate that my trip reports have just evolved into um, I had to watch soooo much of what I say, because I travel with other people, and they're so personal about their stuff, and I've had to watch what I say about Jamaican people and how I say it, what I photograph, and what I put on the board. Everything has been so difficult that I'm almost at the point where I don't even want to do trip reports. Yet I've had people walk up to me on the beach in Negril, who I've never met in my whole life and say "Excuse me, but are you Marilyn from Jamaicans.com?" "Yeah." "Oh, I've read everything you've written, I hang on your every word, I love what you . . ." I feel like a book author or something. [*Voice rises*] *And I like that,* I'm not gonna lie! I am *not* gonna lie [*drags this sentence out*]. I'm not gonna sit here and try to tell you that I don't like that. I *do* like that. I feel like some kinda damn celebrity. But now I don't feel the muse to write like I used to write. Because I don't like the criticism and the fellow travelers going "Well, I didn't want everybody to know that it was a young man that was in the ocean with me." I'm tired of picking my words, and trying to decide what's going to make someone mad or what's going to be too much to reveal. So I'm just about at the point where I don't even want to do them anymore.

Here, Marilyn describes the pros and cons of being a semi-famous cultural broker and the pressures associated with representing Americans and Jamaicans in her reports. Although she appreciates the authority and celebrity status her advice and written reports give her, she abhors the spotlight some in the community put on her words. She is stressed by those she views as cultural police— American and Jamaican boardites who critique trip reports or postings for things they deem racist, classist, nationalist, sexist, or sexually explicit. Yet, Marilyn herself was part of the cultural police squad. As a moderator of the Jamaicaholics forum, she was responsible for keeping the peace and protecting each poster's right to speak without being "flamed" by other members. As long as posters were responsible and acted like good board citizens (according to the rules outlined by the board's creator), each member had the right to speak freely. However, in the previous quote one sees that culturally policing other boardites, and boardites policing her, was exhausting.

At times, Marilyn would take off her official Jamaicans.com moderator hat and act as an American cultural broker who simply disliked the way Jamaica was being portrayed, or who stood up for Jamaicans she saw as fellow Black people and diasporic kin. However, on Jamaicans.com, the authority of the cultural police worked multidirectionally, as Jamaicans and other Americans could speak back to one another and engage in a variety of quick responses where some were protected by their anonymity. In her interview, Marilyn mentions a controversy that arose from the criticisms she received for stopping Jamaicans on the street, taking pictures of their hairstyles and outfits, and posting them in a trip report. These pictures generated a long conversation about whether she, and other foreigners and tourists should receive permission from these individuals to post their images on the World Wide Web. Additionally, peer travelers upset with Marilyn for revealing details of a shared trip would send her private messages critiquing her openness and accusing her of violating their privacy. Marilyn, however, was not the only boardite dealing with the criticism of the cultural police.

A post titled "Mi Gat Sum Questions Fi Deh Ooman Dem" (or "I Have Some Questions for the Women") by a boardite named Wahalla, on May 27, 2006, brought many of the cultural police out of their lurking. Dumbfounded by the American obsession with Jamaica prevalent in the Trip Reports section, Wahalla, a person who claimed Jamaica as home, asked a series of questions to the women tourists, encouraging them to compare their experiences in Jamaica with those in the United States. Dripping with sarcasm and written in patois, the post made fun of some of the tourists' practice of complimenting everything Jamaican, such as the beauty of Jamaican trees, the better-tasting Jamaican fruits, and the enlightenment they received from homeless people while in Jamaica.[24] I include a reconstruction of some of the thirty-four pages of discussion here:

1 What is the spiritual fulfillment you get from Jamaica? Can't you get it in your own country?
2 Are the fruits from Jamaica different from those in your own country?
3 Is the grass greener and the trees prettier in Jamaica?
4 How com unno cyan get spiritual fulfillment inna unno country????
   Unno tink sey people wey nuh ha nuthun wisa den people wid sintig???
   ["Why can't you get spiritual fulfillment in your own country?
   You think people that don't have anything wiser than people with something?"]

Then Wahalla asks, "Do people on here understand the dynamic??? Is the grass not green in the West????...I am Jamaican but don't grant Jamaica some mystical allusion. It is no more spiritual than India." Marilyn responded,

Being one of the great offenders in many of these categories . . . I admit it. . . . The things you mention . . . no many of them are not the same in my world . . . here in Tennessee. When I get on that plane at breakfast time, and am transported to Jamaica by lunch time it is a shock to my whole system. It takes me about 48 hours of constantly repeating "I can't believe I'm here" to really believe I am there. Within my stay, I marvel and cherish . . . every single atom that is NOT like Memphis. . . . Everything . . . that is what I go there for. . . . If it were the same . . . grass as green, trees as pretty, fruit as sweet (and NO there ain't nothing in this world like a Jamaican grow banana), then I could just stay home and keep these thousands of dollars in my bank account. The spirit of your post says basically that . . . stay home. . . . So if that were to happen . . . what then of the Jamaican economy . . . what then of those thousands of hotels, resorts, jerk stands . . . craft markets . . . taxi driver legal and illegal . . . you name it. . . . What then???? Just wondering.

Marilyn writes in again:

By the way . . . while we are at it, we could disband many parts of this board as well, and just leave it for the diaspora and folks at home to chat with one another about things Jamaican, and the rest of us could just go away . . . have a feeling you would like that too. Maybe you need to alert Xavier.

Wahalla writes back:

Aw I've offended you. . . . I am so sorry. . . . Now where did I say you not to visit?????? Where did I say to stop gushing? Where did I say not to use a Rent-ta Dred???? All I did was ask some questions that struck me as odd. . . . Don't you like the questions? . . . Let me be clear, I want all ah unno fi come Jamaica and have a good time . . . Have a rent a dred . . . No two a day, please spend generously. Some of my best friends are renta-dreds. . . . You expect guilt or gratitude from me for the thousand of dollars you spend? . . . Do you want me to tell you you are different from the million or so people who visit? Well you are. You are a shining beacon, an example of social conscience, who without whom Jamaicans morwn [mourn].

Blackstar begins by stating that she has traveled to several countries, including Cuba, Puerto Rico, and Haiti. She writes,

Clearly there must be *something* about Jamaica. How many non-Jamaicans are listening to Bob Marley as opposed to Compay Segundo and Celia Cruz or Gilberto Gil or King Sunny Ade? How many wannabee Rastas are out there compared to "non-native" Vodun or Santeria practitioners? For whatever reason, JA has an influence on the world that is disproportionate to its size and population.

SugarShug says,

I think that people have an "ah ha" moment when they realize that they don't have to wrap their happiness in things. I think that seeing people with less things than you have, and they are in some way happier than you are—makes you think of how you define your happiness. I think this comes from being in a culture that is always focused on getting more versus appreciating what you have now. I also think that the wisdom that you speak of again comes from slowing down. Life seems to have so much clarity when you are not rushing and have the chance to be reflective. What someone in JA says may just seem more wise because we actually have the time to fully ingest it and just not kinda gloss over it because we have some other deadline, meeting, or crisis to attend to.

Wahalla responds to SugarShug:

The suspension of problems is not the solution to problems. That one fails to address the perturbations in life on holiday does not engender a solution. Rather it simply adds to it as the loan shark credit rates afforded by cards does in the end merely acerbate the situation. . . . It is not location that is important rather it is the fact that the oppressive issues related to a post industrial urban environment has been relegated, and the brains resources are focused on the pursuit of hedonistic desires. . . . Paradise bought for 2 weeks is a mere facsimile not a permanent Vahalla. . . . As for wisdom from material poverty . . . There must be a hell of a lot of wise people in Congo Brazaville.

SugarShug responds,

I agree that the suspension of problems does not in and of itself solve the problem. Sometimes just stepping away from the problem can help you see it more clearly. I also think that the location is a big factor for me. Being in a place where I can feel comfortable and relaxed will affect my mood and my frame of mind. Being physically, spiritually and mentally recharged will also help me deal with my problems more effectively.

Here, one gets an idea of the type of cultural critique and policing that took place on the website: arguments about how Jamaica and the United States should be experienced and understood. While the content of this post is interesting for a multitude of reasons significant to this project (the discussion of Jamaican diaspora versus African diaspora; the politics of tourism and political economy; the value of reflection while on vacation; and constructions of happiness), I want to spend some time analyzing the politics that surround the text itself.

The post is interesting because Wahalla chose to post their questions as a separate thread in the Trip Reports section. By posting as a separate thread and not within a trip report, Wahalla kept this post from getting lost in the shuffle. Normally boardites post questions about someone's trip in "Discovering Jamaica" or within a trip report itself. Wahalla's posting of these questions in "Trip Reports" may have been an attempt to gain a larger audience than they would have received in "Discover Jamaica" or "Jamaicaholics." Posting in "Trip Reports" could also have been a strategy to get other Jamaicans to post their comments or critiques about these tourists' Jamaica obsession, subsequently corralling a critical mass of Jamaican cultural police. However, only a few fellow Jamaicans posted in this thread. Nevertheless, the thread had over one hundred views, and although many Jamaicans chose not to post in this particular thread, many were commenting on the conversation in the General Discussion forum, private-messaging behind virtual walls, and (according to Sasha in an interview) calling each other on the phone to talk about it. Furthermore, the decision to post much of their responses in patois (despite the change in language in the response to SugarShug at the end) meant that the tourists Wahalla was targeting were not newcomers or first-time visitors, as those boardites would possibly have found it difficult to decipher the written patois. It was evident that Wahalla wanted to engage veteran travelers, true Jamaicaholics, because they saw some repeated patterns they wanted to bring into question.

A year earlier on June 26, 2005, Orbra, a boardite from St. Louis, provided a warning to fellow tourists and cultural brokers, imploring them to remember their place and defer to the "experts." In a conversation about ganja use and the possibility of getting arrested in Jamaica, Orbra wrote,

> [Whether it's] 4 times or 45 times the one thing we should all remember is that we are still visitors/tourists. Yes we like to think that we are embraced and made privy to all aspects of Jamaica thru the "Friends" we make there. But I feel that if you don't know the answer to questions that can get a fellow visitor into a mountain load of trouble the best thing is to sit back and Learn from the Experts. . . . So many of us from the Board are heading down to the Island weekly and the MISCONCEPTION

AND INEPT information we get from those who have been there 3 times or more and feel that they know all that there is to know can lead to an UNNECESSARY LOAD OF HEARTACHE AND EXPENSE. Let us remember to RESPECT THE LAWS AND PEOPLE OF ANY LAND WE CHOSE [*sic*] TO TRAVEL TO.

These two excerpts of web conversations between board members illustrate how some individuals became aware of their nationalized differences online, affirming the view that these explorations of diasporic diversity were not relegated to physical spaces in Jamaica. In this virtual space, members of the African and Jamaican diasporas engage in conversations that interrogate and illuminate their various racialized, classed, gendered, sexualized, nationalized, and religious differences, while still attempting to construct an online community.

Yet, for all of the controversy surrounding the trip reports and threads posted by international tourists and a few Jamaicans in the Trip Reports forum, it was commonly recognized that these vacation reflections were often the catalyst for bringing new Jamaican and non-Jamaican visitors into the community. In a way, by posting trip reports and sharing their experiences, American and Jamaican boardites were "marketing" Jamaican culture and the tourist industry to tourists on the website as potential consumers and investors. Visitors to this virtual Jamaica became intrigued by the stories others were telling about their experiences in Jamaica, and they either posted questions and comments that expressed their desire to have the same experiences or wanted to share their expert advice on how the author could plan a better trip for next time. Each board member, like Marilyn, had the potential to become a cultural broker or ambassador for Jamaica.

For me, trip reports were the most interesting part of the website because the interactions that took place between tourists and Jamaicans within the forum provided numerous opportunities to examine how complicated the relationship between producer and consumer becomes when Internet technologies are utilized. Members present at one event would post their perspectives and add their two cents on what took place, sometimes filling in gaps in the story. Additionally, other boardites who did not get to travel on a particular trip could post about past experiences in the same city, hotel, or restaurant, or simply ask a question to push the story along. Finally, the arguments, comments, and rebuttals surrounding the representations of Jamaica when the cultural police showed up made the analysis of these reports even more enlightening. In this space, authors of trip reports go through a system of cultural checks and balances, where peer travelers, and Jamaicans who believe they have a say, attempt to police how one represents Jamaica and its people. Here, everyday ethnographers have direct access to their reading audience and those they represent in their texts, immediately opening themselves up to praise or critique.

Consequently, the boardites on Jamaicans.com blur the line between producer and consumer, constantly and continuously transforming what Jamaica means or looks like through people's questions, comments, and narratives. In this virtual space, tourists from all over the world, Jamaican diasporic peoples, and Jamaican residents co-produce what Jamaica means and how it is represented. This is not to say that these boardites in particular have full control over how representations of Jamaica circulate online. However, because it is one of the top five websites resulting when individuals do a web search on Jamaica, for those accessing the website, the members of Jamaicans.com have some influence on how Jamaica is represented and constructed in the global imaginary.

Throughout fieldwork, I was quite aware that some of the Girlfriends were uncomfortable talking about their sexual lives with me or in front of me. Over the past four years, we had formed relationships similar to those between a mother and daughter or aunt and niece. My age (I was twenty-two when I started fieldwork) was the primary factor in their hesitancy to discuss their boyfriends, lovers, and sexual partners with me, particularly since I was the same age as some of their daughters, who they would never give such details. Some of them were conflicted as they stated they did not want to "corrupt" me (their words) with their fantasies and sexual and intimate relationships. However, they wanted to be open and honest with their life stories, since the wisdom to avoid their mistakes is the gift they desired to pass on to future generations of Black women. Although I knew they sometimes censored their discussions or activities when I was around, I did not realize the extent to which my presence caused anxiety for some individuals until one summer day with Jennifer. Immediately after her primary interview in the United States, as Jennifer drove through the busy streets, we had a comical conversation about an upcoming tour we were taking around Jamaica. Jennifer asked me about a recent conference call the Girlfriends and I had about the accommodations in Portland, where the five of us would share a house.

I began to report the conversation to her. "So Gayle said to me on the phone, 'I'm sorry, Bianca. But I have to tell you that your mommas have sex!' I said, 'I know. I've been around you guys. I know you all have sex.' And Maya was like, 'No we don't!! Don't tell her that stuff!'"

"Well Maya called me after you all had that conversation, and she said to me, 'I'm not sure if Bianca should come, because I don't want us having sex with Bianca in the house—,'" Jennifer tattled with a chuckle.

"*Why?!?!* Are you serious?!" I was shocked and somewhat disappointed. Apparently I was not as accepted into the group as I thought I was. Then a thought flashed across my mind. "Oh my goodness. She's going to miss out on sex 'cause I'm in the house?!" I asked.

"Well no, but having sex with you in the house was certainly part of her concern. I mean, like that was the first thing she said to me. I said, 'You're talking like she's twelve.'" Jennifer let out a laugh.

"Right! I'm grown! It's not like I don't know what sex is."

"I told her, 'I don't think Bianca cares.' And she said, 'Well, I just don't want to bring it up with her.' I said, 'I wouldn't think you need to! I mean, Bianca might say 'I don't want you to have sex in the same room I'm sleeping in, but didn't you say there were different rooms?'" Jennifer and I burst into laughter. She continued, 'She was like, 'Nah. It doesn't feel right.' I said to her, 'Well look. I guess I just have no morals.'" With her hands on the steering wheel, Jennifer glanced at me for a moment to catch my facial expression. I think she was checking to see if I agreed with her. "So then Maya said, 'I don't want my man to come, because then I'll look like all the other women that come to get a man.' Now Bianca, I gotta tell you, I don't care. This is my thing, and my life. I'm grown! Unless you're paying my bills, or you're my mother, then I could care less. So I kept asking her, 'Who really cares?'"

"I'm so mad she was worried about me."

"I mean it was like the first thing out of her mouth," Jennifer said. She let out a sigh.

"And you know I wouldn't have cared."

"Yes, I know. I reminded her that you were grown, with your own relationships. And she said, 'Yeah I know. But she's still young.' I said, 'She's not young like thirteen! I could see if she was thirteen, but she's twenty-five. Do you think she's going to think less of you?' She said, 'Well, no.'"

In a quiet, concerned voice, I responded, "I think that's what they're worried about. And I don't care. I just want them to enjoy themselves."

Jennifer turned to me and yelled, "But I mean, who *cares*?!"

EPILOGUE. Lessons Learned

Feelings of being overwhelmed, exhausted, and invisible push the women of Girlfriend Tours International to repeatedly escape the United States (virtually and physically). They travel to Jamaica in pursuit of happiness, love, girlfriendship, relaxation, and diasporic connectivity. Their desire to make their lives better, to "get happy," to enjoy the fruits of their hard labor, to exercise hope in the search for intimacy and friendship—these are what propel them to live to the fullest. For them, staying at home rather than finding strategies to pursue happiness is in a sense a form of social death, emotional distress, and a lifelong sentence of invisibility. For the forty- and fifty-something Black American women of GFT, repeatedly traveling to Jamaica to enjoy themselves as beautiful, Black sexual beings and to "give back" to those seen as diasporic kin is in fact resisting and speaking back to U.S. racism and sexism, a part of a political project. When they realized that their voices were not being heard, and that their social and economic opportunities in the United States could no longer fulfill their desires for life satisfaction, they found an alternative space where their stories and experiences could be appreciated. Their individual and collective tears of joy, sadness, desperation, frustration, and exhilaration tell a great deal about the toll racism and sexism take in their lives and in the lives of other Black women.

Their entire journey toward happiness is significant, as the events along the way help form the lens through which they encounter Jamaica and interact with Jamaicans. Their experiences—as children of the civil rights movement who marched in children's rallies and went to segregated schools; as Black women who were told that leisure and travel were luxuries they could not afford; and as romantics who half-believed they could find the love and companionship that Stella found—all lead up to that first walk down the stairs of the plane in Jamaica. In Jamaica the ladies of GFT encounter a liminal space where they experience the complexity of their diasporic subjectivity and the paradox of American Blackness. They take in the blue water and the sweet smells of Jamaica, while feeling the confidence and validation of being in the racial majority. They arrive to see a sea of Black people they believe look like them and have experienced the same burdens of racism; yet frequently Girlfriends have their diasporic dream shattered or at least disrupted by their American privilege and hegemonic understandings of Blackness.

These African American women find themselves deeply located in the enigma of American Blackness—a space where their race, nationality, and pursuits of happiness converge. Their ability to travel (by obtaining a passport and having access to "disposable" income) signifies a certain achievement of the American dream. However, these particular Americans are traveling specifically because it seems that successfully accomplishing their pursuit of happiness is almost impossible within U.S. borders. The gendered and racialized contours of their lived experiences are often what trigger the tracks of their tears. In Jamaica, their Blackness ushers them into new networks of relationships, even if these relationships are at times tense with power differentials linked to their nationality. Their Americanness continually gets in the way, disrupting these friendships and the fulfillment of their diasporic dreams. In the end, they seem "Black" enough but too "American" to be situated comfortably within the diasporic relationships they seek with Jamaicans. Furthermore, their experiences with historical and contemporary racism make them too "Black," and arguably too much "woman," to exhale comfortably within the embrace of American society. Perhaps these contradictions, ambiguities, and mistranslations are embedded in being Black, woman, and American. And perhaps it only gets more complicated if you have the audacity to try to be Black, woman, American, and happy.

Returning Home: Lessons For and From the Field

Fieldwork is hard work. Becoming a good ethnographer is even harder. And I am not sure you can confidently know when you have done either correctly or well. The years of coursework, grant proposal writing, reading of ethnographies, and preliminary, short-term research trips that compose the pre-doctoral training process for anthropologists provide you with tools for pushing your way through primary research. But they don't necessarily prepare you for the highs and lows, the twists and turns of the long-term fieldwork experience.[1] There is so much you learn only by committing to the process and throwing yourself fully into the work.

During this research, I learned significant lessons about participant observation, analysis, and writing, all key aspects of the ethnographic process. (Instead of being three distinct components of the ethnographic experience—which is sometimes how we are taught about them—these three parts often overlap.) I learned that a great deal of ethnography is the process of seeing, observing, and connecting, while being constantly aware that the gazes of those being observed are looking back. Pick any of the voices in this text, and ask them what they saw and experienced at a particular moment, and you might get a different book. I realize that while seeing and observing are essential to participant observation, what is truly the meat of the ethnographic method is relationship building. I discovered that it is a balancing act to analyze your data with the theoretical frameworks and concepts held in your mind, while also analyzing the data—those relationships you created—with your heart. And finally, figuring out the audience you are writing to—the people you are writing that final ethnographic product for—is a tough decision and one that will affect your writing process.

PARTICIPANT OBSERVATION

It wasn't until I began to try to connect with Jamaicans in Jamaica and follow the Girlfriends during their trips that I truly got a sense of how important relationships are during the fieldwork process. Initiating, building, maintaining, and nurturing relationships are the currency of this process; yet, this is part of the research that we are the least trained to do. Thankfully, Jamaicans like those on Fisherman's Beach in Ocho Rios and some individuals who worked in the transportation and tourism industries in Montego Bay and Negril took me in. They taught me all about the "runnings" in their cities and introduced me to parts of Jamaica's history that dovetailed with my own family's history there, while I conversed with them about race, politics, and life in the United States.[2]

I am also grateful that the Girlfriends were such a gracious group of women, who saw something in me that convinced them that they wanted to have me around. I did my best to make myself useful, so they would not feel that I was a burden to them or a killjoy during their vacations. As a Jamaican American, and as an anthropologist who stayed in Jamaica for periods after the Girlfriends returned home, I was viewed as an insider-outsider.[3] I embodied a set of ever-changing positionalities when were together—intermediary, confidant, translator, and tour guide. I tried to do whatever they might ask of me to the best of my ability. I wanted them to feel like there was a purpose to me being there that was connected to, but distinguishable from, my research purpose. I wanted them to know that I cared about their experiences, their stories, and their friendships.

As is wont to happen in the ethnographic relationship, the Girlfriends did a disproportionate amount of teaching. While I explained parts of Jamaica to them, they taught me valuable lessons, many of which are evident in this text. In addition to all that I came to understand about the significance of Black women pursuing happiness, I also learned these two lessons: (1) Age truly ain't nothing but a number. We are agentive beings that get to choose how we want to live our lives, and it is never too late to experience new things, connect with new people, and gain new insights into who we are. Girlfriends modeled this for me. Some told me that they decided to participate in this project because they wanted me and other Black women to learn this lesson about choice and action earlier than they did. They pushed me to ask myself frequently if I was happy and content with the decisions I was making about my life, and if I wasn't, then I needed to get up and take action. (2) It is important to create space for inter-generational Black women conversations. While my own girlfriends and peers have always been invaluable to me, sitting at the feet of older Black women willing to share their generational knowledge changed me. We didn't always get along, and there were definitely tough moments when I knew some of our relationships would never be the same. But as they made room for me within their group, Girlfriends demonstrated the importance of Black women friend-ships and showed me that we don't need permission from anyone else to create those spaces. Even if the pursuit of girlfriendship entails us leaving our country to find quiet in the midst of racist and sexist madness, the labor required to make that happen will be worth it. Relationships are not only the currency of ethnographic work. For Black women, they are also the key to our collective survival.

Acquiring these lessons required hard work. Staying up late, trying to be fully present to not only observe, but also participate in activities and discus-sions, while noting who is saying and doing what is no easy feat. My students laugh when I tell them that taking regular bathroom breaks to write down field-notes is normal behavior for an ethnographer. But in all seriousness, being an ethnographer requires you to be a more public version of yourself, to get out of your comfort zone and initiate conversations and relationships with people your "real self" might not encounter. You are asked to participate in activities you would normally never do, eat foods you wouldn't eat, think deeply about things you would might not want to engage, question parts of yourself that you've never had to interrogate. As a researcher, you are aware that the research is not about you. All of this is done to connect with research participants and complete this process we call "fieldwork." Yet, building relationships with others in the pursuit of knowledge will push you to also become more aware of yourself. Your mind and body may become exhausted from the deep listening and detailed observation you are doing daily, while trying to understand the language, beliefs, traditions, values, and practices of your research participants, which may differ from your own. It is a type of emotional labor that I wish anthropologists spoke about more, especially to our students.

ANALYSIS

At the end of fieldwork, one returns home to begin analyzing the data collected. Leaving the field and coming home can be a bumpy process, not only for you, but also for your research participants. Doing fieldwork taught me that your participants get to know a version of you really well. It is a true "you"—an "ethnographer self" that is authentic—but a "you" that is centered on the work. This "you" will be different from who you are at home, when you're not focused on observing and participating, and the research participants do not drive your day. In a way, you are performing your ethnographer self as your participants are performing the version of themselves that they want to make visible to you.

In Jamaica, the Girlfriends knew me as a twenty-something, easy-going, kind of quiet woman who was open to accompanying them on all types of excursions and adventures, and who always had time for a conversation. In the United States, I was a stressed-out, outspoken, married graduate student with a dissertation to write, family and work obligations, and little time to spare. What added an extra layer of complexity to leaving my fieldsite was that my project was multisited. During fieldwork, the Girlfriends believed that my "home self" and my "ethnographer self" were one in the same, since I returned to the United States frequently, and they still had access to my ethnographer self. The weeks I spent at home in Florida during my fieldwork, I would prioritize their phone calls and emails, spend a significant amount of time interacting with them on Jamaicans.com while doing virtual ethnography, and visit them in their hometowns, where the method of them taking the lead continued, just like in Jamaica. Once my fieldwork was completed, however, my real life came rushing back and my home self had to face this new post-fieldwork reality. Participant observation could no longer be my priority; I had to move on to the analysis phase.

Few people teach you how to leave the field. In this contemporary period of experimental ethnographic methods and increasing communication through digital technologies, ending research and leaving the field are more complicated than in previous moments. Even less is taught about how to explain your exiting the field to your research participants so they can understand what is happening as the ethnographer shifts from observation to analysis. Which day is the right one to leave from your virtual fieldsite and stop doing virtual ethnography? How do you explain to your participants that previously you would answer calls at all times, but in "real life" you have other things you must also attend to? How do you make clear that though you've traveled to your fieldsite numerous times in the past couple of years, you won't be able to attend the next trip because, in contrast to the ethnographer life they've witnessed, in real life you are a graduate student living under the poverty line? When the relationships you create with participants become the "fieldsite," how do you ever leave it? If leaving is possible, how do you do it responsibly?

In the absence of answers to these questions, I admit I did not leave the field well. As I moved into analyzing the data I collected during my four years of virtual ethnography and two years of traditional ethnography, my relationships with the Girlfriends changed. The point of ethnography is to take everything that you saw, everything you observed, all the things you heard, and interpret them to make sense and learn something new, different, or significant about human traditions and practices. I was overwhelmed by all of the data. I was anxious about figuring out how to write a dissertation about these relationships while trying to fit back into my familial relationships and community. I was unprepared for gossip and unpleasant (and untrue) interpretations of past interactions and choices in the field, which seemed to affect my relationships with some Girlfriends. Whether as a result of these events or as a part of the process of concluding fieldwork, my communication with the Girlfriends decreased as I returned to my real life—completing the dissertation, finishing graduate school, surviving a divorce, moving across the country, starting an academic job, writing this book—and our relationships fell by the wayside. I imagine some version of this shift happens to many ethnographers when they leave the field. However, my inability to better articulate the transition to the Girlfriends is one of my biggest regrets.

Returning home from fieldwork requires you to make sense of not only the data you collected and the experiences of your research participants, but also your own experiences in the field. As I wrote this book, I began to better understand how vulnerable the Girlfriends had to be to trust me to tell parts of their stories and to have someone observing them during some of their most vulnerable moments. To be subject to an anthropological gaze is not easy. The discipline has been at pains to find ways to make the process more dialogical and multivocal than in previous eras. Nonetheless, after a few Girlfriends read the dissertation version of my research, one expressed her displeasure with my analysis of her narratives and experiences. I understood why she was upset, and it pained me that my interpretations had hurt her; but I also knew that what I had written was anchored in truth. The writing became more difficult as I sifted through the data and my interpretations, trying to find ways to both represent what I had seen and protect the women who had become so important to me. The analysis phase of ethnographic research is one that may entail physical, mental, and relational shifts, as it is not only about analyzing the fieldnotes you have written, but also about making sense of the ethnographic process as a whole.

WRITING

There are enough articles and books written on the complexities and phases of ethnographic writing to fill multiple shelves in any library. I am sure in the future I will contribute to that canon. Here I will simply mention a few things from my own experience writing about Girlfriend Tours International and Black women's pursuits of happiness. As I began to move from analysis to writing, I quickly recognized that everyone's understanding of what happened in the field was going to be different, and no one's, including my own, was going to be holistic. I understood that once the book was published, I had no control over the reader's interpretation of the text. Knowing this did not make the writing less difficult. No matter whether the (imagined) audience is the research participants, a dissertation committee, colleagues, a tenure review committee, a broader racialized and gendered community, or all of the above, many ethnographers are trying to write narratives that interweave the experiential knowledge that comes from their fieldwork with the critical and theoretical knowledge that comes from their disciplinary training. How do you hold the (emotional) intricacies and ambiguities of fieldwork and the decisiveness of theory and critique concurrently? How do you represent multiple, sometimes conflicting truths while leaving space for new and different interpretations? I do not purport to have the answers to these questions. But I did write with them in mind, and I became ever more aware of how they drove the writing process.

I imagine every ethnographer has a list of things they wish they had known before they started the process, things they wish they could go back and do better, things they missed, and things they could better represent in the final ethnography. This is why some ethnographers continue to return to their fieldsites, year after year. It is difficult to get the dynamism of the fieldwork process onto paper. I would argue that the dynamism of the Girlfriends, their sisterhood, and their fantastical trips to Jamaica was exceptionally difficult to put in writing. There is so much that I experienced—that we experienced—that cannot be captured here. But I understand that writing ethnography is about highlighting snapshots of a time period and letting the narrative reveal itself.

Conclusion

On December 30, 2015, I came to the end of my research project during a trip to Jamaica. Of course my project had been over well before this date, as it had been almost eight years since I officially finished fieldwork with GFT. However, because of the complicated departures just described, I had never felt closure. For this trip, I had traveled to Jamaica to attend a friend's wedding in Kingston. Instead of going directly there, I stopped in Negril for a couple of days of vacation. It was the first time I had been back to the city since I ended fieldwork in 2007, and it wasn't without some trepidation. The night before I departed for Kingston I found myself back in the cliffs, having dinner with my then partner and reflecting on my fieldwork experience. Then I saw her—one of the Girlfriends was having dinner at a nearby table. Out of all the hotels in the cliffs, she was there on the last night of my trip in Negril, and so I felt that our encounter was destined.

However, I was anxious and started to hyperventilate. Literally. It wasn't just the presence of the Girlfriend; everything that had happened during my research came rushing back—writing anxieties, a love lost, my imagining of the Girlfriends' disappointment and anger with me, the loss of some of their friendships, the urgency to finish the book—everything came up in my body at the same time. It was sensory overload. I took a few deep breaths and tried my best to calm myself down. Then I walked over to the Girlfriend's table to say "hello."

She was shocked to see me, and I could tell that a similar processing of all the previous years before, our time together, flew through her mind. "Bianca, is that really you? It's been forever." She took a deep breath. I took one also. I wanted to hug her, but I wasn't sure how she would receive it. She looked behind me. "Who are you here with?" she asked. Her face changed, and there was a brief moment of apprehension. I quickly realized she was worried that I was still doing research, still studying her. I tried to put her at ease. "I'm just here on vacation. For a wedding. I'm here with my boyfriend. He's back there." I pointed, and her eyes followed my hand. "Oh, well he's handsome. Take me to meet him!" I chuckled, as this was reminiscent of our old selves, our old relationship. I understood that this gesture was a small demonstration of our connection, an acknowledgment of the love we still had for one another. It was an olive branch.

Still in shock and having an out-of-body experience, I walked her over to my partner. I was speechless. I may have gotten five or six words out as she carried on a conversation with him, asking about our trip. There was so much I wanted to say. I wanted to apologize for losing touch and clear up rumors that had circulated within the group. I wanted to thank her again for opening up to me, for letting me in her life, and for the lessons I learned listening to her stories. I wished to inquire how she and the other Girlfriends were doing, and how it felt for her to finally live in Jamaica, a place I knew had called to her for a long time. Was she happy? In that moment, I wanted to introduce her to me, "Bianca" the home self, and not "Bianca" the ethnographer self. I needed to tell her that both missed her terribly.

But then the moment passed. I broke away from the thoughts in my head and listened as my partner said it was nice to meet her and that he enjoyed finally putting a face with a name. I looked on with tears forming in my eyes as she grabbed his hand and said, "Take good care of her," waved at me, and walked away to rejoin dinner with her friends. I continue to be thankful for her well wishes and her grace, and for giving me the closure that I needed that night. There are times when I want to pick up the phone or get online to hear all about the adventures, shenanigans, and fabulousness that are taking place as she and the other Girlfriends continue to pursue happiness in the country they love, as Black women who know that they deserve that happiness and will work hard to experience it regularly, even in the face of obstacles, disconnects, troubling realities, and difficult truths. Because home is where the heart is, and for the Girlfriends, Jamaica will always and forever have a piece of their hearts.

Notes

INTRODUCTION. *"Jamaica Crawled Into My Soul"*

1 Throughout the book, I use the term "Black Americans" to describe those individuals who reside in the United States and are of African descent. This includes African, Caribbean, and African American peoples—individuals who are ascribed the racialized identity of "Black" by individuals and the State. "African Americans" is used specifically to refer to those individuals native to the United States. This distinction is important as the particular nationalized history and relationship that many African Americans have with the trans-Atlantic slave trade and U.S. racialized politics is central to the diasporic imaginary explored in this text. When I use the term "Black Americans," it is often used in reference to a process or experience that Black peoples encounter regardless of their ethnic background.

2 Wolf, "Family Secrets."

3 Harvey, *Condition of Postmodernity.*

4 Anderson, *Imagined Communities.*

5 Anderson, *Imagined Communities,* 6.

6 Anderson, *Imagined Communities,* 7.

7 However, see Davies, "Pan-Africanism"; Drake, *Critical Appropriations*; and Pinto, *Difficult Diasporas.*

8 James, "John Henryism."

9 Mullings, "Resistance and Resilience," 79.

10 Mullings, "Resistance and Resilience," 87.

11 Mullings, "Resistance and Resilience," 87.

12 Dent, *Black Popular Culture,* 1.

13 Dent, *Black Popular Culture,* 11.

14 McMillan, *How Stella Got Her Groove Back*; Sullivan, *How Stella Got Her Groove Back.*

15 If I could do this research over, I would have more purposely and actively initiated discussions and interviews with Jamaican women for their responses to what I was observing with the ladies of GFT. While I did spend some time with Jamaican women

in hair salons, in the administrative offices of the accommodations we stayed at, and during the few times I saw some on Fisherman's Beach, I did not usually initiate long-term relationships with them. The Jamaican women I befriended were often friends of friends I had from the United States and were mostly people I interacted with when Girlfriends returned home or when I wasn't in tourist areas.

CHAPTER 1. *More Than a Groove*

1 Du Bois, *Souls of Black Folk.*
2 Cooper, *Voice from the South*; Davis, *Women, Race, and Class*; Giddings, *When and Where I Enter*; White, *Too Heavy a Load*; Guy-Sheftall, *Words of Fire*; and Smith, *Home Girls.*
3 Crenshaw, "Demarginalizing the Intersection of Race and Sex."
4 "Jamaicaholism" was the word that Girlfriends and Jamaicans.com boardites used to describe their obsession with Jamaica and its culture. Because I recognize the ableist nature of this term, I try to use it sparingly throughout the text.
5 Hall, "What Is This 'Black' in Black Popular Culture?"
6 Harris-Perry, *Sister Citizen.*
7 Harris-Perry, *Sister Citizen*, 106–107.
8 Harris-Perry, *Sister Citizen*, 215.
9 Stewart, *Ordinary Affects*, 43.
10 Stewart, *Ordinary Affects*, 107.
11 Harris-Perry, *Sister Citizen*, 5
12 Morgan, *When Chickenheads Come Home to Roost*, 59.
13 Berlant, *Cruel Optimism*; Cvetkovich, *Depression.*
14 Ahmed, *Promise of Happiness.*
15 McGlotten, *Virtual Intimacies*, 11.
16 Angelia Hairston and Marilyn Williams are the real names of the owners of Girlfriend Tours International. I have chosen to use their real names when I discuss them in their professional capacities, as the website for their business made their names public in Jamaica and in the virtual community Girlfriends participated in. However, throughout the rest of the book, I use pseudonyms for Girlfriends and Jamaican interviewees to protect their anonymity as they discuss more personal perspectives on their visits to Jamaica and their thoughts on race and racism.
17 All-inclusive resort hotels in Jamaica clearly had a preference for couples, as single occupants often had to pay a pretty steep supplement fee for their room. Girlfriends saw this as a sort of penalty for wanting to travel on their own. They also were aware through conversations with Jamaicans who worked at these hotels that gay, lesbian, and queer couples were often discouraged from booking rooms, particularly if they were understood to be a couple. However, hotels that were not all-inclusives, which were more frequently owned by Jamaicans, were more welcoming to solo women travelers and would generally allow guests to participate in the informal economy of hospitality and romance tourism. Subsequently, heterosexual male companions might be allowed entrance at these hotels, which was mostly forbidden at all-inclusives. Still, during my time completing fieldwork, none of the local hotels Girl-

friends stayed at seemed to explicitly welcome queer couples, especially if they were participating in hospitality or romance tourism for same-gender individuals.

18 The journals played an important function, as I observed many Girlfriends pulling them out throughout the trip, on bus rides, on the beach, and at breakfast, recording their thoughts and documenting their experiences. Excerpts from these journal entries were often included in their online trip reports on Jamaicans.com. It may seem a bit out of place for a journal to be given such emphasis on vacation; however, its inclusion in the GFT welcome gift bag indicates the emphasis on self-reflection the founders encouraged during these annual trips to Jamaica.

19 Dancehall is a genre of Jamaican music that is faster than reggae and is often created for the intention of dancing in a club or party. Started in the 1970s, the music is frequently deejay based.

20 "Lyrics" is a word that many Jamaicans and veteran tourists employ to describe the pick-up lines Jamaican men use to compliment, come on to, or begin intimate or romantic relationships with women of all nationalities, including Jamaican women. Most Jamaican men attempt to create beautifully poetic lines, filled with metaphors and similes that make the woman at the receiving end smile and blush. These lines are known to be so lyrical that they are compared to lyrics of a song, hence the slang term. Oftentimes, Girlfriends claimed that Jamaican men were more gifted at this particular "performance" than any other men they had come across in other countries, including Caribbean men on other islands. Frequently, they would request that Jamaican men teach African American men the gift of lyrics, arguing that understanding the needs and wants of a woman was at the heart of a Jamaican man's mastery of lyrics. Thus, to give good lyrics was to speak the language of love, connection, and acceptance to women.

21 This initiation is described in the introduction of the book.

22 Each year there was one Black man on the tour (a partner or husband of a Girlfriend) who was often dubbed the Girlfriends' "mascot." He usually did not join in the cliff initiation or the visit to Jackie's on the Reef, as these spaces were held as women-only sacred spaces. However, he was generally present while eating dinner at 3 Dives. More often than not, this American man and his partner would choose to join the Girlfriends for the main events on the itinerary and then disappear to pursue their own interests during the rest of the tour. Additionally, one white American woman was present on earlier GFT tours. However, during the years I observed GFT annual tours, no white American women participated as official Girlfriends. There was a white American man and several white American women Jamaicans.com members who would meet up with Girlfriends during the tour to have dinner, go clubbing, or climb the waterfalls. This interaction between official Girlfriends and some members of Jamaicans.com was often how Girlfriends who were not already web-board members became introduced to the virtual community.

23 Collins, *Black Feminist Thought*.

24 Collins, *Black Feminist Thought*, 114.

25 Once, Jacqueline's refrigerator needed repair, and she held an online conversation with Jamaicans.com neighbors about whether it was worth sacrificing a trip to Ja-

maica to fix the fridge in the next few weeks. She was due for a trip to Jamaica (as she tried to visit every three months) and the fridge's malfunction was threatening her travel budget.

26 Alexander, "Erotic Autonomy as a Politics of Decolonialization," 64.

27 During my research period, most of the women I studied had adult children (over eighteen) or left their younger children with family members during their trips to Jamaica. At no time was I aware of a mother actually abandoning her child to visit Jamaica. In fact, during some small group trips, mothers would bring their children with them. However, these were seen as times when they were still playing the mother role Gayle refers to, and not relaxing trips for themselves. Oftentimes the frequency of their trips to Jamaica would increase as their children grew older and were responsible for taking care of themselves in the United States.

28 Jones and Shorter-Gooden, *Shifting*, 7.

29 Collins, *Black Feminist Thought*, 111.

30 This trip and conversation took place in 2007, before the election of the first Black president of the United States, Barack Obama.

31 The Jamaica Labour Party (JLP) and the People's National Party (PNP) are the two main political parties in Jamaica. From discussions with Jamaicans including Kevon, I learned that there are frequently close ties between certain gangs and leaders of these organizations (also known as "dons") and the political parties, particularly in Kingston, the political and economic capital of Jamaica.

32 I volunteered to ride along during several of these rides to the airport, as I usually stayed for a few days after the last Girlfriend departed. I wanted to support those leaving, spend more time with them one-on-one, and provide a hand to hold when necessary. This is how I knew what was happening during the drives to the airport.

CHAPTER 2. *"Giving Back" to Jamaica*

1 Pratt, *Imperial Eyes*.

2 Pratt, *Imperial Eyes*.

3 Pratt, *Imperial Eyes*, 4.

4 Pratt, *Imperial Eyes*, 6.

5 Pratt, *Imperial Eyes*, 4–5.

6 Pratt, *Imperial Eyes*, 6.

7 Pratt, *Imperial Eyes*, 6.

8 While not all of them necessarily use the term "contact zone" in their work, scholars such as Lena Sawyer (Sweden), Jacqueline Nassy-Brown (United Kingdom), Paulla Ebron (Ghana), and E. Patrick Johnson (Australia) exemplify the utility of the concept by using ethnography to document the ways that nationalized, racialized, and gendered subjectivities and the power associated with them can lead to tensions within communities and various forms of contact zones.

9 Campt and Thomas, "Gendering Diaspora."

10 Edwards, *Practice of Diaspora*.

11 Edwards, *Practice of Diaspora*, 64.

12 Dollar amounts are quoted in American dollars and prices from 2004–2007; how-

ever, during fieldwork the exchange rate averaged about 60 Jamaican dollars for each American dollar.

13 Caribbean Tourism Organization, "Jamaica Tourism Statistics," accessed May 20, 2009, http://www.onecaribbean.org/content/files/2004JamaicatoStKittsreport.pdf.

14 All of the drivers I observed during the Girlfriend Tours were men.

15 Holsey, "Transatlantic Dreaming," 171.

16 Holsey, "Transatlantic Dreaming," 177.

17 Holsey, "Transatlantic Dreaming," 167.

18 Dent, *Black Popular Culture*, 15–16.

19 Campt and Thomas, "Gendering Diaspora"; see also Saidiya Hartman, *Lose Your Mother*.

20 Sawyer, "Racialization, Gender, and the Negotiation of Power," 398.

21 Sawyer, "Racialization, Gender, and the Negotiation of Power," 408.

22 Ganja is a term for marijuana.

23 In Jamaica, the obeah woman described a woman who utilizes magic, sorcery, and other supernatural forces to heal, provide medicine, and curse others. She is greatly influenced by West African culture, particularly Igbo peoples. Historically, the nine night was a tradition of holding several nights of mourning, grieving, and celebration for a person after their death. The body was prepared with particular rituals and the funeral was held on the tenth day. Currently, the nine night may not actually last nine nights but is a celebration of the person's life with family, friends, and community members. There is usually lively music, food, and drink as people share memories of the person who passed away.

24 Girlfriends were clearly not always successful in practicing their mantra of "doing Jamaica right," as I discuss throughout the book. However, many times the intention was there. This was particularly apparent when dealing with American customer service expectations in banks or grocery stores, or wait times for food in restaurants. Newcomers from the United States would often complain about the long wait for their order to be taken or for the food to arrive, or about rudeness when dealing with some workers in different establishments, stating that there were no customer service standards in Jamaica. Veteran travelers like Maya, Gayle, and Jacqueline would frequently joke and say that Jamaicans worked on a different understanding of time and that it was best to have patience and give into the "soon come" mentality many Jamaicans claimed to have. Newcomers successfully succumbing to this "soon come" way of thinking was one sign to Girlfriends that they were finally releasing the United States and beginning to "get" Jamaica in the right way.

25 Clarke and Thomas, *Globalization and Race*, 27.

26 "Reasoning" is a word used to describe a conversation where people (particularly Jamaican men) theorize, hypothesize, and debate about the ways of the world and various philosophies. Most often the word is formally used to describe the intense political and theological discussions those who practice Rastafari engage in; however, I would observe (and sometimes participate) in these deep, intentional discussions in a variety of places throughout my trips.

27 "Dutty" is Jamaican patois for "dirty," while "bwoy" means "boy."

28 I am clear that many Black Americans have very different relationships to the racial epithet "nigger" and to the word "nigga," which is sometimes used as an intra-community term of endearment. Devan used the word "nigga" in this interview, and I was unclear about which version of the word he was invoking, or whether he was aware of the distinction between the two words in the United States.

29 In her book, *Black Identities: West Indian Immigrant Dreams and American Realities*, Mary C. Waters does a good job of explicating these different relationships to race and racism for African Americans and Jamaicans, particularly as it relates to their countries' histories. She explains that since Jamaicans grow up in a predominantly Black country, where at every level of occupation, status, and power there are Black people, they are less inclined to see a barrier as connected to race. However, African Americans, who are constantly taught and experience the fact that white people are structurally at the top of the racial hierarchy and therefore have access to more power and privilege, and who are navigating their lives within a country with a white majority, are more inclined to see a barrier to equity as connected to racism and white supremacy.

30 Ebron, *Performing Africa*, 188.

CHAPTER 3. *Why Jamaica?*

1 "Irie" means feeling good, relaxed.

2 Appadurai, *Modernity at Large*; Brodkin, "Global Capitalism"; Freeman, *High Tech and High Heels*; Harvey, *Condition of Postmodernity*.

3 Appadurai, "Disjuncture and Difference"; Basch, Glick Schiller, and Szanton Blanc, *Nations Unbound*; Glick Schiller and Fouron, *Georges Woke Up Laughing*; Ong, introduction to *Flexible Citizenship*; Trouillot, "Anthropology of the State."

4 Much of the early work on globalization has been critiqued for having a celebratory tone, praising the ways in which the creation of new financial markets, the reorganization of temporal and spatial boundaries, and new systems of trade, social reproduction, and communication have drastically changed the way people experience and view the world, including their imaginings of self and community. Appadurai, "Disjuncture and Difference," specifically, has been critiqued by numerous scholars (including Inda and Rosaldo, "World in Motion"; Ong, *Flexible Citizenship*; and Trouillot, "Anthropology of the State") who claim that he has prematurely praised technological advances, the transcendence of national boundaries, and the weakening of state power that have accompanied the expansion of capitalism since the 1970s. Furthermore, his use of "scapes" (ethnoscapes, mediascapes, technoscapes, financescapes, and ideoscapes) as a concept to describe the increased mobility of transnational flows of capital, goods, people, and information has been critiqued for not taking into account the various political, social, and economic specificities of the locales these "scapes" inhabit. In contrast, scholars hesitant to embrace the "newness" of globalization, such as Trouillot, "Anthropology of the State," use the history of the transatlantic slave trade and the work of theorists such as Wallerstein, *Modern World System*; Abu-Lughod, *Before European Hegemony*; and Wolf, *Europe and the People without History*, to point to older histories of global interconnectedness that reach

back to the thirteenth century. In "The Anthropology of the State in the Age of Globalization," Trouillot identifies previous analyses of capital flows and labor divisions, while arguing that "capitalism has always been transnational" (128). He suggests that what is new about this era of globalization is "not the internationalization of capital as such but changes in the spatialization of the world economy and changes in the volume, and especially, the kinds of movements that occur across political boundaries" (128). Contrasting Appadurai's argument that the power of the nation-state is weakening, Troulliot encourages anthropologists to examine areas where the individual and state-like processes and effects are visible (125). Pointing toward the ways NGOs, corporations, and other agencies produce state-like effects such as isolation, identification, legibility, and spatialization, Trouillot critiques the "idyllic vision of a global village" by showing how the "polarization and entanglement" of contemporary globalization creates a "fragmented globality" (129). In this study, my analysis of tourism in Jamaica attempts to take Trouillot's critiques seriously, by paying particular attention to the unevenness of globalization and transnationalism and discussing these processes in a way that makes *people* relevant and present in the local and global. This is in contrast to studies that discuss these developments as a set of abstract processes that push individuals or groups of people into the background. For more on these debates, see Appadurai, "Global Ethnoscapes"; Comaroff and Comaroff, "Millennial Capitalism"; Hannerz, "Notes on the Global Ecumene"; Tsing, "The Global Situation."

5 Hine, *Virtual Ethnography*; Miller and Slater, *Internet*; Hakken, *Cyborgs @ Cyberspace?*

6 Alexander and Mohanty, *Feminist Genealogies*; Comaroff and Comaroff, "Millennial Capitalism"; Friedman, *Cultural Identity and Global Process*. But see also Clarke and Thomas, *Globalization and Race*; Hall, "Local and the Global"; Holt, *Problem of Race in the 21st Century*; Winant, *The World Is a Ghetto*. Hall, in particular, claims that although identities have always been constituted through negotiations with difference (including the exclusion or absorption of racialized, gendered, nationalized, classed, sexualized, and regional "Others"), this contemporary stage of capitalism does not attempt to complete the process of homogenization (where cultural differences are erased and sameness is created), but in fact feeds off of the proliferation of these differences, paradoxes, and contradictions in cultural and economic arenas ("Local and the Global," 29–30). Pointing toward Appadurai's premature celebration of the weakening of the state, Hall argues that although these differences may be under pressure, racism and nationalism are still being maintained and fiercely policed.

7 See Basch, Glick Schiller, and Szanton Blanc, *Nations Unbound*; Glick Schiller and Fouron, *Georges Woke Up Laughing*; Foner, *Islands in the City*; Sutton and Chaney, "The Caribbeanization of New York City"; Waters, *Black Identities*.

8 Glick Schiller, Basch, and Blanc-Szanton, "Transnationalism."

9 Basch, Glick Schiller, and Szanton Blanc, *Nations Unbound*.

10 Sutton and Chaney, "The Caribbeanization of New York City"; Basch, Glick Schiller, and Szanton Blanc, *Nations Unbound*, 3. While some observers would point out that immigrants have always maintained networks of interconnection with their

home country, it is important to recognize that the methods used to maintain these ties change as technologies such as telephones, the Internet, and airplanes are created and improved. Transnational studies, with its history in borderland and migration studies, forces anthropologists to look at the specificities of globalization when observing the new tools people use to make sense of the world, negotiate their relationship to hegemonic ideologies, and execute a response to oppressive structures.

11 Ong, *Flexible Citizenship*, 5.

12 Ong, *Flexible Citizenship*, 5.

13 To get an in-depth analysis of this state-sanctioned surveillance of Black peoples, see Simone Brown's *Dark Matters: On the Surveillance of Blackness*.

14 Urry, *Tourist Gaze*.

15 Coleman and Crang, *Tourism*.

16 See MacCannell, *The Tourist*; Strain, *Public Places, Private Journeys*; Urry, *Tourist Gaze*. Also, there is a long history of theorizing various gazes in anthropology and other disciplines to explore issues regarding representation, authenticity, and desire (including a male gaze, oppositional gaze, and ethnographer's eye; Allison, *Permitted and Prohibited Desires*; Bhabha, "Of Mimicry and Man"; Fanon, *Black Skin, White Masks*; Frank, *G-strings and Sympathy*; Grimshaw, *The Ethnographer's Eye*; Hall, "The Local and the Global"; hooks, "Oppositional Gaze"; Kincaid, *Small Place*; Rony, *Third Eye*). However, there has not been as much theorizing of the gaze and its role in shaping racial identity formations within the context of tourism specifically. This gap in the scholarship on processes of racialization and racial identities in tourism is surprising (especially in American-Caribbean tourist interactions), since theorists have primarily studied tourism from an "acculturation studies" perspective, which has significant links to the acculturation and integration studies of Melville Herskovits (*Acculturation* and *Myth of the Negro Past*) and E. Franklin Frazier (*Black Bourgeoisie* and *Negro Family in the U.S.*) and the plural society debates of Caribbean scholars, such as Raymond T. Smith (*British Guiana*) and Michael G. Smith ("Social and Cultural Pluralism"). These historical analyses of contact and creolization between peoples of different races, ethnicities, and cultures—during and after slavery and colonialism—illuminate the ways in which processes of racialization are always shaped by, and constantly shaping, political and economic relations within societies and between nations.

17 See Hall, "Local and the Global"; Holt, *Problem of Race in the 21st Century*; Clarke and Thomas, *Globalization and Race*; and Winant, *World Is a Ghetto*.

18 Clarke and Thomas, *Globalization and Race*, 8.

19 In chapter 3 I examine the idea of "giving back" and how it affects the consumption practices of these tourists.

20 Frohlick and Jacobs, "Intimate Subjects," 1.

21 Frohlick and Jacobs, "Intimate Subjects," 1.

22 Alexander and Mohanty, *Feminist Genealogies*, xxii.

23 Alexander and Mohanty, *Feminist Genealogies*, xxiii.

24 Brennan, *What's Love Got to Do With It?*; Gregory, "Men in Paradise"; Seabrook, *Travels in the Skin Trade*.

25 Mintz, "Enduring Substances, Trying Theories"; Trouillot, "Caribbean Region."

26 Taylor, *To Hell with Paradise*, 7.

27 Taylor, *To Hell with Paradise*, 58.

28 Stolzoff, *Wake the Town and Tell the People*, 39–40.

29 Cooper, *Sound Clash*, 46.

30 Thomas, "Blackness across Borders," 113.

31 Fanon, *Black Skin, White Masks*.

32 Berlant, *Cruel Optimism*, 93.

33 Major tourist attractions in Ocho Rios included Dolphin Cove, where one can swim with dolphins, and Dunns River Falls, where visitors could climb the waterfalls.

34 In her analysis of emotional transnationalism, Celia J. Falicov writes about the ways immigrants have always had to negotiate living with part of their heart "at home" in the country they left, and a part of their heart in the country where they build their new lives. They had to live with "one's heart divided" ("Emotional Transnationalism and Family Identities," 399). As globalization and transnationalism have enabled immigrants to stay connected with those back home through new technologies, they are able to remain linked (at least on some level) with families and communities while crossing borders. In this way, they can imagine the possibility of "living with two hearts rather than one divided heart," even if it comes with some economic, political, and social complexities (399). Again, the costs of mobility and border crossings are different for transmigrants and tourists like the Girlfriends. However, they experience some of the same motivations, desires, and emotions during their movements and establishing of multisited communities.

Interlude

1 A sound made with the mouth that signifies distaste or frustration. Thanks to David Kennedy for assistance with the Jamaican patois translation.

CHAPTER 4. *Breaking (It) Down*

1 Higginbotham, *Righteous Discontent*, 1994.

2 A "rent-a-dread" is a stereotype of a sex worker in the romance industry in Jamaica who has locs and capitalizes on Rastafarian culture to draw in women customers. This person may or may not actually practice Rastafari. But this stereotypical person would listen to conscious reggae music, usually smoke weed, and embody tourists' fantasies of being close to nature and Africanness. For a discussion about the terms women use to describe their lovers, mates, and friends in the context of sex tourism in the Caribbean, see Amelia Cabezas, "Between Love and Money."

3 Columbus Heights is a hotel and apartment complex located directly at the entrance of the city of Ocho Rios. It sits on top of three escalating hills, surrounded by a stone wall, and faces Fisherman's Beach, which is across the street. The complex is frequently filled with Jamaica's elite residents from Ocho Rios and Kingston, or Jamaican diasporic peoples from the United States and Europe who own their apartments. Since some of the units can be rented nightly or for short-term housing, Columbus Heights is also a popular spot for returning tourists from the United States and Canada. The establishment was the central location for GFT visits to Ocho Rios.

4 This may have been the wrong decision—and it is one I am conflicted about until today. I understand that other anthropologists, in the search for a truth or at least an alternative truth, may have chosen differently, but at the time I thought it was the best decision. Part of being in the field, particularly when doing research on something as messy and complicated as emotions, is the need to make calls in the field that are the best for the context you find yourself in. However, now, as a more seasoned anthropologist and ethnographer, I probably would have found a sensitive and careful way to broach the topic with Maya to ensure that she had a chance to tell her version of the story.

5 In Jamaica, the term "loving" often refers to sex, but it does not always refer to sex alone. The term could be used to describe the physical act of sexual intercourse, sexual intimacy, or love.

6 Taylor, "Dollars Are a Girl's Best Friend?," 759–760.

7 Taylor, "Dollars Are a Girl's Best Friend?," 760.

8 Kempadoo, *Sun, Sex, and Gold* and *Sexing the Caribbean*.

9 Kempadoo, *Sexing the Caribbean*, 28–29. Additionally, feminists like Kempadoo encourage anthropologists to examine the ways in which the language (and theorization) of globalization itself is gendered. Anne Allison points to this in her research when she discusses the prevalence of commodity fetishism and phallic fetishism within capitalist systems, where the hierarchical ideology of masculinism reinforces gendered labor divisions (*Permitted and Prohibited Desires*, xx). As money becomes the standard of value, she argues, "gendered ideologies operate to differentiate between the wage-earning labor males and the unpaid domestic labor of (primarily) women in ways that come to be symbolized in a sexual language of phallic power" (xix).

10 O'Connell Davidson and Sanchez Taylor, "Fantasy Islands," 37.

11 Gayle King is Oprah Winfrey's best friend and also the editor-in-chief of Oprah's *O* magazine.

12 Brown, "Black Liverpool." In this essay, Brown discusses how Black Liverpudlian women felt excluded from "local black male desire" and turned to dating, marrying, and migrating to the United States with the American GIs based in the area during World War II. Brown writes, "We may begin to see that it is exclusionary racial practices occurring within the category *black,* along distinctly gendered lines, that send some black Liverpudlians down the diasporic path" ("Black Liverpool," 307).

13 At times, the GFT ladies did not know that the women they befriended were sex workers. I often discovered this after the women left Jamaica, as I stayed behind to interview Jamaican lovers and friends.

14 To "ice grill" someone is to stare them down with icy eyes.

15 This "master's complex" is discussed in chapter 2.

16 Rollins, *Between Women*.

17 Collins, *Black Feminist Thought*, 113.

18 Jamaican women are not trying to seduce, date, or have sex with American women, which is what could be assumed if the same interactions were between Jamaican men and American women.

CHAPTER 5. *Navigating (Virtual) Jamaica*

1 For a race-focused analysis of the virtual context, see Dines and Humez, *Gender, Race, and Class in Media*; Kolko, Nakamura, and Rodman, *Race in Cyberspace*; Nakamura, *Cybertypes*.

2 Scholars in various locations—such as Abu-Lughod in Egypt and Ginsburg in Australia (Ginsburg, Abu-Lughod, and Larkin, *Media Worlds*); Mankekar, "National Texts and Gendered Lives," in India; and Mahon, *Right to Rock*, in the United States—have undertaken this type of research.

3 See Fox and Starn, *Resistance and Revolution*; Thomas, "Emancipating the Nation (Again)."

4 Hine, *Virtual Ethnography*.

5 Castells, *Internet Galaxy*; Howard and Jones, *Society Online*; Jones, *CyberSociety*; Rheingold, *Virtual Community*; Smith and Kollock, *Communities in Cyberspace*.

6 Kaplan, "Transporting the Subject," 34.

7 Kaplan, "Transporting the Subject," 35. David Harvey's discussion of "time-space compression" and "flexible accumulation" in *The Condition of Postmodernity* theorizes how the move from the rigid Fordist era of overaccumulation to a new regime of post-Fordist capitalism (deterritorialization of capital and flexibility of labor processes and labor markets, such as outsourcing of jobs to international sites and the increase in hiring temporary workers) has affected class-based divisions and patterns of consumption. In striking contrast to the rigidity of the Fordist era, Harvey argues that this new stage of capitalism has "permitted the revival of domestic, familial, and paternalistic labour systems" (187) and has "re-emphasized the vulnerability of disadvantaged groups" (152). He argues that these changes in global capital accumulation could actually put historically underprivileged groups in an even more disadvantaged economic position. Although Harvey alludes to the power differentials—specifically the inequalities in access to technology and mobility inherent in capitalist systems—he doesn't actually engage in an analysis of these power relations.

8 Cherny and Weise, *Wired Women*; Harcourt, *Women@Internet*; Terry and Calvert, *Processed Lives*.

9 But see Kolko, Nakamura, and Rodman, *Race in Cyberspace*.

10 Nakamura, *Cybertypes*.

11 On white supremacist rhetoric and communities in the virtual world, see McPherson, "I'll Take My Stand in Dixie-Net." On constructing racially mixed avatars, see Gonzalez, "Appended Subject." On white masculinities, see Kendall, *Hanging Out in the Virtual Pub*.

12 Scholars (such as Bell, *Introduction to Cybercultures*; Kaplan, "Transporting the Subject"; Kendall, *Hanging Out in the Virtual Pub*; Miller and Slater, *Internet*) from other disciplines—like cultural studies, communication studies, new media theory, and sociology—have also been engaged in this conversation.

13 See Chevannes, *Rastafari*; Cooper, *Sound Clash*; Ebron, *Performing Africa*; Hope, "The British Link-Up Crew"; and Stolzoff, *Wake the Town and Tell the People*, for analyses of music and Black community and identity formations. However, see also

Campt, *Other Germans*; Thomas, *Modern Blackness*; Clarke and Thomas, *Globalization and Race*.

14 Miller and Slater, *Internet*.

15 Although see work on the Indian diaspora (Mitra and Watts, "Theorizing Cyberspace") and queer Asian diaspora (Berry et al., *Mobile Cultures*).

16 McGlotten, *Virtual Intimacies*, 1.

17 McGlotten, *Virtual Intimacies*, 7.

18 McGlotten, *Virtual Intimacies*, 7.

19 Turkle, *Life on the Screen*.

20 Kolko, *Race in Cyberspace*.

21 I hesitate to use the word "real," since my argument in this section is that these boardites' participation in the web community *is* a part of their real life. Although some questioned the "realness" of friendships created in this virtual space, for all intents and purposes, most behaved as if the friends, enemies, and experiences within this online community were a part of their "real" lives. Subsequently, terms like "real," "geographic," and "territorial" do not seem adequate and appear to perpetuate the dichotomy between the virtual and real that I am attempting to shift away from.

22 Sasha was one of the few boardites I interviewed who admitted that she was on the board every day. In fact, during my fieldwork Sasha was often one of the top three board citizens with the most posts on the website. Despite her dedication to participating in the board, this woman in her late twenties stated that the board did not mean much to her, although it enabled her to meet "a lot of cool people."

23 Remittances from Jamaican diasporic peoples are commonly known to be the largest part of Jamaica's GNP, with tourism being the second-largest moneymaker. Although these tourists contribute significantly to Jamaica's economy while they are on the island, they frequently maintain these material connections to Jamaica by sending gifts, loans, and other valuable resources to friends and lovers on the island between their multiple visits.

24 Patois, or patwa, is an English-African dialect spoken in Jamaica. Although commonly understood as an oral language, there have been numerous discussions about making patois a formalized written language for use in schools and other institutions. Furthermore, there is a very rich body of literature written in patois, particularly poetry written by the famous Jamaican poet Louise Bennett, also known as Miss Lou.

EPILOGUE. *Lessons Learned*

1 I have written about some of my gendered fieldwork challenges in "Don't Ride the Bus!"

2 "Runnings" is a Jamaican patois word for practices and happenings, meaning "the way things work and are done." It also can refer to "what's going on."

3 Brown, "Negotiating the Insider/Outsider Status."

Abu-Lughod, Janet L. *Before European Hegemony: The World System A.D. 1250–1350.* New York: Oxford University Press, 1989.

Ahmed, Sara. *The Promise of Happiness.* Durham, NC: Duke University Press, 2010.

Alexander, M. Jacqui. "Erotic Autonomy as a Politics of Decolonialization: An Anatomy of Feminist Practice in the Bahamas' Tourist Economy. In *Feminist Genealogies, Colonial Legacies, Democratic Futures,* edited by M. Jacqui Alexander and Chandra Talpade Mohanty, 63–100. New York: Routledge, 1996.

Alexander, M. Jacqui, and Chandra Talpade Mohanty, eds. *Feminist Genealogies, Colonial Legacies, Democratic Futures.* New York: Routledge, 1996.

Allison, Anne. *Nightwork: Sexuality, Pleasure, and Corporate Masculinity in a Tokyo Hostess Club.* Chicago: University of Chicago Press, 1994.

———. *Permitted and Prohibited Desires: Mothers, Comics, and Censorship in Japan.* Berkeley: University of California Press, 2000.

Anderson, Benedict. *Imagined Communities.* 1983; repr. London: Verso, 2006.

Appadurai, Arjun. "Disjuncture and Difference in the Global Cultural Economy." *Public Culture* 2, no. 2 (1990): 1–24.

———. "Global Ethnoscapes: Notes and Queries for a Transnational Anthropology." In *Recapturing Anthropology: Working in the Present,* edited by Richard G. Fox, 191–210. Santa Fe, NM: School of American Research Press, 1991.

———. *Modernity at Large: Cultural Dimensions of Globalization.* Minneapolis: University of Minnesota Press, 1996.

Auslander, Philip. *Liveness: Performance in a Mediatized Culture.* London: Routledge, 1999.

Axel, Brian. "The Diasporic Imaginary." *Public Culture* 14, no. 2 (2002): 411–428.

Barnes, Riche J. *Raising the Race: Black Career Women Redefine Marriage, Motherhood, and Community.* New Brunswick, NJ: Rutgers University Press, 2016.

Basch, Linda, Nina Glick Schiller, and Cristina Szanton Blanc. *Nations Unbound: Transnational Projects, Postcolonial Predicaments, and Deterritorialized Nation-States.* Langhorne, PA: Gordon and Breach, 1994.

Beauboeuf-Lafontant, Tamara. *Behind the Mask of the Strong Black Woman: Voice and the Embodiment of a Costly Performance.* Philadelphia: Temple University Press, 2009.

Bell, David. *An Introduction to Cybercultures.* London: Routledge, 2001.

Berlant, Lauren. *Cruel Optimism.* Durham, NC: Duke University Press, 2011.

Berry, Chris, Fran Martin, Audrey Yue, and Lynn Spigel. *Mobile Cultures: New Media in Queer Asia.* Durham, NC: Duke University Press, 2003.

Bhabha, Homi K. "Of Mimicry and Man: The Ambivalence of Colonial Discourse." In *The Location of Culture*, edited by Homi Bhabha, 85-92. 2nd ed. London: Routledge, 2004.

Bolles, A. Lynn. *Sister Jamaica: A Study of Women, Work, and Households in Kingston.* Lanham, MD: University Press of America, 1996.

———. "Of Mules and Yankee Gals: Struggling with Stereotypes in the Field." *Anthropology and Humanism Quarterly* 10, no. 4 (1985): 114-119.

Brennan, Denise. *What's Love Got to Do with It? Transnational Desires and Sex Tourism in the Dominican Republic.* Durham, NC: Duke University Press, 2004.

Brodkin, Karen. "Global Capitalism: What's Race Got to Do with It?" *American Ethnologist* 27, no. 2 (2000): 237–256.

Brown, Nadia E. "Negotiating the Insider/Outsider Status: Black Feminist Ethnography and Legislative Studies." *Journal of Feminist Scholarship* 3 (2012): 19–34.

Brown, Jacqueline Nassy. "Black Liverpool, Black America, and the Gendering of Diasporic Space." *Cultural Anthropology* 13, no. 3 (1998): 291–325.

Browne, Simone. *Dark Matters: On the Surveillance of Blackness.* Durham, NC: Duke University Press, 2015.

Cabezas, Amelia L. "Between Love and Money: Sex, Tourism, and Citizenship in Cuba and the Dominican Republic." *Signs: Journal of Women in Culture and Society* 29, no. 4 (2004): 987–1015.

Campt, Tina. *Other Germans: Black Germans and the Politics of Race, Gender, and Memory in the Third Reich.* Ann Arbor: University of Michigan Press, 2004.

Campt, Tina M., and Deborah A. Thomas. "Gendering Diaspora: Transnational Feminism, Diaspora, and Its Hegemonies." *Feminist Review* 90 (2008): 1–8.

Castells, Manuel. *The Internet Galaxy: Reflections on the Internet, Business, and Society.* Oxford: Oxford University Press, 2001.

Chambers, Erve. *Native Tours: The Anthropology of Travel and Tourism.* Long Grove, IL: Waveland Press, 2010.

Cherny, Lynn, and Elizabeth Reba Weise. *Wired Women: Gender and New Realities in Cyberspace.* Seattle: Seal Press, 1996.

Chevannes, Barry. *Rastafari: Roots and Ideology.* Syracuse, NY: Syracuse University Press, 1994.

Clarke, Kamari Maxine, and Deborah A. Thomas, eds. *Globalization and Race: Transformations in the Cultural Production of Blackness.* Durham, NC: Duke University Press, 2006.

Clifford, James. "Diasporas." *Cultural Anthropology* 9, no. 3 (1994): 302–338.

Cobb, William Jelani. "Blame It on Rio." *Essence*, September 2006.

Codrington, Ray. "The Homegrown: Rap, Race, and Class in London." In *Globalization and Race: Transformations in the Cultural Production of Blackness*, edited by Kamari Maxine Clarke and Deborah A. Thomas, 299–315. Durham, NC: Duke University Press, 2006.

Cohen, Erik. "Authenticity and Commoditization in Tourism." *Annals of Tourism Research* 15 (1988): 371–386.

Coleman, Simon, and Mike Crang. *Tourism: Between Place and Performance.* New York: Berghahn, 2002.

Collins, Patricia Hill. *Black Feminist Thought: Knowledge, Consciousness, and the Politics of Empowerment.* London: Routledge, 2008.

———. *Black Sexual Politics: African Americans, Gender, and the New Racism.* London: Routledge, 2005.

Comaroff, Jean, and John L. Comaroff. "Millennial Capitalism: First Thoughts on a Second Coming." In *Millennial Capitalism and the Culture of Neoliberalism*, 1–56. Durham, NC: Duke University Press, 2001.

Cooper, Anna Julia. *A Voice from the South by a Black Woman of the South.* New York: Oxford University Press, 1988.

Cooper, Carolyn. *Noises in the Blood: Orality, Gender, and the "Vulgar" Body of Jamaican Popular Culture.* Durham, NC: Duke University Press, 1995.

———. *Sound Clash: Jamaican Dancehall Culture at Large.* New York: MacMillan, 2004.

Craven, Christa and Dana-Ain Davis. *Feminist Activist Ethnography: Counterpoints to Neoliberalism in North America.* Lanham, MD: Lexington Books, 2013.

Crenshaw, Kimberlé Williams. "Demarginalizing the Intersection of Race and Sex: A Black Feminist Critique of Antidiscrimination Doctrine, Feminist Theory, and Anti-racist Politics." *University of Chicago Legal Forum* (1989): 139–167.

Crick, Malcolm. "Representations of International Tourism in the Social Sciences: Sun, Sex, Sights, Savings and Servility." *Annual Review of Anthropology* 18 (1989): 307–344.

Cvetkovich, Ann. *Depression: A Public Feeling.* Durham, NC: Duke University Press, 2012.

Davies, Carole Boyce. "Pan-Africanism, Transnational Black Feminism and the Limits of Cultural Analyses in African Gender Discourses." *Feminist Africa* 19 (2014): 78–93.

Davis, Angela Y. *Women, Race, and Class.* New York: Vintage, 1983.

Dent, Gina. *Black Popular Culture.* New York: New Press, 1983.

Dines, Gail, and Jean H. Humez. *Gender, Race, and Class in Media: A Text Reader.* Thousand Oaks, CA: Sage, 2002.

Drake, Simone C. *Critical Appropriations: African American Women and the Construction of Transnational Identity.* Baton Rouge: Louisiana State University Press, 2014.

Du Bois, W. E. B. *The Souls of Black Folk.* 1903; repr. Oxford: Oxford University Press, 2007.

duCille, Ann. "The Occult of True Black Womanhood: Critical Demeanor and Black Feminist Studies." *Signs* 19, no. 3 (1994): 591–629.

Ebron, Paulla A. *Performing Africa.* Princeton, NJ: Princeton University Press, 2002.

Edwards, Brent Hayes. *The Practice of Diaspora: Literature, Translation, and the Rise of Black Internationalism.* Cambridge, MA: Harvard University Press, 2003.

———. "The Uses of *Diaspora.*" *Social Text* 66, vol. 19, no. 1 (spring 2001): 45–73.

Enloe, Cynthia H. *Bananas, Beaches, and Bases: Making Feminist Sense of International Politics.* Berkeley: University of California Press, 1990.

Falicov, Celia J. "Emotional Transnationalism and Family Identities." *Family Process* 44, no. 4 (2005): 399–406.

Fanon, Frantz. *Black Skin, White Masks.* 1969; repr. New York: Grove Press, 1991.

Foner, Nancy. *Islands in the City: West Indian Migration to New York.* Berkeley: University of California Press, 2001.

Frank, Katherine. *G-strings and Sympathy: Strip Club Regulars and Male Desire.* Durham, NC: Duke University Press, 2002.

Frazier, E. Franklin. *Black Bourgeoisie.* New York: Free Press, 1965.

———. *Negro Family in the U.S.* Chicago: University of Chicago Press, 1966.

Frederick, Marla F. *Between Sundays: Black Women and Everyday Struggles of Faith.* Berkeley: University of California Press, 2003.

Freeman, Carla. *High Tech and High Heels in the Global Economy: Women, Work, and Pink-Collar Identities in the Caribbean.* Durham, NC: Duke University Press, 2000.

———. "Is Local:Global as Feminine:Masculine? Rethinking the Gender of Globalization." *Signs* 26, no. 4 (2001): 1007–1037.

Friedman, Jonathan. *Cultural Identity and Global Process.* Thousand Oaks, CA: Sage, 1994.

Frohlick, Susan and Jessica Jacobs. "Intimate Subjects: Women's Erotic Desires, Travels, and Consumption in the Twenty-First Century." Unpublished manuscript, 2010.

Gauntlett, David, and Ross Horsley. *WebStudies.* London: Oxford University Press, 2004.

Giddings, Paula J. *When and Where I Enter: The Impact of Black Women on Race and Sex in America.* New York: Harper Collins, 1984.

Gilroy, Paul. *Against Race: Imagining Political Culture beyond the Color Line.* Cambridge, MA: Belknap Press of Harvard University Press, 2000.

———. *The Black Atlantic: Modernity and Double Consciousness.* Cambridge, MA: Harvard University Press, 1993.

Ginsburg, Faye, Lila Abu-Lughod, and Brian Larkin. *Media Worlds: Anthropology on New Terrain.* Berkeley: University of California Press, 2002.

Glick Schiller, Nina, and Georges Fouron. *Georges Woke Up Laughing: Long Distance Nationalism and the Search for Home.* Durham, NC: Duke University Press, 2001.

Glick Schiller, Nina, Linda Basch, and Cristina Blanc-Szanton. "Transnationalism: A New Analytic Framework for Understanding Migration." In *Towards a Transnational Perspective on Migration: Race, Class, Ethnicity, and Nationalism Reconsidered*, edited by Nina Glick Schiller, Linda Basch, and Cristina Blanc-Szanton, 1–24. New York: New York Academy of Sciences, 1992.

Gobe, Marc. *Emotional Branding: The New Paradigm for Connecting Brands to People.* New York: Allworth Press, 2001.

Gonzalez, Jennifer. "The Appended Subject: Race and Identity as Digital Assemblage." In *Race in Cyberspace*, edited by Beth E. Kolko, Lisa Nakamura, and Gilbert B. Rodman, 27–50. New York: Routledge, 2000.

Gregg, Melissa, Gregory J. Seigworth. *The Affect Theory Reader*. Durham, NC: Duke University Press, 2010.

Gregory, Steven. *The Devil behind the Mirror: Globalization and Politics in the Dominican Republic*. Berkeley: University of California Press, 2007.

———. "Men in Paradise: Sex Tourism and the Political Economy of Masculinity." In *Race, Nature, and the Politics of Difference*, edited by Donald S. Moore, Jake Kosek, and Anand Pandian, 323–355. Durham, NC: Duke University Press, 2003.

Grimshaw, Anna. *The Ethnographer's Eye: Ways of Seeing in Modern Anthropology*. Cambridge, MA: Cambridge University Press, 2002.

Guy-Sheftall, Beverly. *Words of Fire: An Anthology of African-American Feminist Thought*. New York: The New Press, 1995.

Haidt, Jonathan. *The Happiness Hypothesis: Finding Modern Truth in Ancient Wisdom*. New York: Basic Books, 2006.

Hakken, David. *Cyborgs @ Cyberspace? An Ethnographer Looks to the Future*. New York: Routledge, 1999.

Hall, Stuart. "The Local and the Global: Globalization and Ethnicity." In *Culture, Globalization, and the World-System: Contemporary Conditions for the Representation of Identity*, edited by Anthony King, 19–39. Minneapolis: University of Minnesota Press, 1997.

———. "Thinking the Diaspora: Home-Thoughts from Abroad." *Small Axe* 3 (1999): 1–18.

———. "What Is This 'Black' in Black Popular Culture?" In *The Black Studies Reader*, edited by Jacqueline Bobo, Cynthia Hudley, and Claudine Michel, 255–264. New York: Routledge, 2004.

Hannerz, Ulf. "Notes on the Global Ecumene." *Public Culture* 1, no. 2 (1989): 66–75.

Harcourt, Wendy. *Women@Internet: Creating New Cultures in Cyberspace*. London: Zed Books, 1999.

Harris-Perry, Melissa. *Sister Citizen: Shame, Stereotypes, and Black Women in America*. New Haven, CT: Yale University Press, 2011.

Harrison, Faye V. *Decolonizing Anthropology: Moving Further Toward an Anthropology for Liberation*. Arlington, VA: American Anthropological Association, 1997.

Harvey, David. *The Condition of Postmodernity: An Enquiry into the Origins of Cultural Change*. Oxford: Blackwell, 1989.

Hernandez-Reguant, Ariana. "Havana's Timba: A Macho Sound for Sex." In *Globalization and Race: Transformations in the Cultural Production of Blackness*, edited by Kamari Maxine Clarke and Deborah A. Thomas, 249–278. Durham, NC: Duke University Press, 2006.

Herskovits, Melville. *Acculturation: The Study of Culture Contact*. New York: J. J. Augustin, 1938.

———. *The Myth of the Negro Past*. New York: Harper & Brothers, 1941.

Higginbotham, Evelyn Brooks. *Righteous Discontent: The Women's Movement in the Black Baptist Church, 1880–1920*. Rev. ed. Cambridge, MA: Harvard University Press, 1994.

Hine, Christine M. *Virtual Ethnography*. Thousand Oaks, CA: Sage, 2000.

Holsey, Bayo. "Transatlantic Dreaming: Slavery, Tourism, and Diasporic Encounters." In

Homecomings: Unsettling Paths of Return, edited by Anders H. Stefansson and Fran Markowitz, 166–182. Lanham, MD: Lexington Books, 2004.

Holt, Thomas. *The Problem of Race in the 21st Century*. Cambridge, MA: Harvard University Press, 2000.

hooks, bell. "The Oppositional Gaze." In *Black Looks: Race and Representation*. Boston: South End Press, 1992.

Hope, Donna. "The British Link-Up Crew: Consumption Masquerading as Masculinity in the Dancehall." *Interventions* 6, no. 1 (2004): 101–117.

Horkheimer, Max, and Theodore W. Adorno. "The Culture Industry: Enlightenment as Mass Deception." In *Dialectic of Enlightenment: Philosophical Fragments*, edited by Gunzelin Schmid Noerr, 94–136. Translated by Edmund Jephcott. Stanford, CA: Stanford University Press, 2002. Original German version 1944; repr. 1969.

How Stella Got Her Groove Back. Film. Directed by Kevin Rodney Sullivan. Los Angeles: Twentieth Century Fox, 1998.

Howard, Philip N., and Steve Jones. *Society Online: The Internet in Context*. Thousand Oaks, CA: Sage, 2004.

Hurston, Zora Neale. *Mules and Men*. Philadelphia: J. B. Lippincott, 1935.

———. *Tell My Horse: Voodoo and Life in Haiti and Jamaica*. Philadelphia: J. B. Lippincott, 1938.

Inda, Jonathan Xavier, and Renato Rosaldo. "A World in Motion." In *Anthropology of Globalization: A Reader*, edited by Jonathan Xavier Inda and Renato Rosaldo, 1–34. Malden, MA: Blackwell, 2002.

Jackson, John L. *Harlemworld: Doing Race and Class in Contemporary Black America*. Chicago: University of Chicago Press, 2001.

James, Joy. *Shadowboxing: Representations of Black Feminist Politics*. New York: Palgrave Macmillan, 2002.

James, Sherman A. "John Henryism and the Health of African-Americans." *Culture, Medicine and Psychiatry* 18 (1994): 163–182.

Jeffreys, Sheila. "Sex Tourism: Do Women Do It Too?" *Leisure Studies* 22 (2003): 223–238.

Johnson, E. Patrick. *Appropriating Blackness: Performance and the Politics of Authenticity*. Durham, NC: Duke University Press, 2003.

Jones, Charisse, and Kumea Shorter-Gooden. *Shifting: The Double Lives of Black Women in America*. New York: Harper Perennial, 2004.

Jones, Steve. *CyberSociety: Computer-Mediated Communication and Community*. Thousand Oaks, CA: Sage, 1995.

Kaplan, Caren. "Transporting the Subject: Technologies of Mobility and Location in an Era of Globalization." *PMLA* 117, no. 1 (2002): 32–42.

Kelsky, Karen. *Women on the Verge: Japanese Women, Western Dreams*. Durham, NC: Duke University Press, 2001.

Kempadoo, Kamala. *Sexing the Caribbean: Gender, Race, and Sexual Labor*. New York: Routledge, 2004.

———, ed. *Sun, Sex, and Gold: Tourism and Sex Work in the Caribbean*. Lanham, MD: Rowman & Littlefield, 1999.

Kendall, Lori. *Hanging Out in the Virtual Pub: Masculinities and Relationships Online.* Berkeley: University of California Press, 2002.

Kincaid, Jamaica. *A Small Place.* New York: Penguin, 1988.

Kolko, Beth, Lisa Nakamura, and Gilbert B. Rodman. *Race in Cyberspace.* New York: Routledge, 2002.

Kozinets, Robert V. *Netnography: Doing Ethnographic Research Online.* Thousand Oaks, CA: Sage, 2010.

MacCannell, Dean. *The Tourist: A New Theory of the Leisure Class.* Berkeley: University of California Press, 1999.

Mahon, Maureen. *Right to Rock: The Black Rock Coalition and the Cultural Politics of Race.* Durham, NC: Duke University Press, 2004.

Mankekar, Purninma. "National Texts and Gendered Lives: An Ethnography of Television Viewers in a North Indian City." In *The Anthropology of Media: A Reader*, edited by Kelly Askew and Richard R. Wilk, 299–322. Malden, MA: Blackwell, 2002.

Marchand, Marianne, and Anne Runyon. "Feminist Sightings of Global Restructuring: Conceptualizations and Reconceptualizations." In *Gender and Global Restructuring: Sightings, Sites and Resistances*, 1–22. New York: Routledge, 2000.

Mazzeralla, William. "Culture, Globalization, Mediation." *Annual Review of Anthropology* 33 (2004): 345–367.

McClaurin, Irma. *Black Feminist Anthropology: Theory, Politics, Praxis, and Poetics.* New Brunswick, NJ: Rutgers University Press, 2001.

McGlotten, Shaka. *Virtual Intimacies: Media, Affect, and Queer Sociality.* Albany: State University of New York Press, 2013.

McKittrick, Katherine. *Demonic Grounds: Black Women and the Cartographies of Struggle.* Minneapolis: University of Minnesota Press, 2006.

McLuhan, Marshall. "Medium Is the Message." In *Understanding Media: The Extensions of Man*, 7–21. 1964; repr. Cambridge, MA: MIT Press, 1994.

McMillan, Terry. *How Stella Got Her Groove Back.* New York: Viking, 1996.

McPherson, Tara. "I'll Take My Stand in Dixie-Net: White Guys, the South, and Cyberspace." In *Race in Cyberspace*, edited by Beth E. Kolko, Lisa Nakamura, and Gilbert B. Rodman, 117–132. New York: Routledge, 2000.

Miller, Daniel, and Don Slater. *The Internet: An Ethnographic Approach.* Oxford: Berg, 2000.

Mintz, Sidney. "Enduring Substances, Trying Theories: The Caribbean Region as Oi Koumene." *Journal of the Royal Anthropological Institute* 2, no. 2 (1996): 289–312.

Mitra, Ananda. "Marginal Voices in Cyberspace." *New Media & Society* 3, no. 1 (2001): 29–48.

Mitra, Ananda, and Eric Watts. "Theorizing Cyberspace: The Idea of Voice Applied to the Internet Discourse." *New Media and Society* 4, no. 4 (2002): 479–498.

Morgan, Joan. *When Chickenheads Come Home to Roost: My Life as a Hip-Hop Feminist.* New York: Simon & Schuster, 1999.

Munoz, Jose Esteban. "Feeling Brown, Feeling Down: Latina Affect, the Performativity of Race, and the Depressive Position." *Signs: Journal of Women in Culture and Society*, 31 no. 3 (2006): 675–688.

Mullings, Leith. "Resistance and Resilience: The Sojourner Syndrome and the Social Context of Reproduction in Central Harlem." *Transforming Anthropology* 13, no. 2 (2005): 79–91.

Nakamura, Lisa. *Cybertypes: Race, Ethnicity, and Identity on the Internet.* New York: Routledge, 2002.

Nash, Dennison. *Anthropology of Tourism.* Kidlington, Oxford: Elsevier Science, 1996.

O'Connell Davidson, Julia. "The Sex Tourist, The Expatriate, His Ex-Wife and Her 'Other': The Politics of Loss, Difference, and Desire." *Sexualities* 4, no. 1 (2001): 5–24.

O'Connell Davidson, Julia, and Jacqueline Sanchez Taylor. "Fantasy Islands: Exploring the Demand for Sex Tourism." In *Sun, Sex, and Gold: Tourism and Sex Work in the Caribbean*, edited by Kamala Kempadoo, 37–54. Lanham, MD: Rowman & Littlefield, 1999.

Ong, Aihwa. *Flexible Citizenship: The Cultural Logics of Transnationality.* Durham, NC: Duke University Press, 1999.

Parks, Sheri. *Fierce Angels: The Strong Black Woman in American Life and Culture.* New York: One World/Ballantine, 2010.

Pattullo, Polly. *Last Resorts: The Cost of Tourism in the Caribbean.* London: Cassell, 1996.

Perry, Marc. "Global Black Self-Fashionings: Hip Hop as Diasporic Space." *Identities: Global Studies in Power and Culture* 15, no. 6 (2008): 635–664.

Pew Research Center. "Blacks See Growing Values Gap between Poor and Middle Class: Optimism about Black Progress Declines." November 13, 2007. http://www.pew socialtrends.org/2007/11/13/blacks-see-growing-values-gap-between-poor-and -middle-class/.

Phelan, Peggy. *Unmarked: The Politics of Performance.* London: Routledge, 1994.

Pierre, Jemima. *The Predicament of Blackness: Postcolonial Ghana and the Politics of Race,* Chicago: University of Chicago Press, 2012.

Pinto, Samantha. *Difficult Diasporas: The Transnational Feminist Aesthetic of the Black Atlantic.* New York: New York University Press, 2013.

Pratt, Mary Louise. *Imperial Eyes: Travel Writing and Transculturation.* 2nd ed. New York: Routledge, 2007.

Pruitt, Deborah, and Suzanne LaFont. "For Love and Money: Romance Tourism in Jamaica." *Annals of Tourism Research* 22, no. 2 (1993): 422–440.

Rheingold, Howard. *The Virtual Community: Homesteading on the Electronic Frontier.* Reading, MA: Addison-Wesley, 1993.

Rodriguez, Cheryl R. *Transtlantic Feminisms: Women and Gender Studies in Africa and the Diaspora.* Lanham, MD: Lexington Books.

Roland, L. Kaifa. *Cuban Color in Tourism and La Lucha: An Ethnography of Racial Meanings.* New York: Oxford University Press, 2011.

Rollins, Judith. *Between Women: Domestics and Their Employers.* Philadelphia: Temple University Press, 1985.

Rony, Fatimah Tobing. *The Third Eye: Race, Cinema, and Ethnographic Spectacle.* Durham, NC: Duke University Press, 1996.

Rubin, Gayle. "The Traffic in Women: Notes on the 'Political Economy' of Sex." In *Toward an Anthropology of Women,* edited by Rayna Reiter, 157–210. New York: Monthly Review Press, 1975.

Ruby, Jay. *Picturing Culture: Explorations of Film & Anthropology.* Chicago: University of Chicago Press, 2000.

Sassen, Saskia. *Globalization and Its Discontents: Essays on the New Mobility of People and Money.* New York: New Press, 1998.

Sawyer, Lena. "Racialization, Gender, and the Negotiation of Power in Stockholm's African Dance Courses." In *Globalization and Race: Transformations in the Cultural Production of Blackness,* edited by Kamari Maxine Clarke and Deborah A. Thomas, 316–334. Durham, NC: Duke University Press, 2006.

Seabrook, Jeremy. *Travels in the Skin Trade: Tourism and the Sex Industry.* London: Pluto, 1996.

Sharpley-Whiting, T. Denean. "Video Vixens, Beauty Culture, and Diasporic Sex Tourism." In *Pimps Up, Ho's Down: Hip-Hop's Hold on Young Black Women,* 23–52. New York: New York University Press, 2007.

Slocum, Karla, and Deborah A. Thomas. "Introduction: Locality in Today's Global Caribbean: Shifting Economies of Nation, Race, and Development." *Identities: Global Studies in Culture and Power* 14, no. 1 (2007): 1–18.

———. "Rethinking Global and Area Studies: Insights from Caribbeanist Anthropology." *American Anthropologist* 105, no. 3 (2003): 553–565.

Smith, Barbara, ed. *Home Girls: A Black Feminist Anthology.* New Brunswick, NJ: Rutgers University Press, 2000.

Smith, Marc A., and Peter Kollock. *Communities in Cyberspace.* New York: Routledge, 1999.

Smith, Michael. G. "Social and Cultural Pluralism" in *Social and Cultural Pluralism in the Caribbean.* Annals of the New York Academy of Sciences 83, art. 5 (1960): 763–777.

Smith, Raymond T. *British Guiana.* London: Oxford University Press, 1962.

———. "Review of Social and Cultural Pluralism in the Caribbean." *American Anthropologist* 63, no. 1 (1961): 155–157.

Smith, Valerie. *Hosts and Guests: The Anthropology of Tourism.* Philadelphia: University of Pennsylvania Press, 1989.

Stewart, Kathleen. *Ordinary Affects.* Durham, NC: Duke University Press, 2007.

Stolzoff, Norman C. *Wake the Town and Tell the People: Dancehall Culture in Jamaica.* Durham, NC: Duke University Press, 2000.

Strain, Ellen. *Public Places, Private Journeys: Ethnography, Entertainment, and the Tourist Gaze.* New Brunswick, NJ: Rutgers University Press, 2003.

Sutton, Constance R., and Elsa M. Chaney. "The Caribbeanization of New York City and the Emergence of a Transnational Sociocultural System." In *Caribbean Life in New York City: Sociocultural Dimensions,* edited by Constance Sutton and Elsa M. Chaney, 15–29. New York: Center for Migration Studies of New York, 1987.

Takeda, Atsushi. "Emotional Transnationalism and Emotional Flows: Japanese Women in Australia." *Women's Studies International Forum* 35 (2012): 22–28.

Taylor, Frank Fonda. *To Hell with Paradise: A History of the Jamaican Tourist Industry.* Pittsburgh: University of Pittsburgh Press, 1993.

Taylor, Jacqueline Sanchez. "Dollars Are a Girl's Best Friend? Female Tourists' Sexual Behaviour in the Caribbean." *Sociology* 35, no. 3 (2001): 749–764.

Terry, Jennifer, and Melodie Calvert. *Processed Lives: Gender and Technology in Everyday Life*. London: Routledge, 1997.

Thomas, Deborah A. "Blackness across Borders: Jamaican Diasporas and New Politics of Citizenship." *Identities: Global Studies in Culture and Power* 14, no. 1 (2007): 111–133.

———. "Emancipating the Nation (Again): Notes on Nationalism, 'Modernization,' and Other Dilemmas in Post-Colonial Jamaica." *Identities: Global Studies in Culture and Power* 5, no. 4 (1999): 501–542.

———. *Modern Blackness: Nationalism, Globalization, and the Politics of Culture in Jamaica*. Durham, NC: Duke University Press, 2004.

Trouillot, Michel-Rolph. "The Anthropology of the State in the Age of Globalization: Close Encounters of the Deceptive Kind." *Current Anthropology* 42, no. 1 (2001): 125–138.

———. "The Caribbean Region: An Open Frontier in Anthropological Theory." *Annual Review of Anthropology* 21 (1992): 19–42.

Tsing, Anna. "The Global Situation." *Cultural Anthropology* 15, no. 3 (2000): 327–360.

———. *Friction: An Ethnography of Global Connection*. Princeton: Princeton University Press, 2005.

Turkle, Sherry. *Life on the Screen: Identity in the Age of the Internet*. New York: Simon & Schuster, 1995.

Ulysse, Gina. *Downtown Ladies: Informal Commercial Importers, a Haitian Anthropologist and Self-Making in Jamaica*. Chicago: University of Chicago Press, 2008.

———. "Uptown Ladies and Downtown Women: Female Representations of Class and Color in Jamaica." In *Representations of Blackness and the Performance of Identities*, edited by Jean Rahier, 147–172. Westport, CT: Bergin & Garvey, 1999.

Urry, John. *The Tourist Gaze*. 2nd ed. Thousand Oaks, CA: Sage, 2002.

Vance, Carole S. "Pleasure and Danger: Towards a Politics of Sexuality." In *Pleasure and Danger: Exploring Female Sexuality*, edited by Carole S. Vance. London: Pandora, 1989.

Wallerstein, Immanuel. *The Modern World-System: Capitalist Agriculture and the Origins of the European World-Economy in the Sixteenth Century*. New York: Academic Press, 1974.

Wanzo, Rebecca. *The Suffering Will Not Be Televised: African American Women and Sentimental Political Storytelling*. Albany: State University of New York Press, 2009.

Waters, Mary. *Black Identities: West Indian Immigrant Dreams and American Realities*. Cambridge, MA: Harvard University Press, 2001.

Weston, Kate. "The Virtual Anthropologist." In *Anthropological Locations: Boundaries and Grounds of Field Science*, edited by Akhil Gupta and James Ferguson, 163–184. Berkeley: University of California Press, 1997.

White, Deborah Gray. *Too Heavy a Load: Black Women in Defense of Themselves, 1894–1994*. New York: W. W. Norton, 1999.

Williams, Bianca C. "'Giving Back' to Jamaica: Experiencing Community and Conflict While Traveling with Diasporic Heart." *Souls: A Critical Journal of Black Politics, Culture, and Society* 19, no. 1 (2017): 24–38.

———. "'Don't Ride the Bus!': And Other Warnings Women Anthropologists Are Given During Fieldwork." *Transforming Anthropology* 17, no. 2 (2009): 155–158.

Williams, Erica Lorraine. *Sex Tourism in Bahia: Ambiguous Entanglements.* Chicago: University of Illinois Press, 2013.

Williams, Terrie M. *Black Pain: It Just Looks Like We're Not Hurting.* New York: Scribner, 2008.

Winant, Howard. *The World Is a Ghetto: Race and Democracy Since World War II.* New York: Basic Books, 2001.

Wolf, Diane. "Family Secrets: Transnational Struggles among Children of Filipino Immigrants." *Sociological Perspectives* 40, no. 3 (1997): 457–482.

Wolf, Eric R. *Europe and the People without History.* Berkeley: University of California Press, 1982.

Collins, Patricia Hill, 46, 53, 151–52
Columbus Heights complex, 205n3
communal spaces, 39–40, 43
competition and sisterhood, 154–55
contact zones: diasporic, 67–68; in ethnography, 200n8; Jamaicans.com, 163, 168; Pratt and, 65, 77–78; significance of, 17
Cooper, Carolyn, 110
Crenshaw, Kimberlé, 32
Cruel Optimism (Berlant), 114
crying and tears, 3–4, 6–7, 45–46, 59–60
cultural policing, 178–84
customs officers, Jamaican, 95–96
Cvetkovich, Ann, 37
cyberspace, identities in, 166
cyberspace, scholarship on, 168
Cybertypes (Nakamura), 170

dancehall music, 199n19
dancing, role of, 136
Dent, Gina, 13–14, 76–77
Devan (Jamaican hotel worker), 84–85, 202n28
diaspora: in cyberspace, 163, 168; diasporic and nationalized difference, 159–61; diasporic contact zones, 67–68; diasporic kinship and connectivity, 56–57, 65–66, 92–93, 146–56; diasporic nostalgia, 7, 23; diasporic spaces, 23, 68–74; hegemonic, 67; Jamaican, 86; race gender and, 8–11; in sex and romance tourism, 141–46; traveling with a diasporic heart, 66, 68–74. *See also* emotional transnationalism; race and racism
difference: diasporic, 141–46; Gayle on, 82–85; nationalized, 23, 80–82, 93; racial, 23, 59–61
"Disjuncture and Difference" (Appadurai), 202n4
Dolphin Cove, 115, 205n33
drivers and tour guides, 72–73
Du Bois, W. E. B., 31–32
"dutty" defined, 201n26

Ebron, Paulla, 92
Edwards, Brent Hayes, 67
emotional costs of desiring happiness, 47–57
emotional knowledges, 38

emotional transnationalism: concept of, 4–5; Falicov on, 205n34; racism linked to, 61–62; significance of, 6–7, 9, 104, 118. *See also* diaspora
Eric (male girlfriend), 81–82
erotic autonomy, 48
ethnography: contact zones in, 200n8; on cyberspace, 168; on diasporic difference, 141; fieldwork, 188–91; multisited, 19, 24; participant observation, 188–91; significance of, 14; virtual, 17–19, 101. *See also* methodology, research

fantasies, Black paradisal thinking, 66, 100, 110–14
fantasies, limits of, 114–17
fantasies, romantic, 129, 132–37
"Fantasy Islands" (O'Connell Davidson), 141
fishermen, relations with, 124
Flexible Citizenship (Ong), 102
friendships with Jamaican men, 131
Frohlick, Susan, 106–7

ganja, 182, 201n22
gay, lesbian, and queer tourists, 198n17
Gayle (girlfriend): on difference, 82–85; introduction of, 2; on Jamaica, 54; Jamaica connection of, 50–52; on Jamaicans.com, 173; on master complex, 91; on McMillan, 139–40; on power dynamics, 144–45; romances of, 132; on transactional relationships, 130–31
gaze, the collective, 105
gaze, the role in racialization, 204n16
gaze, the tourist, 88
gender, conceptualizations of, 125–26
gender and class relations, 146–47
gender and power dynamics, 142–45
gender and sexuality in cyberspace, 166
gendered aspects of diasporic kinship and connectivity, 148–56
generational social positions, 13–14
girlfriends: arrival stories of, 74; attitudes toward, 147–48; Black paradisal thinking of, 66, 100, 110–14; children of, 200n27; class of, 68–69; community of, 8; criticism of, 48, 50–51, 128, 152–53; expenses of, 69;

labor of, 53, 55, 62; relations with Jamaican women, 206n13; romantic moments, 54; significance of, 157; as Stella, 112–13; Thanksgiving in Jamaica, 123–24; transnationalism of, 102–3

Girlfriend Tours International (GFT): cliff initiation, 2; "doing Jamaica right," 82, 201n24; founders, 2, 40–41, 72, 198n16; Hairston of, 72; happiness and, 3; use of journals, 199n18; journals of, 199n18; men on, 81–82, 199n22; nature of, 1–2; origin and nature of, 21, 40–46; participants, 2–3; rates of, 69; significance of, 157, 187–88; strategies of, 11–12; white women and husbands-partners on, 199n22. *See also* Williams, Marilyn

"giving back" practices, 68–74, 106

Glick Schiller, Nina, 101–2

globalization, gender and race, 106–7, 202n4

gold diggers, 155–56

Hairston, Angelia, 2, 40–41, 72, 198n16

"Half House Sue," 141–42

Hall, Stuart, 33, 87, 203n6

happiness: costs related to desiring, 47–57; declarations of, 39–40; as a political project, 32–33, 35, 38, 60; as process, 40–47; representation in relation to, 3–4; scholars, 118. *See also* diaspora; emotional transnationalism; race and racism

Harris-Perry, Melissa, 33–36, 58

Hartman, Saidiya, 75

Harvey, David, 6–7, 166, 207n7

Hine, Christine, 101

Holsey, Bayo, 75–76

homecoming stories, 74–75

hotels, all-inclusive resort, 198n17

How Stella Got Her Groove Back (McMillan): girlfriends on, 138–40; impact of, 111–12; plot of, 15–16; response to, 99; visibility politics and, 113

identity: American, 23, 88–89; emotion in relation to, 37; formation of, 204n16; on Jamaicans.com, 164, 168–69; Nakamura on, 166; racial, 87, 126. *See also* difference; race and racism

Imagined Communities (Anderson), 8

imagined community, 8–11

immigrants, divided hearts of, 205n34

immigrants and technology, 203n10

Imperial Eyes (Pratt), 66–67

interludes, 27–30, 63–64, 95–97, 121–22, 159–61, 185–86

Internet. *See* Jamaicans.com

intersectionality, 3, 12–14, 32, 107–8

Jacobs, Jessica, 106–7

Jacqueline (girlfriend): on Afrocentrism, 79–80; characteristics of, 47–48; on economics, 2; emotional costs of, 55–57; fears of, 114–15; happiness declaration of, 39; Jamaica connection of, 49–50, 59; Jamaicaholism of, 199n35; on Jamaicans.com, 173–74; on Jamaican women, 153–54; politics of, 32; on relations with Jamaican men, 129; relations with Maya, 133–34; sentiments of, 118–19; trip report of, 18–19

Jamaica and Jamaicans: attitudes of, 55–57; as Black paradise, 66, 100; as commodity free, 117; on diaspora, 86; doing Jamaica right, 201n24; economy of, 70–71; government of, 56, 200n27; lived experiences of, 82–83; racial experiences of, 79–80; romance tourism in, 15–16; stereotypes of, 73; tourist industry, 109. *See also* Jamaican men; Jamaican women

Jamaicaholics and Jamaicaholism, 172–74, 198n4

Jamaican men: African American men compared to, 129, 145–46; attitudes toward, 144; characteristics of, 54–55, 136; drivers and tour guides, 56, 72–73; fishermen, 124; friendships with, 131; hotel worker, 84–86, 202n28; Jennifer and Jacqueline on, 128–29; "lyrics" of, 199n20; Michael on, 135–37, 142, 153–54; relations with, 127–28; sexuality of, 139–40; as sex workers, 130

Jamaicans.com: as a diasporic space, 163, 168; as ethnographic site, 19; forums, 174–75; gender relations on, 152–53; GFT on, 41; identities on, 164, 166, 168–69; Maya on, 173; Murphy, 174–76; origin and nature of, 17–19; policing on, 163, 178–84; reunions, 20–21; role and purpose of, 47, 172–73;

Jamaicans.com (*continued*)
    Sasha on, 208n22; segregation on, 175; trip reports, 18–19, 71, 99n18, 182–83, 199n18. *See also* trip reports
Jamaican Union of Travelers Association (JUTA), 72
Jamaican women: airport singers, 71–72; attitudes of, 57, 147–49, 155; attitudes toward, 145–46, 153–54; baby mamas, 135; customs officers, 95–97; economic aspects, 155–56; mothers, 150; in relation to visibility politics, 151–52; role of, 24, 126, 197n15; sex workers, 130, 206n13
James, Sherman, 12
Jennifer (girlfriend), 73–74, 128–29, 143, 170–72, 185–86
John Henryism, 11–12
Jones, Clarissa, 52–53, 58
Jungle club, 42–45
JUTA (Jamaican Union of Travelers Association), 72

Kaplan, Caren, 166
Keisha and Rob (boardites), 159–61, 172
Kempadoo Kamala, 141, 206n9
Kevon (Jamaican driver), 56
King, Gayle, 206n11

labor, emotional, 150, 156, 190–91
labor of girlfriends, 53, 55, 62
leisure class, 108
LGBTQ tourists, 198n17
lived experiences, 9–10, 31–32, 82–87
local politics, 115
Lorde, Audre, 1, 38, 46
"loving" defined, 206n5
"lyrics" defined, 138, 199n20

Marilyn. *See* Williams, Marilyn
master complex, 65, 89–92
Maya (girlfriend): fears of, 116–17; introduction of, 3; on power dynamics, 143; Sam and, 132–35; as trip organizer, 80–82; on trip reports, 173
McGlotten, Shaka, 167–68
McMillan, Terri. *See How Stella Got Her Groove Back* (McMillan)

media representation, 33, 35
methodology, research: analysis, 191–93; Black feminist, 11; challenges, 206n4; daughter figure in, 134; fieldwork, 188–91; interludes, 27–30, 63–64, 95–97, 121–22, 159–61, 185–86; intersectionality, 14; Jamaican women and, 24; limitations of, 23–24; multisited, 19; origin and nature of, 3–5; participant observation, 188–91; research questions, 4–5; respectability politics in, 134; subjects, 21–22, 25; writing, 193–94. *See also* ethnography
Michael (British Jamaican tour guide), 135–37, 142, 153–54
Miller, Daniel, 167
Miriam (girlfriend), 54
misrecognition, politics of, 33–36, 58
mobility methods, 9–10
Mohanty, Chandra Talpade, 107
Morgan, Joan, 36
mothers and mothering, 150
Mullings, Leith, 12–13
multisited research, 19, 24
Murphy, Xavier, 17, 174–76
music, Black, 109

Nakamura, Lisa, 166, 170
nationalized difference, encountering, 80–82
nigger, use of, 202n28
nine night tradition, 201n23

"obeah" woman, 201n23
Obra (boardite), 182
O'Connell Davidson, Julia, 144
Ong, Aihwa, 102
Ordinary Affairs (Stewart), 35–36
"Other" Blackness, 80–82

patois, 208n24
Petagaye (young Jamaican woman), 155
policing, cultural, 178–84
policing Black women, 48
politics: of authenticity and respectability, 127–32; of happiness, 32–33, 35, 38, 60; local, 115; of misrecognition, 33–36; of transnationalism, 105–8; of visibility, 24–25, 113
power and privilege, Jamaicans on, 88–90

power dynamics with Jamaican women, 146–48

The Practice of Diaspora (Edwards), 67

Pratt, Mary Louise, 65–67, 77–78

privilege, Black American, 55, 61

privilege, class and nationalized, 76–77

privilege, Jamaicans on, 88–90

problemhood, Black, 31–32

The Promise of Happiness (Ahmed), 37

race and racism: attitudes toward, 202n29; capitalism and, 105–6; Du Bois on, 31–32; emotional transnationalism linked to, 61–62; gender, diaspora and, 8–11; globalization and, 106; intersection of sexism and, 3, 12–14, 32, 107–8; in Jamaica, 79–80, 126; master complex in relation to, 89–92; racial difference, 23, 59–61, 141; racial subjectivities, 164–65; resistance to, 12–14, 187; shared experiences of, 82–87; subjectivities, racialized, 4, 16–17, 22–23, 164–67. *See also* diaspora; emotional transnationalism

"Racialization, Gender, and the Negotiation of Power in Stockholm's African Dance Courses" (Sawyer), 77–78

Rastafari, 201n26, 205n2

"real" selves vs. the virtual, 168–72

"reasoning" defined, 201n26

"rent-a-dread," 205n2

representation, politics of, 3, 10, 33

resistance. *See* race and racism

"Resistance and Resilience" (Mullings), 12–13

respectability and authenticity, politics of, 127–32, 134

Rollins, Judith, 148–49

"runnings" defined, 208n2

safe spaces, 46–47, 151–52

Sam and Maya, 132–35

Sangster International Airport, 71–72

Sarah (girlfriend), 74–75

Sasha (Jamaican American boardite), 85–86, 131, 152–53, 155–56, 175, 208n22

Sawyer, Lena, 77–79

sex and romance tourism: affective and transactional aspects, 126–31, 134–39;

Black women's role in, 107; breakups, 138; diasporic difference in, 141–46; in Jamaica, 15–16; nature of, 126–27, 130–31; sex workers, 205n2, 206n13; Stella in, 112–13

sexism and racism. *See* Black feminism and feminists; intersectionality; race and racism

sexual agency, 128–29, 137

sexuality and gender in cyberspace, 166

Shifting (Jones and Shorter-Gooden), 52–53

Shorter-Gooden, Kumea, 52–53, 58

single women travelers, 106–7, 177, 198n17

Sister Citizen (Harris-Perry), 33–34

sisterhood, diasporic, 146–56

Slater, Don, 167

slave trade, 103–4

Sojourner Syndrome, 11–12

"soon come" mentality, 201n24

The Souls of Black Folk (Du Bois), 31–32

Stella. See How Stella Got Her Groove Back (McMillan)

Stewart, Kathryn, 35–36

Stolzoff, Norman, 109–10

subjectivities, diasporic, 68

subjectivities, racialized and gendered, 4, 16–17, 22–23, 164–65

SugarShug (boardite), 181

Taylor, Frank Fonda, 109, 140

Taylor, Jacqueline Sanchez, 141, 144

technology. *See* Jamaicans.com

Thomas, Deborah, 67, 106, 110

time-space compression transformation, 6–7

tipping practices, 73–74, 150

To Hell with Paradise (Taylor), 109

tourism: identity, 166, 169; Jamaican, 109–10; as a lens into transnationalism, 105–8; tourist gaze, 88, 105–6. *See also* sex and romance tourism

"Transatlantic Dreaming" (Holsey), 75–76

transatlantic slave trade, 103–4

transnationalism and transnational studies: on black women, 10; of girlfriends, 102–3; intersectionality in, 107–8; methodologies, 9; politics of, 105–6; scholarship on, 101–2. *See also* diaspora; emotional transnationalism trip reports: on ganja use, 182; Jacqueline's, 18–19, 71, 178; Marilyn's, 169–73, 175; role and purpose of, 199n18; significance of, 183

Trouillot, Michel Rolph, 202n4

United Fruit Company, 109
Urry, John, 105

Veblen, Thorstein, 108
Vera (girfriend), 138–39
Virtual Ethnography (Hine), 101
virtual fieldwork and community, 17–20
virtual media, anthropology of, 165–68

virtual overlapping with the real, 168–72
visibility politics, 24–25, 58, 61, 113, 146–56

Wahalla (Jamaican boardite), 179–82
Walker, Alice, 1
Waters, Mary C., 201n29
web tools. *See* Jamaicans.com
Williams, Marilyn: of GFT, 2, 40–41, 198n16; on Jamaicans.com, 180; job controversy of, 170–72; role of, 176–78; trip reports of, 168–69. *See also* Girlfriend Tours International (GFT)
Winfrey, Oprah, 145
Wolf, Diane, 4

CPSIA information can be obtained
at www.ICGtesting.com
Printed in the USA
BVHW041624280821
615439BV00002B/238